BENJAMIN FRANKLIN'S
The ART *of* VIRTUE

BENJAMIN FRANKLIN'S

The ART *of* VIRTUE

His Formula for Successful Living

EDITED BY GEORGE L. ROGERS

THIRD EDITION

Library of Congress Cataloging-in-Publication Data

Franklin, Benjamin, 1706-1790.
Benjamin Franklin's the art of virtue: his formula for
successful living / edited by George L. Rogers. -- 3rd ed.
p. cm.
Includes bibliographical references and index.
ISBN 0-938399-10-1
1. Franklin, Benjamin, 1706-1790--Quotations. 2. Franklin,
Benjamin, 1706-1790--Views on conduct of life. 3. Conduct of
life--Quotations, maxims, etc. I. Rogers, George L. 1938-
E302.F82 1996
973.3'092--dc20 96-15076
CIP

CHOICESKILLS
MIDVALE, UTAH

CONTENTS

Contents

ILLUSTRATIONS

by John Hamer

Cover Design, Foster and Foster, Fairfield, IA

Cover Franklin by Charles Wilson Peale, permission of the American Philosophical Society

The primary source material for Franklins writings has been "The Works of Benjamin Franklin", (referred to as WBF in the chapter notes) edited by John Bigelow and published by G.P. Putnam's Sons in 1904. The only alterations from the text in Bigelow's edition are some modernization of punctuation and spelling, the replacement of a few archaic words, and the use of italics to emphasize particular ideas or statements.

Quotes taken directly from *Poor Richard's Almanack* adhere as closely as possible to the original text in punctuation, spelling, and use of italics for emphasis.

PREFACE

The other night, I had a dream in which my children came to me, all in a group, filing in from the oldest to the youngest. Each wore a serious expression and it was obvious they wanted to talk with me about something. I was surprised when they said they wanted to know why I was writing a book about Benjamin Franklin. Believing my "discussion" with them to be a useful introduction to Dr. Franklin's eminently practical, often fun, and always sound counsel for leading a happier and more fulfilling life, I decided to include it as a preface to *The Art of Virtue.*

CHILDREN: Dad, why are you writing a book about Benjamin Franklin? Hasn't everything been said about him already that could be said?

FATHER: Actually children, the book is not so much about Benjamin Franklin as it is by him. Essentially, it contains his formula for successful living.

CHILDREN: What is a formula for successful living?

FATHER: Well, suppose you want to bake a chocolate cake. You know that if you vary too much from the recipe, you're not likely to end up with a good cake. Success in other aspects of life is really not much different. Just as there are rules for baking cakes, there are also rules for successful living.

CHILDREN: But Dad, you know how old-fashioned we think you are, and Benjamin Franklin lived a long time before you. How could his ideas on successful living be very useful now? The world is a lot different than when he was alive.

FATHER: Sure, a lot has changed. But, there are certain things that never really change. For example, it may be easier to make a cake in our modern stoves than it used to be, and perhaps box cakes are easier to make than starting from scratch. Still, the underlying principles of cake making have not changed. Neither have the underlying principles of successful living changed. Benjamin Franklin seemed to understand those rules better than most people, and in my opinion, his ideas about them are as relevant and beneficial today as when they were written over two hundred years ago.

CHILDREN: Dad, you said the book is by Benjamin Franklin. What do you mean? Did he write another book besides his autobiography?

FATHER: He wanted to. Franklin first planned the work in 1732, about the age of twenty-six. He had earlier developed a method for self-improvement from which he was deriving considerable benefit and thought it could be useful to others as well. For many years he nurtured the idea of writing this book. In 1760, he wrote to a close friend, Lord Kames:

> I propose. . . . a little work for the benefit of youth, to be called *The Art of Virtue*. From the title I think you will hardly conjecture what the nature of the book may be. I must therefore explain it a little. Many people lead bad lives that would gladly live good ones, but do not know how to make the change. They have frequently resolved and endeavored it; but in vain, because their endeavors have not been properly conducted. To expect people to be good, to be just, to be temperate, &c., without showing them how they should become so, seems like the ineffectual charity mentioned by the Apostle, which consists in saying to the hungry, the cold, and the naked, "Be ye fed, be ye warmed, be ye clothed," without showing them how they should get food, fire, or clothing.
>
> Most people have naturally some virtues, but none have naturally all the virtues. To acquire those that are wanting, and secure what we acquire, as well as those we have naturally, is as properly an art as painting, navigation, or architecture. If a man would become a painter, navigator, or architect, it is not enough that he is advised to be one, that he is convinced by the arguments of his adviser that it would be for his advantage to be

one, and that he resolves to be one, *but he must also be taught the principles of the art, be shown all the methods of working, and how to acquire the habits of using properly all the instruments; and thus regularly and gradually he arrives, by practice, at some perfection in the art.* If he does not proceed thus, he is apt to meet with difficulties that discourage him, and make him drop the pursuit.

My *Art of Virtue* has also its instruments and teaches the manner of using them. . . . Such as are naturally well disposed, and have been so carefully educated, as that good habits have been early established, and bad ones prevented, have less need for this art; but all may be more or less benefited by it. It is, in short, to be adapted for universal use.[1]

In writing his autobiography in 1785, Franklin described the self-improvement method he had employed in his life, and then explained why he was never able to complete *The Art of Virtue*:

. . . .being fully persuaded of the utility and excellence of my method, and that it might be serviceable to people in all religions. . . .I purposed writing a little comment on each virtue, in which I should have shown the advantages of possessing it, and the mischiefs attending its opposite vice; and I should have called my book *The Art of Virtue*. . . .

But it so happened that my intention of writing and publishing this comment was never fulfilled. . . .the necessary close attention to private business in the earlier part of my life, and public business since, have occasioned my postponing it; for it, being connected in my mind with a *great and extensive project* that required the whole man to execute, and which an unforeseen succession of employs prevented my attending to, it has hitherto remained unfinished.[2]

So you can see, that Franklin maintained his interest in writing and publishing this book for well over fifty years.

CHILDREN: But if he didn't complete it, where did you get it?

FATHER: As you know, a few years ago, I obtained a set of Franklin's works. In reading his private letters, personal notes, essays, satires, and other materials, I found so much of benefit to me personally and so much that I wanted to share with you children, that I began to think in terms of extracting and organizing some of his ideas for our personal use. It then occurred to me the result would be very similar to what he had in mind with *The Art of Virtue*, and that it could possibly be of interest to others as well.

CHILDREN: That's interesting, Dad, but what did Franklin mean about people living bad lives that would gladly live good lives if they could only make the change? Do you think we live bad lives?

FATHER: No, of course not. But, there is still much we can all learn from him. Franklin was a close observer of human conduct, and recognized at an early age that certain attitudes and behaviors are more conducive to success and happiness than others. He had observed that happiness seemed to be more related to what went on within a person than without. He had also come to believe that success could be better measured by the good a person does than by any other means.

CHILDREN: Dad, we hate to ask this, but do you think a book on virtue by Benjamin Franklin will be very believable?

FATHER: What do you mean?

CHILDREN: Well Dad, surely you've noticed that while Franklin's biographers all acknowledge his greatness, most seem willing to question his personal virtue. For example, some suggest that for all Franklin had to say about frugality, it was a virtue he practiced only so long as he had to. Many writers present him as a womanizer, charging him with everything from fathering an illegitimate son when he was young to chasing the ladies of France when he was old. Some writers insinuate that Franklin was an ambitious man, somewhat ruthless in his business affairs and self-serving in his political activities. Even his relationships with his wife and children are often portrayed in unflattering terms. Frankly Dad, based on what they say, Benjamin Franklin doesn't seem like a very virtuous person.

FATHER: It's true, many of Franklin's biographers have said those kinds of things about him, but I would suggest that you examine closely what they have said. In my opinion, many writers have been extremely unfair to Franklin, as well as to their readers. It seems to me that several of them have attempted to build up their own reputations by tearing his down.

CHILDREN: Do you really feel you're on solid ground in challenging these experts?

FATHER: I'll let you judge for yourselves. Rather than attempt to address all of the things you mentioned, however, let's just consider the one of the most frequent allegations made about Franklin—that he fathered an illegitimate son. Nearly all of Franklin's biographers claim that William, his first son, was born out of wedlock. Most simply make the statement, as though it were a matter of known fact. Few make any attempt to document their sources of information and it's easy to see why. In fact, I have been absolutely amazed at their willingness to give these sources any credibility whatsoever, much less present them as valid documentation. It seems to me these authors follow a pattern. First, they make a bold statement which has the appearance of fact. Then, after the damage is done, they interject some uncertainty with respect to the details, which gives them an air of objectivity. Personally, I find a great deal of inconsistency between the different biographers, and sometimes even within a given biographer's own statements. For example, in one biography the author makes the following statement as though it were an undisputed fact:

> In Britain, where Franklin had spent a formative
> eighteen months, and where he was to spend many
> years, bastards were as thick on the family trees as fruit
> in a good year. He was to have his own, William,
> believed to have been born in 1731.[3]

What is this author's authority for making the statement, "he was to have his own"? He documents it as follows:

> The bastardy of Franklin's own son has remained
> covered in mystery. It was first claimed in a political
> pamphlet that the mother was a young servant in the

Franklin household; then in London's *The Morning Post and Daily Advertiser,* that he "had this son by an oyster wench in Philadelphia, whom he left to die in the streets of disease and hunger." The second statement, written at a time when Franklin was considered by many Englishmen as a traitor about whom any calumny might be spread, need not be taken too seriously. . . . There is also the unscotched rumor that William Franklin was in fact the son by Franklin of the Deborah Read whom Benjamin married in September 1730.[4]

In reading this, I wonder how a responsible historian can be so willing to injure Franklin's reputation on basis of the above information. After declaring, as though it were a known fact, that William was a bastard son, this writer acknowledges, "The bastardy of Franklin's own son has remained covered in mystery." He discounts the oyster wench possibility reported in a newspaper because Franklin had enemies who were willing to spread any form of calumny concerning him, but apparently thinks it less likely that Franklin's enemies would use a political pamphlet for the same purpose. He then relegates the idea that Deborah, Franklin's wife, was William's real mother to the status of an unscotched rumor even though he acknowledges they were married in September 1730 and *believes* William to have been born sometime in 1731.

CHILDREN: Gee, Dad, it just doesn't seem fair, does it?

FATHER: Obviously, this author believed what he chose to believe. Based on the same information, I would not choose to believe the same thing. Unfortunately, he has passed off his beliefs as knowledge and, in the process, has adversely prejudiced the minds of many people, like yourselves, with respect to an important aspect of Franklin's life. Let me give you one more example, equally amazing for it's inconsistency. Another writer has produced two biographies on Benjamin Franklin. In both of them, he unequivocally stated that William was an illegitimate child, but chose not to document his information. In the first biography, published in 1971, this author wrote in terms that would suggest he knew who the mother was:

Another factor added extra urgency to Franklin's concern for William. He was illegitimate, the product of a liaison with a working-class woman, into which Franklin had stumbled during his first unmarried years in Philadelphia. William had apparently been born six months <u>before</u> Franklin married Deborah Read.[5]

In his second biography on Benjamin Franklin, published in 1972, just one year later, this same gentleman wrote with equal positive assurance, the following contradictory statement:

Not long after his marriage, Franklin brought home one of the results of his intrigues with low women that he did not mention in his Autobiography. . . . His illegitimate son, William, had been born about six months <u>after</u> his marriage.[6]

It is bad enough that this author expects his readers to equate "a liaison with a working-class woman" to "intrigues with low women", but to state so presumptuously in one that the event was six months before his marriage, and in the other that it was six months after is, in my opinion, simply irresponsible.

CHILDREN: If people like these biographers can write whatever they want about a man like Benjamin Franklin, how can someone really know the truth about him?

FATHER: I have come to believe that you can tell a lot more about people by what they have to say themselves than by what someone else has to say about them. More important than the inconsistencies of these authors is the fact that what they have said is inconsistent with Franklin's own writings and with the quality of his life. Over the course of a long life, in private letters as well as public documents, Franklin was wholly consistent in the values he espoused and in the beliefs that guided him. In every respect they are contrary to the things of this kind that have been written about him. Furthermore, the nature of his achievements and the contributions he made to the world are all evidence of the nobility of his soul. That is why the bulk of my book is to be by Benjamin Franklin rather than about him. While it is possible to provide similar refutations to other statements damaging to Franklin's character, I think you will find, in his own writings, adequate reason to believe otherwise about him if you wish.

CHILDREN: We do have another problem Dad.

FATHER: What's that?

CHILDREN: Benjamin Franklin's writings aren't always easy to read, and, well, sometimes you use big words too

FATHER: I recognize the truth of what you are saying, but you are old enough to realize that worth while things often require extra effort. Franklin's ideas on happiness are perhaps more substantive than many you may have encountered, and may require more effort to read and understand than other things you may have read. If necessary, keep a dictionary by, and read the book in segments. If you were only to read the quotes in italics and the summaries at the end of each section you would find a wealth of useful and inspiring ideas on successful living. Your greatest benefit in reading the book will be realized when you understand particular ideas and attempt to apply them in your own lives. I have found these ideas so beneficial I come back to them again and again. If you will make the effort to read and ponder Franklin's writings, I am confident you, too, will find much that will enrich your life and increase your happiness.

So ended my dream, but I have another. It is that in a troubled world where happiness is often elusive and hard to find, *The Art of Virtue* will be a means of helping many people, including my own family, to enjoy more successful and fulfilling lives, and in some small way, bring added luster to the career of a great man who was also good—Benjamin Franklin.

INTRODUCTION

Lives of great men all remind us
We can make our lives sublime
And departing, leave behind us
Footprints on the sands of time
Longfellow

Rung by rung, Benjamin Franklin slowly but surely climbed the ladder of success. To him, each rung on the ladder was a well-defined principle of general application to all people. Studiously he applied those principles throughout his life, and to them he attributed his accomplishments. In his ascent, there came no accidents of fortune, no sudden windfalls to catapult him forward. From small things to great, he progressed step by step, patiently mastering the details, industriously performing the necessary duties, and persistently pursuing his objectives. Now, some two hundred years after his death, there is scarcely a living person untouched and unimproved by his contributions.

A printer by trade, Franklin began his apprenticeship at the age of twelve. From sweeping floors to setting type; from keeping books to delivering flyers; from writing articles to publishing newspapers, he learned and performed every aspect of his trade. Little by little, over many long years, he progressed from the status of an apprentice printer to publisher of one of America's foremost newspapers, *The Pennsylvania Gazette*, and of one of its most successful periodicals, *Poor Richard's Almanac*.

As a writer Benjamin practiced long hours, turning poetry into prose and prose into poetry. When he met with writings he thought particularly excellent, he would make brief notes of the ideas, reconstruct the piece in his own words, and then compare his with the original. Sometimes he would jumble his notes, set them aside for a time, and then reorganize the thoughts for greater effect. As he grew in confidence, he sought opportunities to express his own thoughts in writing, even though they were not always welcome. By this tedious process, his skill increased until the time when his pen became, as it were, the Voice of America to a generation of Europeans and a formidable weapon in the cause of American freedom.

Sir Humphry Davy, an accomplished English chemist, said of Franklin's scientific accomplishments, "By very small means he established very grand truths." His interest in science, said Davy, was to make it "a useful inmate and servant in the common habitations of man." By trial and error, Franklin forged new paths in science. While learning to understand and harness the powerful force of electricity, Franklin encountered many setbacks including electrical shocks, failed experiments, and even ridicule and criticism. But, he pressed forward. Now the whole world is blessed by discoveries he made. In addition to electricity, Franklin made significant contributions in medicine, meteorology, and even oceanography. His inventions are numerous and some, like bifocal glasses, have made life easier for literally millions of people. His papers include topics ranging from proposals as menial as cleaning and lighting streets to proposals as novel as making watertight compartments in ships. Wherever Franklin saw a human need, and this is a grand key to understanding his life, he sought to provide a solution.

When war erupted between America and England, Franklin was appointed by the Continental Congress as the first Postmaster General for the United States. Prior to this time he had served for forty years in the postal service of England. During this period, he rose by a succession of inferior degrees from Deputy Postmaster of Pennsylvania to Deputy Postmaster of North America. His first appointment came to him because of his knowledge of bookkeeping; successive appointments came because of his contributions in making the service profitable.

Although Benjamin Franklin only had two years of formal education himself, his interest in youth and his influence in establishing educational institutions make his one of the foremost names in American education. As a printer, he utilized his business as a means of furthering education in the new country. He was largely responsible for founding the first circulating library in America. The American Philosophical Society, established to foster scientific studies in the new world, was the offspring of his imagination. He was also instrumental in founding an academy which eventually became the University of Pennsylvania.

As a statesman, Franklin began his career as clerk of the Pennsylvania assembly in 1736. Beginning with small things, his involvement and influence increased until he became one of America's first, and greatest, ambassadors. His signature is on the Declaration of Independence, the Articles of Confederation, and the Constitution of the United States, as well as treaties of peace with England and several other European nations.

One of seventeen children of a Boston candle maker, Benjamin Franklin's rise from humble beginnings to rank as one of the most influential men in history is as instructive as it is impressive. Whatever natural gifts Franklin possessed, whatever skills he developed, and whatever his accomplishments, the outstanding characteristic of his life was none of these. Franklin's greatness lay not in either his talents or his achievements, as extraordinary as they were, but in his character. Benjamin Vaughan, a close friend of Franklin and one of England's representatives in negotiating the treaty of peace, wrote in the preface to a collection of Franklin's writings: "Yet he who praises Dr. Franklin for mere *ability*, praises him for that quality which stands lowest in his own esteem. Reader, whoever you are and how much soever you think you hate him, know that this great man loves *you* enough to wish to do you good. His 'country's friend, but *more* of human kind.'"[1]

The mainspring of motivation that energized Franklin's life was an unquenchable desire to do good and to live usefully. Virtually every endeavor to which he put his hand and heart had as its objective the betterment of human existence. To his mother he once wrote, "So the years roll round, and the last will come, when I would rather have it said, *He lived usefully*, than *He died rich.*"[2] Near the end of his life, in a letter to Samuel Mather, he revealed how he happened on this way of thinking:

> When I was a boy, I met with a book entitled *Essays to do Good*, which I think was written by your father [Cotton Mather]. It had been so little regarded by a former possessor, that several leaves of it were torn out; but the remainder gave me such a turn of thinking, as to

have an influence on my conduct through life; for I have always set a greater value on the character of a *doer of good*, than any other kind of reputation; and if I have been, as you seem to think, a useful citizen, the public owes the advantage of it to that book.[3]

Think how Benjamin Franklin must have felt when, as an obscure young boy, with nothing to commend him but an active mind, he read the following passage from this wonderful book:

> Reader, though, perhaps, thou art one who makest but a little figure in the world, "a brother of low degree," yet behold this vast encouragement; a little man may do a great deal of harm; and pray, why not a little man do a great deal of good? It is possible that "the wisdom of a poor man" may start a proposal which may "save a city," serve a nation![4]

While yet in his boyhood, Franklin made important decisions as to the kind of person he wanted to be; "a doer of good", "one who lived usefully." In early manhood, he developed formalized goals, plans, and methods specifically designed to help him become that kind of person. In the process of attempting to live a useful life, he was led more or less naturally into the activities which have made his one of the most revered names in history.

The Art of Virtue attempts to capture, in his own words, the guiding principles of Franklin's life. Like rungs on a ladder, these principles provided the footing by which Franklin rose, step by step, from apprentice to master in all that he undertook. Demonstrated through centuries of common human experience, these are principles that can be applied, with benefit, by anyone who wishes to make the effort. To help youth understand what may be achieved through a consistent application of these principles was one of the greatest desires of Franklin's life. These principles, as presented in *The Art of Virtue,* are:

GUIDING PRINCIPLE NUMBER ONE
There is no happiness but in a virtuous and self-approving conduct.

GUIDING PRINCIPLE NUMBER TWO
Acquiring the qualities of virtue requires a good plan and consistent effort.
GUIDING PRINCIPLE NUMBER THREE
Religion is a powerful regulator of human conduct.
GUIDING PRINCIPLE NUMBER FOUR
Correct action is dependent upon correct opinion.
GUIDING PRINCIPLE NUMBER FIVE
Motives of personal gain tend to be opposite of one's true self interest.
GUIDING PRINCIPLE NUMBER SIX
Where truth and honesty are wanting, everything is wanting.
GUIDING PRINCIPLE NUMBER SEVEN
The proper acquisition and use of money may be a blessing, but the opposite is always a curse.
GUIDING PRINCIPLE NUMBER EIGHT
It is, by far, much easier to preserve health than to regain it.
GUIDING PRINCIPLE NUMBER NINE
Happiness springs immediately from the mind.
GUIDING PRINCIPLE NUMBER TEN
Life is immeasurably more satisfying to those who get along well with others than to those who do not.
GUIDING PRINCIPLE NUMBER ELEVEN
Of all human relationships, the most enduring and satisfying are those of family.
GUIDING PRINCIPLE NUMBER TWELVE
In the process of aging and dying the fruits of a virtuous life are most sensibly felt.

The above concepts represent the general format of this book. To communicate these principles to others, and especially youth, was the primary objective of Benjamin Franklin's autobiography and his hope for the work he never completed, *The Art of Virtue.* In a day and an age when there is, perhaps, an even greater need to understand these principles of successful living, this work will hopefully complete, at least in part, the one remaining ambition of his life.

GUIDING PRINCIPLE
NUMBER ONE

THERE IS NO HAPPINESS BUT IN A
VIRTUOUS AND SELF-APPROVING CONDUCT

"The masterpiece of man," wrote Franklin in *Poor Richard's Almanack* of 1737, "is to live to the purpose." But what is that purpose? Is there more than one purpose? Do we all have the same purpose or do we each have different purposes? Although there are perhaps many possible answers to these questions, Franklin cut close to the root when he wrote, "The desire of happiness in general is so natural to us that all the world is in pursuit of it; all have this one end in view, though they take such different methods to attain it, and are so much divided in their notions of it." In other words, the one purpose or goal for which most people, most consistently strive is simply to be happy.

If, then, happiness is a major goal of so many, why is it that so few seem to fully attain it? Perhaps one reason may be that many of us fail to ask, as did Franklin, "Wherein lies the happiness of a rational creature?" And, not having asked, we don't understand, as did he, "That there is no happiness then but in a virtuous and self-approving conduct." And, because we don't understand this basic, fundamental principle of happiness, we fail to live to the purpose.

For example, *Poor Richard's Almanack* is riddled with comments like; "*Many a Man thinks he is buying Pleasure, when he is really selling himself a Slave to it.*" (1750) "*If Man could have Half his wishes, he would double his troubles.*" (1752) "*Is there any thing Men take more pains about than to render themselves unhappy?*" (1738) "*If what most men admire, they would despise, 'Twould look as if mankind were growing wise.*" (1735) and "*Many a Man would have been worse, if his Estate had been better.*" (1751)

Franklin realized that, in making choices and decisions, we attach the greatest value or importance to those things we believe will make us happy or improve our well-being. Those things to which we attach the greatest importance, in essence, become our governing values, or the values that govern how we think and what we do. If we believe that wealth is what will make us happy, then our actions will be governed by decisions calculated to help us accumulate wealth. If pleasure is our principle objective, then we will choose those things that we think will bring us the greatest pleasure.

As evidenced by the above statements from *Poor Richard's Almanack*, Franklin's observations of people convinced him that the obtaining of wealth or pleasure or similar things not only could not assure happiness, but on the contrary, were frequently, the very causes of much unhappiness. Thus, in writing to a friend, Franklin said, "In short, I conceive that a great part of the miseries of mankind are brought upon them by the false estimates they have made of the value of things."

Having made these observations at an early age, Benjamin Franklin deliberately chose a course of life which, in the long run, proved to be extraordinarily beneficial to others and personally satisfying to himself. The course he chose may be found in the following pages of *The Art of Virtue*. The governing value that placed him upon and guided him in that course perhaps may best be capsulized by this statement from a prayer book which he carefully prepared for his own personal devotions. "I believe," Franklin wrote, "he [God] is pleased and delights in the Happiness of those he has created; and since without Virtue Man can have no happiness in this world, I firmly believe he delights to see me Virtuous because he is pleased when he sees Me Happy."

BE CAREFUL WHAT YOU WANT

YOU MAY GET IT

1

DON'T PAY TOO MUCH FOR THE WHISTLE

Benjamin Franklin was a wonderful correspondent. His private letters contain a wealth of wisdom and insight. He often included in them accounts of personal experiences and lessons learned. The following letter to a friend, Madame Brillon, provides both delightful reading and valuable instruction. In it he observes that, "A great part of the miseries of mankind are brought upon them by the false estimates they have made of the value of things, and by their giving too much for their whistles."

I am charmed with your description of Paradise, and your plan of living there; and I approve much of your conclusion, that, in the meantime, we should draw all the good we can from this world. In my opinion we might all draw more good from it than we do, and suffer less evil, if we would take care not to give too much for *whistles*. For to me it seems that most of the unhappy people we meet with are become so by neglect of that caution.

You ask what I mean? You love stories, and will excuse my telling one of myself.

When I was a child of seven years old, my friends on a holiday, filled my pocket with coppers. I went directly to a shop where they sold toys for children; and being charmed with the sound of a *whistle*, that I met by the way in the hands of another boy, I voluntarily offered and gave all my money for one. I then came home, and went whistling all over the house, much pleased with my *whistle*, but disturbing all the family. My brothers, and sisters, and cousins, understanding the bargain I had made, told me I had given four times as much for it as it was worth; put me in mind what good things I might have bought with the rest of the money; and laughed at me so much for my folly, that I cried with vexation; and the reflection gave me more chagrin than the whistle gave me pleasure.

This, however, was afterwards of use to me, the impression continuing on my mind; so that often, when I was tempted to buy some unnecessary thing, I said to myself, *Don't give too much for the whistle*; and I saved my money.

As I grew up, came into the world, and observed the actions of men, I thought I met with many, very many, who *gave too much for the whistle*.

When I saw one too ambitious of court favor,

sacrificing his time in attendance on levees, his repose, his liberty, his virtue, and perhaps his friends to attain it, I have said to myself, *This man gives too much for his whistle.*

When I saw another fond of popularity, constantly employing himself in political bustles, neglecting his own affairs, and ruining them by that neglect, *He pays, indeed*, said I, *too much for his whistle.*

If I knew a miser, who gave up every kind of comfortable living, all the pleasure of doing good to others, all the esteem of his fellow-citizens, and the joys of benevolent friendship, for the sake of accumulating wealth, *Poor man*, said I, *you pay too much for your whistle.*

When I met with a man of pleasure, sacrificing every laudable improvement of the mind, or of his fortune, to mere corporeal sensations, and ruining his health in their pursuit, *Mistaken man*, said I, *you are providing pain for yourself, instead of pleasure; you give too much for your whistle.*

If I see one fond of appearance, or fine clothes, fine houses, fine furniture, fine equipages, all above his fortune, for which he contracts debts, and ends his career in a prison, *Alas!* say I, *he has paid dear, very dear, for his whistle.*

When I see a beautiful, sweet-tempered girl married to an ill-natured brute of a husband, *What a pity*, say I, *that she should pay so much for a whistle.*

In short, I conceive that a great part of the miseries of mankind are brought upon them by the false estimates they have made of the value of things, and *by their giving too much for their whistles.*

Yet I ought to have charity for these unhappy people, when I consider that, with all this wisdom of which I am boasting, there are certain things in the world so tempting, for example, the apples of King John, which happily are not to be bought; for if they were put to sale by auction, I might very easily be led to ruin myself in the purchase, and find that I had once more *given too much for the whistle.*[1]

THE EPHEMERA: AN EMBLEM OF HUMAN LIFE

In a parable contained in another enchanting letter to Madame Brillon, Franklin considered how quickly life passes and the futility of most human endeavor. He pondered the emptiness of fortune and fame when faced with the ultimate ruin that eventually comes to all earthly things, and concluded that the only real satisfaction in old age is "the reflection of a long life spent in meaning well."

You may remember, my dear friend, that when we lately spent that happy day in the delightful garden and sweet society of the Moulin Joly, I stopped a little in one of our walks, and stayed some time behind the company. We had been shown numberless skeletons of a kind of little fly, called an ephemera, whose successive generations, we were told, were bred and expired within the day. I happened to see a living company of them on a leaf, who appeared to be engaged in a conversation. You know I understand all the inferior animal tongues. My too great application to the study of them is the best excuse I can give for the little progress I have made in your charming language. I listened through curiosity to the discourse of these little creatures; but as they, in their national vivacity, spoke three or four together, I could make but little of their conversation. I found, however, by some broken expressions that I heard now and then, they were disputing warmly on the merit of two foreign musicians, one a cousin, the other a moscheto; in which dispute they spent their time, seemingly regardless of the shortness of life as if they had been sure of living a month. Happy people! thought I; you are certainly under a wise, just, and mild government, since you have no public grievances to complain of, nor any subject of contention but the perfections and imperfections of foreign music. I turned my head from them to an old gray-headed one, who was single on another leaf, and talking to himself. Being amused with his soliloquy, I put it down in writing, in hopes it will likewise amuse her to whom I am so much indebted for the most pleasing of amusements, her delicious company and heavenly harmony.

"It was," said he, "the opinion of learned philosophers of our race, who lived and flourished long before my time, that this vast world, the Moulin Joly, could not itself subsist more than eighteen hours; and I think there was some foundation for that opinion, since, by the apparent motion of the great luminary that gives life to all nature, and which in my time has evidently declined considerably towards the ocean at the end of our earth, it must then finish its course, be extinguished in the waters that surround us, and leave the world in cold and dark- ness, necessarily producing universal death and destruc- tion. I have lived seven of those hours, a great age, being no less than four hundred and twenty minutes of time. How very few of us continue so long! I have seen generations born, flourish, and expire. My present friends are the children and grandchildren of the friends of my youth, who are now, alas, no more! And I must soon follow them; for, by the course of nature, though still in health, I cannot expect to live above seven or eight minutes longer. What now avails in all my toil and labor in amassing honey-dew on this leaf, which I cannot live to enjoy! What the political struggles I have been engaged in for the good of my compatriot inhabit- ants of this bush, or my philosophical studies for the benefit of our race in general! *for in politics what can laws do without morals?* Our present race of ephemerae will in a course of minutes become corrupt, like those of other and older bushes, and consequently as wretched. And in philosophy how small our progress! Alas! art is long, and life is short! My friends would comfort me with the idea of a name they say I shall leave behind me; and they tell me I have long enough to nature and glory. But what will fame be to an ephemera who no longer exists? And what will become of all history in the eighteenth hour, when the world itself shall end, even the whole Moulin Joly, shall come to its end and be buried in universal ruin?"

To me, after all my eager pursuits, no solid pleasures now remain, but the reflection of a long life spent in meaning well, the sensible conversation of a few good lady ephemerae, and now and then a kind smile and a tune from the ever amiable Brillante.[2]

IF WE WERE AS INDUSTRIOUS TO BECOME GOOD

Prior to launching his own printing business, Benjamin Franklin contributed a series of articles, titled *The Busy-Body*, to Philadelphia's first newspaper, the *Weekly Mercury*. In *Busy-Body III*, he challenged his readers to examine their values and reconsider their goals. This article is one of his earliest published writings and reflects his thinking at the age of twenty-two. Little did he realize that some forty-six years later he would stand himself before great and powerful men under the most extraordinary circumstances, sustained only by a consciousness of his own innate worth and unshaken integrity. (See 152, 153) In a real sense, Franklin's description of Cato was a role model he had chosen for his own. To him, "there was never yet a truly great man that was not at the same time truly virtuous."

It is said that the Persians, in their constitution, had public schools in which virtue was taught as a liberal art or science; and *it is certainly of more consequence to a man, that he has learnt to govern his passions in spite of temptation, to be just in his dealings, to be temperate in his pleasures, to support himself with fortitude under his misfortunes, to behave with prudence in all his affairs and every circumstance of life; I say, it is of much more real advantage to him to be thus qualified, than to be a master of all the arts and sciences in the world beside.*

Virtue alone is sufficient to make a man great, glorious, and happy. He that is acquainted with Cato, as I am, cannot help thinking as I do now, and will acknowledge he deserves the name, without being honored by it. Cato is a man whom fortune has placed in the most obscure part of the country. His circumstances are such as only put him above necessity, without affording him any superfluities; yet who is greater than Cato? I happened but the other day to be at a house in town, where, among others, were met men of the most note in this place. Cato had business with some of them, and knocked at the door. The most trifling actions of a man, in my opinion, as well as the smallest features and lineaments of the face, give a nice observer some notion of his mind. Methought he rapped in such a peculiar manner, as seemed of itself to express there was one who deserved, as well as desired, admission. He appeared in the plainest country garb; his great coat was coarse, and looked old and threadbare; his linen was homespun, his beard, perhaps of seven days' growth; his shoes thick and heavy; and every part of his dress corresponding. Why was this man received with such concurring respect from every person in the room, even from those who had never known him or seen him before? It was not an exquisite form of person or grandeur of dress that struck us with admiration.

I believe long habits of virtue have a sensible effect on the countenance. There was something in the air of his face that manifested the true greatness of his mind, which likewise appeared in all he said, and in every part of his behavior, obliging us to regard him with a kind of veneration. His aspect is sweetened with humanity and benevolence, and at the same time emboldened with resolution, equally free from diffident bashfulness and an unbecoming assurance. *The consciousness of his own innate worth and unshaken integrity renders him calm and undaunted in the presence of the most great and powerful and upon the most extraordinary occasions.* His strict justice and known impartiality make him the arbitrator and decider of all differences that arise for many miles around him, without putting his neighbors to the charge, perplexity, and uncertainty of lawsuits. *He always speaks the thing he means, which he is never afraid or ashamed to do, because he knows he always means well,* and therefore is never obliged to blush, and feel the confusion of finding himself detected in the meanness of a falsehood. He never contrives ill against his neighbor, and therefore is never seen with a lowering, suspicious aspect. A mixture of innocence and wisdom makes him ever seriously cheerful. His generous hospitality to strangers according to his ability, his goodness, his charity, his courage in the cause of the oppressed, his fidelity in friendship, his humility, his honesty and sincerity, his moderation, and his loyalty to the government, his piety, his temperance, his love to mankind, his magnanimity, his public-spiritedness, and, in fine, his consummate virtue, make him justly deserve to be esteemed the glory of his country. . . .

Who would not rather choose, if it were in his choice, to merit the above character, than be the richest, most learned, or the most powerful man in the province without it?

Almost every man has a strong natural desire of being valued and esteemed by the rest of his species, but I am concerned and grieved to see how few fall into the right and only infallible method of becoming so. That laudable ambition is too commonly misapplied and often ill employed. Some, to make themselves considerable, pursue learning; others grasp at wealth; some aim at being thought witty; and others are only careful to make the most of a handsome person; but what is wit, or wealth, or form, or learning, when compared with virtue? It is true we love the handsome, we applaud the learned, and we fear the rich and powerful; but we even worship and adore the virtuous. Nor is it strange; since men of virtue are so rare, so very rare to be found. *If we were as industrious to become good as to make ourselves great, we should become really great by being good, and the number of valuable men would be much increased; but it is a grand mistake to think of being great without goodness; and I pronounce it as certain, that there was never yet a truly great man that was not at the same time truly virtuous.*[3]

THOSE WHO LOVE
THEMSELVES RIGHTLY $\quad 2$

Shortly before his marriage to Deborah Read, Benjamin published two essays on happiness which he titled *Dialogues Concerning Virtue and Pleasure*. The first dialogue appeared on June 23, 1730, in the *Pennsylvania Gazette*, and the second the month following. The dialogues consist of two conversations between Horatio, a lover of pleasure, and Philocles, a wise philosopher. Despite their differing life styles, Philocles and Horatio are good friends with a mutual respect for each other. In the first dialogue, Horatio admits to Philocles that his indiscriminate pursuit of pleasure has plunged him into unhappy difficulties. Admiring Philocles' freedom from similar cares, Horatio wishes to know his secret. Philocles answers Horatio:

> **Philocles:** There are few men in the world I value
> more than you, Horatio; for amidst all your foibles and
> painful pursuits of pleasure I have oft observed in you
> an honest heart and a mind strongly bent towards virtue.
> I wish, from my soul, I could assist you in acting
> steadily the part of a reasonable creature, for if you
> would not think it a paradox I should tell you I love you
> better than you do yourself.[1]

Since Horatio's whole focus is self-gratification, he can't understand how anyone could love him more than he does himself.

Horatio: I think he loves himself very well and very judiciously too, as you call it, who allows himself to do what ever he pleases.

Philocles: What, though it be to the ruin and destruction of that very self which he loves so well? *That man alone loves himself rightly who procures that greatest possible good to himself through the whole of his existence, and so pursues pleasure as not to give for it more than it is worth.*

Horatio: That depends all upon opinion. Who shall judge what the pleasure is worth? Suppose a pleasing form of the fair kind strikes me so much that I can enjoy nothing without the enjoyment of that one object; or that pleasure in general is so favorite a mistress that I will take her as men do their wives, for better, or for worse, minding no consequences nor regarding what is to come. Why should I not do it?

Philocles: Suppose, Horatio, that a friend of yours entered into the world about two-and-twenty, with a healthful, vigorous body, and a fair, plentiful estate of about five hundred pounds a year, and yet before he had reached thirty should, by following his own pleasures and not as you duly regarding consequences, have run out of his estate and disabled his body to that degree that he had neither the means nor capacity of enjoyment left, nor anything else to do but wisely shoot himself through the head to be at rest, what would you say to this unfortunate man's conduct? Is it wrong by opinion or fancy only? Or is there really a right and wrong in the case? Is not one opinion of life and action juster than another? Or one sort of conduct preferable to another? Or does that miserable son of pleasure appear as reasonable and lovely a being in your eyes as a man who by prudently and rightly gratifying his natural passion has preserved his body in full health and his estate entire, and enjoyed both to a good old age, and then died with a thankful heart for the good things he had received, and with an entire submission to the will of Him who first called him into being? Say, Horatio, are

these men equally wise and happy? And is everything to
be measured by mere fancy and opinion, without
considering whether that fancy or opinion be right?[2]

Recognizing that acceptance of this line of reasoning would
require him to make some major changes, Horatio argues:

Sure the wise and good Author of nature could never
make us to plague us. He could never give us passions
on purpose to subdue and conquer them, nor create this
self of mine, or any other self, only that it may be
denied.[3]

Philocles responds:

*You are, Horatio, in a very miserable condition
indeed, for you say you cannot be happy if you control
your passions, and you feel yourself miserable by an
unrestrained gratification of them, so that here is evil,
irremediable evil, either way.*[4]

Philocles points out to Horatio that *self-denial*, as understood
by men of sense, is really the highest form of self gratification
because it *"is never a duty or a reasonable action but as it is a
natural means of procuring more pleasure than you can taste
without it."* In deciding whether this kind of self-denial will give
us more pleasure or not, *all we have to do is consider whether
something we want to do is consistent, "with our happiness
tomorrow, next week, or next year; for as we all wish to live, we
are obligated by reason to take as much care for our future as
our present happiness and not build one on the ruins of the
other."* [5]

After concluding this conversation, Horatio and Philocles take
leave of each other. About three months later, they meet again
and resume their conversation. Dialogue number two begins by
Horatio informing Philocles that since their previous discussion
he had come to an understanding of the proper role of self-
denial. As a result he had made substantial changes in his life.
Still not satisfied, however, Horatio asks Philocles:

Show me to the path that leads up to that constant, durable, and invariable good, which I have heard you so beautifully describe and which you seem so fully to possess. . . . Can anything be constant in a world which is eternally changing. . . . ? What is this constant, durable good, then, of yours? . . . . Begin, then; I am prepared:

Philocles: I will. I believe, Horatio, with all your skepticism about you, you will allow that good to be constant which is never absent from you, and that to be durable which never ends but with your being.

Horatio: Yes, go on.

Philocles: That can never be the good of a creature which when present the creature may be miserable, and when absent is certainly so.

Horatio: I think not; but pray explain what you mean, for I am not much used to this abstract way of reasoning.

Philocles: I mean all the pleasures of sense. *The good of man cannot consist in the mere pleasures of sense, because when any one of those objects which you love is absent or cannot be come at, you are certainly miserable; and if the faculty be impaired, though the object be present, you cannot enjoy it.* So that this sensual good depends upon a thousand things without and within you and all out of your power. Can this then be the good of man? Say, Horatio, what think you, is not this a checkered, fleeting, fantastical good? *Can that, in any propriety of speech, be called the good of man which even while he is tasting he may be miserable, and which when he cannot taste he is necessarily so? Can that be our good which costs us a great deal of pains to obtain, which cloys in possessing, for which we must wait the return of appetite before we can enjoy again? Or is that our good which we can come at without difficulty, which is heightened by possession, which never ends in weariness and disappointment, and which the more we enjoy the better qualified we are to enjoy on?*

Horatio: The latter, I think; but why do you torment me thus? Philocles, *show me this good immediately.*

Philocles: I have showed you what it is not: it is not sensual, but it is rational and moral good. *It is doing all the good we can to others, by acts of humanity, friendship, generosity, and benevolence; this is that constant and durable good which will afford contentment and satisfaction always alike, without variation or diminution.* I speak to your experience now, Horatio. Did you ever find yourself weary of relieving the miserable, or of raising the distressed into life or happiness? Or rather, do not you find the pleasure grow upon you by repetition, and that it is greater in the reflection than in the act itself? Is there a pleasure upon earth to be compared with that which arises from the sense of making others happy? Can this pleasure ever be absent, or ever end but with your being? Does it not always accompany you? Doth it not lie down and rise with you, live as long as you live, give you consolation in the hour of death, and remain with you when all other things are going to forsake you, or you them?

Horatio: How glowingly you paint, Philocles. Methinks Horatio is among the enthusiasts. I feel the passion; I am enchantingly convinced, but I do not know why; overborne by something stronger than reason. Sure some divinity speaks within me. But prithee, Philocles, give me the cause why this rational and moral good so infinitely excels the mere natural or sensual.

Philocles: I think, Horatio, that I have clearly shown you the difference between merely natural or sensual good and rational or moral good. Natural or sensual pleasure continues no longer than the action itself; but this divine or moral pleasure continues when the action is over, and swells and grows upon your hand by reflection. The one is inconstant, unsatisfying, of short duration, and attended with numberless ills; the other is constant, yields full satisfaction, is durable, and no evils preceding, accompanying, or following it. But if you inquire farther into the cause of this difference, and would know why the moral pleasures are greater than the sensual, perhaps the reason is the same as in all other creatures, that their happiness or chief good consists in acting up to their chief faculty, or that faculty which distinguishes them from all creatures of a different species. The chief faculty in man is his reason, and consequently his chief good, or that which may be justly called his good, consists not merely in action, but in reasonable action. *By reasonable actions we understand those actions which are preservative of the human kind and naturally tend to produce real and unmixed happiness; and these actions, by way of distinction, we call actions morally good.*

Horatio: You speak very clearly, Philocles; but, that no difficulty may remain on my mind, pray tell me what is the real difference between natural good and evil and moral good and evil, for I know several people who use the terms without ideas.

Philocles: That may be. The difference lies only in this: that natural good and evil are pleasure and pain; moral good and evil are pleasure or pain produced with intention and design; for it is the intention only that makes the agent morally good or bad.

Horatio: *But may not a man with a very good intention do an evil action?*

Philocles: *Yes; but then he errs in his judgment, though his design be good. If his error is inevitable, or such as, all things considered, he could not help, he is inculpable; but if it arose through want of diligence in forming his judgment about the nature of human actions, he is immoral and culpable.*

Horatio: *I find, then, that in order to please ourselves rightly, or to do good to others morally, we should take great care of our opinions.*

Philocles: *Nothing concerns you more; for as the happiness or real good of men consists in right action, and right action cannot be produced without right opinion, it behooves us, above all things in this world, to take care that our own opinions of things be according* *to the nature of things. The foundation of all virtue and happiness is thinking rightly.* He who sees an action is right—that is, naturally tending to good and does it because of that tendency, he only is a moral man; and he alone is capable of that constant, durable, and invariable good which has been the subject of this conversation.

Horatio: How, my dear philosophical guide, shall I be able to know, and determine certainly, what is right and wrong in life?

Philocles: As easily as you distinguish a circle from a square, or light from darkness. Look, Horatio, into the sacred book of nature; read your own nature, and view the relation which other men stand in to you, and you to them, and you will immediately see what constitutes human happiness, and consequently what is right.[6]

HAPPINESS

A UNIVERSAL DESIRE

3

The one unifying thread through all human endeavor is the quest for happiness. To be happy is, perhaps, the only common objective shared by all people in all ages. Every other human aspiration may be explained in context of its perceived value in contributing to this universal goal. For all its importance, however, few people seem to realize there are laws that govern happiness as surely as there are laws that govern the forces of nature. The better a person understands the laws of happiness, the greater his chances are of doing those things that will bring him happiness. As may be seen from Franklin's description of these laws, there is often an inverse relationship between happiness and things people do to obtain it.

QUERIES

In 1727 Franklin organized a club for mutual improvement which he and his friends called the "Junto". The purpose of this club was to meet on a regular basis to discuss topics of mutual interest. In such meetings, each could benefit from the knowledge and experience of the others. The club was quite successful and had a very important influence on Franklin's life.

As one of the rules for the club, each of the members was to "produce one or more queries on any point of Morals, Politics, or Natural Philosophy, to be discussed by the company."[1] The following queries on happiness, apparently personal notes prepared for discussion purposes and partly missing, were part of Franklin's contribution. It is interesting to note that Franklin prepared these questions as a young man at the beginning of his career. Penetrating and insightful, these questions are well worth the asking, by anyone, at any time.

Question. Wherein consists the happiness of a rational creature?

Answer. In having a sound mind and a healthy body, a sufficiency of the necessaries and conveniences of life, together with the favor of God and the love of mankind.

Q. What do you mean by a sound mind?

A. A faculty of reasoning justly and truly in searching after such truths as relate to my happiness. This faculty is the gift of God, capable of being improved by experience and instruction into wisdom.

Q. What is wisdom?

A. The knowledge of what will be best for us on all occasions, and the best ways of attaining it.

Q. Is any man wise at all times and in all things?

A. No, but some are more frequently wise than others.

Q. What do you mean the necessaries of life?

A. Having wholesome food and drink wherewith to satisfy hunger and thirst, clothing, and a place of habitation fit to secure against the inclemencies of the weather.

Q. What do you mean by the conveniences of life?

A. Such a plenty. . . .[missing]

Whether it is worth a rational man's while to forego the pleasure arising from the present luxury of the age, in eating and drinking, and artful cookery, studying to gratify the appetite, for the sake of enjoying a healthy old age, a sound mind, and a sound body, which are the advantages reasonably to be expected from a more simple and temperate diet?

Whether those meats and drinks are not best, that contain nothing in their natural taste, nor have anything added by art, so pleasing as to induce us to eat or drink when we are not thirsty or hungry, or after hunger and thirst are satisfied; water, for instance, for drink, and bread or the like for meat?

Is there any difference between knowledge and prudence? If there is any, which of the two is most eligible? . . . .What general conduct of life is most suitable for men in such circumstances as most of the members of the Junto are? Or, of the many schemes of living which are in our power to pursue, which will be most probably conducive to our happiness?

Which is best, to make a friend of a wise and good man that is poor, or of a rich man that is neither wise nor good?

Which of the two is the greatest loss to a country if they both die?

Which of the two is happiest in life?

Does it not, in a general way, require great study and intense application for a poor man to become rich and powerful, if he would do it without the forfeiture of his honesty?

Does it not require as much pains, study, and application to become truly wise and strictly virtuous, as to become rich?

Can a man of common capacity pursue both views with success, at the same time?

If not, which of the two is it best for him to make his whole application to?[2]

ON TRUE HAPPINESS

On November 25, 1735, Benjamin Franklin published the following essay on happiness in the Pennsylvania Gazette. Its message is simply that true happiness can only be obtained through virtuous living. In it may be seen how precisely Franklin identified happiness as the major objective of his own life and the means by which it might be obtained. To him, these were fundamental laws or maxims of human behavior. They could be applied with predictable results by anyone wishing to make the effort. This essay deserves careful study.

The desire of happiness in general is so natural to us that all the world is in pursuit of it; all have this one end in view, though they take such different methods to attain it, and are so much divided in their notions of it.

Evil, as evil, can never be chosen; and though evil is often the effect of our own choice, yet we never desire it but under the appearance of an imaginary good.

Many things we indulge ourselves in may be considered by us as evils, and yet be desirable; but then they are only considered as evils in their effects and consequences, not as evils at present and attended with immediate misery.

Reason represents things to us not only as they are at present, but as they are in their whole nature and tendency; passion only regards them in their former light. When this governs us we are regardless of the future, and are only affected with the present. It is impossible ever to enjoy ourselves rightly if our conduct be not such as to preserve the harmony and order of our faculties and the original frame and constitution of our minds; all true happiness, as all that is truly beautiful, can only result from order.

Whilst there is a conflict betwixt the two principles of passion and reason, we must be miserable in proportion to the struggle, and when the victory is gained and reason so far subdued as seldom to trouble us with its remonstrances, the happiness we have then is not the happiness of our rational nature, but the happiness only of the inferior and sensual part of us, and consequently a very low and imperfect happiness to what the other would have afforded us.

If we reflect upon any one passion and disposition of mind abstract from virtue, we shall soon see the disconnection between that and true, solid happiness. It is of the very essence, for instance, of envy to be uneasy and disquieted. Pride meets with provocations and disturbances upon almost every occasion. Covetousness is ever attended with solicitude and anxiety. Ambition has its disappointments to sour us, but never the good fortune to satisfy us; its appetite grows the keener by indulgence, and all we can gratify it with at present serves but the more to inflame insatiable desires.

The passions, by being too much conversant with earthly objects, can never fix in us a proper composure and acquiescence of mind. *Nothing but an indifference to the things of this world, and entire submission to the will of Providence here, and a well-grounded expectation of happiness hereafter, can give us a true satisfactory enjoyment of ourselves.* Virtue is the best guard against the many unavoidable evils incident to us; nothing better alleviates the weight of the afflictions or gives a truer relish of the blessings of human life.

What is without us has not the least connection with happiness only so far as the preservation of our lives and health depends upon it. Health of body, though so far necessary that we cannot be perfectly happy without it, is not sufficient to make us happy of itself. Happiness springs immediately from the mind; health is but to be considered as a condition or circumstance, without which this happiness cannot be tasted pure and unabated.

Virtue is the best preservative of health, as it prescribes temperance and such a regulation of our passions as is most conducive to the wellbeing of the animal economy, so that it is at the same time the only true happiness of the mind and the best means of preserving the health of the body.

If our desires are to the things of this world, they are never to be satisfied. If our great view is upon those of the next, the expectation of them is an infinitely higher satisfaction than the enjoyment of those of the present.

There is no happiness then but in a virtuous and self-approving conduct. Unless our actions will bear the test of sober judgments and reflections upon them, they are not the actions and consequently not the happiness of a rational being.[3]

FRANKLIN'S FORMULA FOR SUCCESSFUL LIVING
NUMBER ONE

"If our desires
are to the things of this world,"
wrote Franklin,
"they are never to be satisfied."

Pleasure,
position,
popularity,
wealth,
and appearance
are among those whistles in life
which cannot satisfy,
and for which many people pay too much.

Happiness is so common a desire
that all the world
is in pursuit of it;
but, since the happiness of man
lies in correct action,
and correct action
flows only from correct opinion,
many never fully experience
the happiness that could be theirs
if they were more careful of their opinions.

To be happy,
it is necessary to possess
an indifference to the things of this world,
to be willing
to submit to the will of Providence,
and to have
a well-grounded expectation of life hereafter.

Formula One

To be happy,
it is necessary to learn how
to govern one's passions and appetites,
to be just in one's dealings with others,
to be temperate in one's pleasures,
to support oneself with fortitude in difficulties,
and to be prudent in one's affairs.

Because those things external to man
have little to do with happiness,
Franklin believed
that happiness can only be found
in a virtuous
and self-approving conduct.

And because,
in old age
the only solid satisfaction
is the reflection
of a long life spent in meaning well,
Franklin believed that,
in this life,
the only constant
and durable source of happiness,
is in acts of
humanity,
friendship,
generosity,
and benevolence.

GUIDING PRINCIPLE
NUMBER TWO

ACQUIRING THE QUALITIES OF VIRTUE REQUIRES A GOOD PLAN AND CONSISTENT EFFORT

It was wise cousel given to a young man, *Pitch upon that course of life which is most excellent, and* CUSTOM *will make it the most delightful.* But many pitch upon no course of life at all, nor form any scheme of living, by which to attain any valuable end; but wander perpetually from one thing to another.

Hast thou not yet propos'd some certain end,
To which thy life, thy every act may tend?
Hast thou no mark at which to bend thy bow?. . . .
[Oh] learn the motions of the mind [and know],
Why you were made, for what you were design'd,
And the great moral end *of [all] human kind. . . .*

So wrote Poor Richard in his almanac of 1749. But, As Franklin had learned many years earlier, it is one thing to set upon a course, and another to make it custom. To this end, Poor Richard commented in his almanac for 1742.

'Tis easy to frame a good bold resolution;
But hard is the Task that concerns execution.

By 1728, Franklin had clearly identified the mark at which to aim his bow. It was no less than to attain moral perfection. It was by this means he felt he could live more usefully, do more good, and achieve greater happiness than any other course he might pursue. However, he discovered,

> . . . .that the mere speculative conviction that it [is] our interest to be completely virtuous, [is] not sufficient to prevent our slipping; and that contrary bad habits must be broken, and good ones established, before we can have any dependence on a steady, uniform rectitude of conduct.

He, therefore, found it necessary to develop a written plan and system to help him achieve his goals. The methods he developed were perhaps, not much different than a coach might use in building a football team, or a farmer in planting crops, or even a scientist in planning a research project. It consisted of clearly stating his objectives and establishing a method by which he could daily monitor his progress against those objectives. He knew few things of significance ever just happen. No one just happens to clilmb Mount Everest. No one just happens to become a skilled musician or mathematician. Neither does one just happen to become a good parent, an honest person, or a useful citizen. Certainly, no one just happens to achieve moral excellence. There are too many pulls in the other direction. Such things can only be achieved when they are established as specific goals and pursued with careful planning and consistent effort.

Once his plan was established, he continued follow it for many years. It was to this process that Franklin attributed the "constant felicity of his life", and although he never fully obtained the "moral perfection" for which he was striving, he was by his own account, a far happier and better man by the endeavor than he would have been had he not attempted it.

A METHOD
FOR PROGRESSING

4

Although Benjamin Franklin worked very hard to develop specific skills and to make good use of his talents, his real attention was given to the perfection of his character, or arriving at what he called "moral perfection". As commendable as it is to excel in a particular field of endeavor, to Franklin excellence in a particular endeavor was subordinate to being a good person. To a young friend who had become interested in the study of insects, he expressed this belief:

> There is, however, a prudent moderation to be used in studies of this kind. The knowledge of nature may be ornamental, and it may be useful; but if, to attain an eminence in that, we neglect the knowledge and practice of essential duties, we deserve reprehension. For there is no rank in natural knowledge of equal dignity and importance with that of being a good parent, a good child, a good husband or wife, a good neighbor or friend, a good subject or citizen—that is, in short a good Christian.[1]

Accordingly, Franklin set his sights much higher than the attainment of mere temporal objectives.

DEFINING OBJECTIVES

The first step in preparing a plan for personal progress is to clearly define one's objectives very specifically. Franklin's approach is exemplary in several respects. First, it illustrates the kind of thinking necessary for clarifying and defining objectives. Second, it demonstrates how to express specific objectives in a succinct manner. Third, it provides us a wonderful example of the kinds of goals most likely to produce a happy and satisfying life. In his own words:

It was bout this time [1728] I conceived the bold and arduous project of arriving at moral perfection. I wished to live without committing any fault at any time; I would conquer all that either natural inclination, custom, or company might lead me into. As I knew, or thought I knew, what was right and wrong, I did not see why I might not always do the one and avoid the other. But I soon found I had undertaken a task of more difficulty than I had imagined. While my care was employed in guarding against one fault, I was often surprised by another; habit took the advantage of inattention; inclination was sometimes too strong for reason. *I concluded, at length, that the mere speculative conviction that it was our interest to be completely virtuous, was not sufficient to prevent our slipping; and that the contrary habits must be broken, and good ones acquired and established, before we can have any dependence on a steady, uniform rectitude of conduct.* For this purpose I therefore contrived the following method.

In the various enumerations of the moral virtues I had met with in my reading, I found the catalogue more or less numerous, as different writers included more or fewer ideas under the same name. Temperance, for example, was by some confined to eating and drinking, while by others it was extended to mean the moderating every other pleasure, appetite, inclination, or passion, bodily or mental, even to our avarice and ambition. I proposed to myself, for the sake of clearness, to use

rather more names, with fewer ideas annexed to each,
than a few names with more ideas; and I included under
thirteen names of virtues all that at that time occurred to
me as necessary or desirable, and annexed to each a
short precept, which fully expressed the extent I gave to
its meaning.

These names of virtues, with their precepts, were:

1. TEMPERANCE

Eat not to dullness; drink not to elevation.

2. SILENCE

Speak not but what may benefit others or yourself;
avoid trifling conversation.

3. ORDER

Let all your things have their places; let each part of
your business have its time.

4. RESOLUTION

Resolve to perform what you ought; perform without
fail what you resolve.

5. FRUGALITY

Make no expense but to do good to others or yourself;
i.e., waste nothing.

6. INDUSTRY

Lose no time; be always employed in something
useful; cut off all unnecessary actions.

7. SINCERITY

Use no hurtful deceit; think innocently and justly; and,
if you speak, speak accordingly.

8. JUSTICE

Wrong none by doing injuries, or omitting the benefits that are your duty.

9. MODERATION

Avoid extremes; forbear resenting injuries so much as you think they deserve.

10. CLEANLINESS

Tolerate no uncleanliness in body, clothes, or habitation.

11. TRANQUILLITY

Be not disturbed at trifles, or at accidents common or unavoidable.

12. CHASTITY

Rarely use venery [sexual intercourse] but for health or offspring, never to dulness, weakness, or the injury of your own or another's peace or reputation.

13. HUMILITY

Imitate Jesus and Socrates.[2]

MEASURING PROGRESS

As Franklin discovered, however, it is not enough merely to establish objectives. There is also a need to provide some means of keeping them in front of us and to measure our progress with re-spect to achieving them. As he noted:

> *My intention being to acquire the habitude of all these virtues, I judged it would be well not to distract my attention by attempting the whole at once, but to fix it on one of them at a time; and, when I should be master of*

that, then proceed to another, and so on till I had gone through the thirteen; and, as the previous acquisition of some might facilitate the acquisition of certain others, I arranged them with that view, as they stand above. Temperance first, as it tends to procure that coolness and clearness of head, which is so necessary where constant vigilance was to be kept up, and guard maintained against the unremitting attraction of ancient habits, and the force of perpetual temptations. This being acquired and established, Silence would be more easy; and my desire being to gain knowledge at the same time that I improved in virtue, and considering that in conversation it was obtained rather by the use of the ears than of the tongue, and therefore wishing to break a habit I was getting into of prattling, punning, and joking, which only made me acceptable to trifling company, I gave Silence the second place. This and the next, Order, I expected would allow me more time for attending to my project and my studies. Resolution, once become habitual, would keep me firm in my endeavors to obtain all the subsequent virtues; Frugality and Industry freeing me from my remaining debt, and producing affluence and independence, would make more easy the practice of Sincerity and Justice, etc., etc. Conceiving, then, that, agreeably to the advice of Pythagoras in his *Golden Verses*, daily examination would be necessary, I contrived the following method for conducting that examination.

I made a little book, in which I allotted a page for each of the virtues. I ruled each page with red ink, so as to have seven columns, one for each day of the week, marking each column with a letter for the day. I crossed these columns with thirteen red lines, marking the beginning of each line with the first letter of one of the virtues, on which line, and in its proper column, I might mark, by a little black spot, every fault I found upon examination to have been committed respecting that virtue upon that day.

Form of the Pages

	S	M	T	W	TH	F	S
TEMPERANCE							
Eat not to dullness; Drink not to elevation.							
T.							
S.	*	*		*		*	
O.	**	*	*		*	*	*
R.			*			*	
F.		*			*		
I.			*				
S.							
J.							
M.							
C.							
T.							
C.							
H.							

I determined to give a week's strict attention to each of the virtues successively. Thus, in the first week, my great guard was to avoid every least offence against Temperance, leaving the other virtues to their ordinary chance, only marking every evening the faults of the day. Thus, if in the first week I could keep my first line, marked T, clear of spots, I supposed the habit of that virtue so much strengthened, and its opposite weakened, that I might venture extending my attention to include the next, and for the following week keep both lines clear of spots. Proceeding thus to the last, I could go through a course complete in thirteen weeks, and four courses in a year. And like him who, having a garden to weed, does not attempt to eradicate all the bad herbs at once, which would exceed his reach and his strength, but works on one of the beds at a time, and, having accomplished the first, proceeds to a second, so I should have, I hoped, the encouraging pleasure of seeing on my pages the progress I made in virtue, by clearing successively my lines of their spots, till in the end, by a number of courses, I should be happy in viewing a clean book, after a thirteen weeks' daily examination.[3]

MAINTAINING MOTIVATION

To help him maintain his resolve to work on these virtues, Franklin included inspirational sayings in his book:

This my little book had for its motto these lines from Addison's Cato:

Here will I hold. If there's a power above us
(And that there is, all nature cries aloud
Through all her works), He must delight in virtue;
And that which He delights in must be happy.

Another from the Proverbs of Solomon, speaking of wisdom or virtue:

Length of days is in her right hand, and in her left
hand riches and honor. Her ways are ways of pleasant-
ness, and all her paths are peace. _iii. 16,17.

And conceiving God to be the fountain of wisdom, I thought it right and necessary to solicit his assistance for obtaining it; to this end I formed the following little prayer, which was prefixed to my tables of examination, for daily use.

*O powerful goodness! bountiful Father! merciful
Guide! Increase in me that wisdom which discovers my
truest interest. Strengthen my resolutions to perform
what that wisdom dictates. Accept my kind offices to thy
other children as the only return in my power for thy
continual favors to me.*

I used also sometimes a little prayer which I took from Thomson's Poems, viz.:

Father of light and life, thou good Supreme!
O teach me what is good; teach me Thyself!
Save me from folly, vanity, and vice,
From every low pursuit; and fill my soul
With knowledge, conscious peace, and virtue pure;
Sacred, substantial, never-fading bliss![4]

FRANKLIN'S PERSONAL EXPERIENCE

The importance of this method of self-improvement in Franklin's life is noted in his autobiography. To it he attributed "the constant felicity of his life." He wrote, not only of its usefulness to him, but also of his hope it might be of use to his descendants and others:

I entered upon the execution of this plan for self-examination, and continued it with occasional intermissions for some time. *I was surprised to find myself so much fuller of faults than I had imagined; but I had the satisfaction of seeing them diminish.* . . . After a while I went through one course only in a year, and afterward only one in several years, till at length I omitted them entirely, being employed in voyages and business abroad, with a multiplicity of affairs that interfered; but I always carried my little book with me.

My scheme of Order gave me the most trouble; and I found that, though it might be practicable where a man's business was such as to leave him the disposition of his time, that of a journeyman printer, for instance, it was not possible to be exactly observed by a master who must mix with the world and often receive people of business at their own hours. Order, too, with regard to places for things, papers, etc., I found extremely difficult to acquire. I had not been early accustomed to it, and, having an exceeding good memory, I was not so sensible of the inconvenience attending want of method. This article, therefore cost me so much painful attention and my faults in it vexed me so much, and I made so little progress in amendment, and had such frequent relapses that I was almost ready to give up the attempt, and content myself with a faulty character in that respect, like the man who, in buying an ax of a smith, my neighbor, desired to have the whole of its surface as bright as the edge. The smith consented to grind it bright for him if he would turn the wheel; he turned while the smith pressed the broad face of the ax hard and heavily on the stone which made the turning of it very fatiguing. The man came every now and then from the wheel to see how the work went on and at length would take his ax as it was, without farther grinding. "No," said the smith, "turn on, turn on; we shall have it bright by and by; as yet, it is only speckled." "Yes," says the man, "but I think I like a speckled ax best." And I believe this may have been the case with many who, having, for want of some such means as I employed, found the difficulty of obtaining good and breaking bad habits in other points of vice and virtue, have given up the struggle, and concluded that "a speckled was best"; for something, that pretended to be reason, was every now and then suggesting to me that such extreme nicety as I exacted of myself might be a kind of foppery in morals, which, if it were known, would make me ridiculous; that a perfect character might be attended with the inconvenience of being envied and hated; and that a benevolent man should allow a few faults in himself, to keep his friends in countenance.

In truth, I found myself incorrigible with respect to Order; and now I am grown old and my memory bad, I feel very sensibly the want of it. *But, on the whole, though I never arrived at the perfection I had been so ambitious of obtaining, but fell far short of it, yet I was, by the endeavor, a better and happier man than I otherwise should have been if I had not attempted it;* as those who aim at perfect writing by imitating the engraved copies, though they never reach the wished-for excellence of those copies, their hand is mended by the endeavor, and is tolerable while it continues fair and legible.

It may be well my posterity should be informed that *to this little artifice, with the blessings of God, their ancestor owed the constant felicity of his life,* down to his 79th year, in which this is written. What reverses may attend the remainder is in the hand of Providence; but, if they arrive, the reflection on past happiness enjoyed ought to help his bearing them with more resignation. *To Temperance he ascribes his long-continued health, and what is still left to him of a good constitution; to Industry and Frugality, the early easiness of his circumstances and acquisition of his fortune, with all that knowledge that enabled him to be a useful citizen, and obtained for him some degree of reputation among the learned; to Sincerity and Justice, the confidence of his country, and the honorable employs it conferred upon him; and to the joint influence of the whole mass of virtues, even in the imperfect state he was able to acquire them, all that evenness of temper, and that cheerfulness in conversation, which makes his company still sought for and agreeable to his younger acquaintances.* I hope, therefore, that some of my descendants may follow the example and reap of the benefit.[5]

FRANKLIN'S FORMULA FOR SUCCESSFUL LIVING
NUMBER TWO

To become more than we are
is a common desire
shared by most of mankind.

It is neither natural
nor fitting that we should be
totally content
with who we are
or what we are.

Without continual growth and progress,
such words as
improvement, achievement, and success
have no meaning.

There are many ambitions
which stir the human soul.

Some aspire to
athletic prowess,
business acumen,
musical talents,
or intellectual skills.

Others have goals more ephemeral
such as position, power,
possessions, or prominence.

But of all ambitions to which
the human heart may aspire,
there are none more noble
nor any of greater worth
than to improve one's
character and capacity to do good.

Formula Two

It is only
in the pursuit of moral perfection
that a full measure
of happiness and achievement
may be obtained.

But the mere speculative conviction
that something
is in our interest
is not sufficient
to prevent us from slipping.

Bad habits must be eliminated
and good ones acquired "before
we can have any dependence
on a steady, uniform rectitude of conduct."

Progress then,
requires not only specific objectives,
carefully chosen and clearly defined,
but also some method
for measuring that progress
and sustaining the needed motivation
to keep moving.

In the life of Benjamin Franklin
may be found
not only the method,
but a marvelous example
of the blessings that can flow
from reaching for the most
excellent of goals,
a virtuous character.

GUIDING PRINCIPLE
NUMBER THREE

RELIGION IS A POWERFUL REGULATOR
OF HUMAN CONDUCT

In the process of establishing our life's objectives and planning how to achieve them, we are forced to examine the underlying values that govern our thoughts and actions. It is these values, the estimates of worth we attach to things, that enable us to determine the importance of any given objective, and to establish the price we are willing to pay for it. Inherently religious in nature, all value systems encompass some concept of the divine essence, the purpose of life, and the laws that govern human existence. To be sure, there are great differences between various systems with respect to these large issues, and as with everything else in life, not all value systems are equally suitable for all objectives. There are value systems that encourage the pursuit of power and wealth at any price, but they are not well suited for the person seeking peace and happiness. There are value systems that are well designed for people in search of sensual pleasure, but they should not be mistaken for those that develop strong family ties or lasting friendships. Whatever the value system and whatever the goals, if they are consistent and pursued with commitment, they are likely to be achieved.

Unfortunately, there are people, not a few, who claim one set of values while adhering to another. Some do so knowingly.

Others seem unable to recognize the inconsistencies between what they say and what they do. Many simply allow their values ebb and flow with the tide of popular opinion. With no set course of their own, their happiness and well-being must ever be subject, with all the uncertainties this entails, to the whims of the crowd. Whatever the case, all too many follow paths inconsistent with their true interests and end up in places and circumstances different from where they wanted to be

Benjamin Franklin, ever thorough in all he undertook, was very clear with himself, not only in the goals he selected, but also with respect to the value system that motivated him to achieve them. Shortly before his death, he wrote to Ezra Stiles, President of Yale College, "As to Jesus of Nazareth, my opinion of whom you particularly desire, I think his system of morals and religion, as he left them to us, the best the world ever saw or is like to see."[1] In religion as in science, however, Franklin's approach was always the same. Unimpressed with the theoretical, he looked for the useful. His sole study in religion was to understand those principles he could apply to make himself a better person, more useful to others, and more acceptable to God. With the desires he had, both to be good and to do good, it was not too difficult for him to discover those principles and find ways to apply them. He called them the essentials of every religion. In their distilled form they were:

> That there is one God, who made all things.
> That he governs the world by his providence.
> That he ought to be worshipped by adoration,
>   prayer and thanksgiving.
> But that the most acceptable service of God is
>   doing good to man.
> That the soul is immortal.
> And that God will certainly reward virtue and
>   punish vice, either here or hereafter.[2]

This belief, to Benjamin Frankln, was indeed a powerful regulator of his conduct, in all that he said and in all that he did.

THERE IS ONE GOD
WHO MADE ALL THINGS 5

I WAS NEVER WITHOUT RELIGIOUS PRINCIPLES

In his autobiography, Franklin recorded that his parents gave
him "early religious impressions" and raised him "piously, in the
Dissenting way." In other words they were faithful Christians
who had broken with the Church of England. About the age of
fifteen, Benjamin came across some books on deism and quickly
adopted many of its concepts. After observing how this belief
system influenced both himself and others to be either unkind or
dishonest, he concluded it "was not very useful."

I doubted whether some error had not insinuated itself
unperceived into my arguments, so as to infect all that
followed, as is common in metaphysical reasonings.
*I grew convinced that truth, sincerity, and integrity in
dealings between man and man were of the utmost
importance to the felicity of life; and I formed written
resolutions, which still remain in my journal book, to
practice them ever while I lived.* Revelation had indeed
no weight with me, as such; but *I entertained an opinion
that, though certain actions might not be bad because
they were forbidden by it, or good because it commanded them, yet probably those actions might be
forbidden because they were bad for us, or commanded*

because they were beneficial to us, in their own natures, all the circumstances of things considered. And this persuasion, with the kind hand of Providence, or some guardian angel, or accidental favorable circumstances and situations, or all together, preserved me, through this dangerous time of youth, and the hazardous situations I was sometimes in among strangers remote from the eye and advice of my father, without any willful gross immorality or injustice that might have been expected from my want of religion. I say willful, because the instances I have mentioned had something of necessity in them, from my youth, inexperience, and the knavery of others. I had therefore a tolerable character to begin with; I valued it properly, and determined to preserve it.[1]

Further on in his autobiography, Franklin summarized the religious convictions that later guided his life as follows:

I had been religiously educated as a Presbyterian; and though some of the dogmas of that persuasion, such as the eternal decrees of God, election, reprobation, etc., appeared to me unintelligible, others doubtful, and I early absented myself from the public assemblies of the sect, Sunday being my studying day, I never was without some religious principles. *I never doubted, for instance, the existence of the Deity; that he made the world, and governed it by his Providence; that the most acceptable service of God was the doing good to man; that our souls are immortal; and that all crime will be punished, and virtue rewarded, either here or hereafter. These I esteemed the essentials of every religion*; and being to be found in all the religions we had in our country, I respected them all, though with different degrees of respect, as I found them more or less mixed with other articles, which, without any tendency to inspire, promote, or confirm morality, served principally to divide us, and make us unfriendly to one another. This respect to all, with an opinion that the worst had some good

effects, induced me to avoid all discourse that might
tend to lessen the good opinion another might have of
his own religion; and as our province increased in
people, and new places of worship were continually
wanted, and generally erected by voluntary contribution,
my mite for such purpose, whatever might be the sect,
was never refused.[2]

A LECTURE ON THE PROVIDENCE OF GOD

Having arrived at the point where he believed that God not
only can, but does intervene in the affairs of man, Franklin
prepared a lecture, probably for the Junto. In it he explored the
relationship between the free agency of man and the intervention
of God. He presented his reasons for believing that Providence
not only has the power but also the interest to intervene in
human affairs, and the kinds of situations in which He might do
so. This belief in the sustaining influence of a loving God was a
constant source of strength to Franklin; and throughout his life,
he acknowledged the blessings of Providence in all of his affairs.

The Characteristics of God

In the first part of the lecture, Franklin considered those
characteristics of God that require our worship and adoration:

I propose, at this time, to discourse on the subject of
our last conversation, the providence of God in the
government of the world. It might be judged an affront
to your understandings, should I go about to prove this
first principle, the existence of a Deity, and that he is the
creator of the universe; for that would suppose you
ignorant of what all mankind in all ages have agreed in. I
shall therefore proceed to observe, that *he must be a
being of infinite wisdom, as appears in his admirable
order and disposition of things*; whether we consider the
heavenly bodies, the stars and planets, and their
wonderful regular motions; or this earth, compounded of
such an excellent mixture of all the elements; to the

admirable structure of animate bodies of such infinite
variety, and yet every one adapted to its nature and the
way of life it is to be placed in, whether on earth, in the
air, or in the water, and so exactly that the highest and
most exquisite human reason cannot find a fault, and say
this would have been better so, or in such a manner;
which whoever considers attentively and thoroughly will
be astonished and swallowed up in admiration.

*That the Deity is a being of great goodness, appears in
his giving life to so many creatures, each of which
acknowledges it a benefit, by its unwillingness to leave
it*; in his providing plentiful sustenance for them all, and
making those things that are most useful, most common
and easy to be had; such as water, necessary for almost
every creature to drink; air, without which few could
subsist; the inexpressible benefits of light and sunshine
to almost all animals in general; and to men, the most
useful vegetables, such as corn, the most useful of
metals as iron, etc., the most useful animals, as horses,
oxen, and sheep, he has made easiest to raise or procure
in quantity or numbers; each of which particulars, if
considered seriously and carefully, would fill us with the
highest love and affection.

*That he is a being of infinite power appears in his
being able to form and compound such vast masses of
matter, as this earth, and the sun, and innumerable stars
and planets, and give them such prodigious motion, and
yet so to govern them in their greatest velocity, as that
they shall not fly out of their appointed bounds, nor dash
one against another for their mutual destruction.* But it
is easy to conceive his power, when we are convinced of
his infinite knowledge and wisdom. For, if weak and
foolish creatures as we are, by knowing the nature of a
few things, can produce such wonderful effects—such
as, for instance, by knowing the nature only of nitre and
sea-salt mixed we can make a water which will dissolve
the hardest iron, and by adding one ingredient more can
make the most solid bodies fluid; and by knowing the
nature of saltpetre, sulphur, and charcoal, with those

mean ingredients mixed we can shake the air in the most terrible manner, destroy ships, houses, and men at a distance, and in an instant overthrow cities, and rend rocks into a thousand pieces, and level the highest mountains, what power must he possess, who not only knows the nature of everything in the universe, but can make things of new natures with the greatest ease and at his pleasure![3]

Four Alternatives

Having established the wisdom, goodness and power of God, Franklin then proceeded to consider the extent of God's continuing involvement in the affairs of men. To him there were only four alternatives.

Agreeing, then, that the world was at first made by a being of infinite wisdom, goodness, and power, which being we call God, the state of things existing at this time must be in one of these four following manners, namely:

1. Either he unchangeably decreed and appointed every thing that comes to pass, and left nothing to the course of nature, or allowed any creature free agency;

2. Without decreeing any thing, he left all to general nature and the events of free agency in his creatures, which he never alters or interrupts; or,

3. He decreed some things unchangeably, and left others to general nature and the events of free agency, which also he never alters or interrupts; or,

4. He sometimes interferes by his particular providence, and sets aside the effects which would otherwise have been produced by any of the above causes.

I shall endeavor to show the first three suppositions to be inconsistent with the common light of reason, and that the fourth is most agreeable to, and therefore most probably true.[4]

The Problems with Alternative One

According to Franklin, if alternative one were true, not only would God cease to be God, having nothing more to do, but He would have been most unwise in many of his decrees:

> In the first place, *if you say he has in the beginning unchangeably decreed all things and left nothing to nature of free agency, these strange conclusions will necessarily follow*: 1. That *he is now no more a God.* It is true, indeed, before he made such unchangeable decree, he was a being of power almighty; but now, having determined every thing, he has divested himself of all further power, he has done and has no more to do, he has tied up his hands and has no greater power than an idol of wood or stone; nor can there be any more reason for praying to him or worshiping of him than of such an idol, for the worshipers can never be better for such worship. Then, 2. *He has decreed some things contrary to the very notion of a wise and good being*; such as, that some of his creatures or children shall do all manner of injury to others, and bring every kind of evil upon them without cause; that some of them shall even blaspheme him, their Creator, in the most horrible manner; and, which is still more highly absurd, he has decreed, that the greatest part of mankind shall in all ages put up their earnest prayers to him, both in private and publicly in great assemblies, when all the while he had so determined their fate that he could not possibly grant them any benefits on that account, nor could such prayers be in any way available. Why then should he ordain them to make such prayers? It cannot be imagined that they are of any service to him. Surely it is not more difficult to believe the world was made by a god of wood or stone, than that the God who made the world should be such a God as this.[5]

The Problems with Alternative Two

If alternative two were true, Franklin concluded that God must hide himself from his creations and have no further interest in them:

In the second place, *if you say he has decreed nothing, but left all things to general nature and the events of free agency, which he never alters or interrupts, then these conclusions will follow: he must either utterly hide himself from the works of his own hands, and take no notice at all of their proceedings,* natural or moral, *or he must be,* as undoubtedly he is, *a spectator of everything, for there can be no reason or ground to suppose the first. I say there can be no reason to imagine he would make so glorious a universe merely to abandon it.* In this case, imagine the Deity looking on and beholding the ways of his creatures. Some heroes in virtue he sees are incessantly endeavoring the good of others; they labor through vast difficulties, they suffer incredible hardships and miseries to accomplish this end, in hopes to please a good God, and attain his favors, which they earnestly pray for. What answer can he make, then, within himself, but this? *Take the reward chance may give you; I do not intermeddle in these affairs. He sees others continually doing all manner of evil, and bringing by their actions misery and destruction among mankind. What can he say here but this? If chance rewards you, I shall not punish you; I am not concerned. He sees the just, the innocent, and the beneficent in the hands of the wicked and violent oppressor, and when the good are at the brink of destruction, they pray to him: Thou, O God, art mighty and powerful to save; help us, we beseech thee! He answers: I cannot help you; it is none of my business, nor do I at all regard these things.* How is it possible to believe a wise and an infinitely good being can be delighted in this circumstance, and be utterly unconcerned what becomes of the beings and things he has created? For thus we believe him idle and inactive, and that his glorious attributes of power, wisdom, and goodness are no more to be made use of.[6]

The Problems with Alternative Three

In the third place, *if you say he has decreed some things, and left others to the events of nature and free agency, which he never alters or interrupts, still you un-God* him, if I may be allowed to use the expression; *he has nothing to do; he can cause us neither good nor harm; he is no more to be regarded than a lifeless image*, than Dagon, or Baal, or Bell and the Dragon; and, as in both the other suppositions foregoing, that being, which from its power is most able to act, from its wisdom knows best how to act, and from its goodness would always certainly act best, is, in this opinion, supposed to become the most inactive of all beings, and remain everlastingly idle; an absurdity which, when considered or but barely seen, cannot be swallowed without doing the greatest violence to common reason and all the faculties of the understanding.[7]

The Reasons to Suppose Alternative Four

Franklin then concludes that while Deity has given agency to His creations, He still remains actively involved in their affairs:

We are then, necessarily driven to the fourth supposition, *that the Deity sometimes interferes by his particular providence, and sets aside events, which would otherwise have been produced in the course of nature, or by the free agency of men*; and this is perfectly agreeable with what we know of his attributes and perfections. But, as some may doubt whether it is possible there should be such a thing as free agency in creatures, I shall offer one short argument on that account, and proceed to show how the duty of religion necessarily follows the belief of a Providence. You acknowledge that God is infinitely powerful, wise, and

good, and also a free agent, and you will not deny that
he has communicated to us part of his wisdom, power,
and goodness; that is, he has made us, in some degree,
wise, potent, and good. And is it, then, impossible for
him to communicate any part of his freedom, and make
us also in some degree free? Is not even this infinite
power sufficient for this? I should be glad to hear what
reason any man can give for thinking in that manner. It
is sufficient for me to show it is not impossible, and no
man, I think, can show it is improbable. Much more
might be offered to demonstrate clearly that men are in
some degree free agents and accountable for their
actions; however, this I may possibly reserve for another
separate discourse hereafter, if I find occasion.

*Lastly, if God does not sometimes interfere by his
providence, it is either because he cannot, or because he
will not. Which of these positions will you choose?
There is a righteous nation grievously oppressed by a
cruel tyrant; they earnestly entreat God to deliver them.
If you say he cannot, you deny his infinite power, which
you at first acknowledged. If you say he will not, you
must directly deny his infinite goodness.* You are of
necessity obliged to allow that it is highly reasonable to
believe a Providence, because it is highly absurd to
believe otherwise.

Now, if it is unreasonable to suppose it out of the
power of the Deity to help and favor us particularly, or
that we are out of his hearing and notice, or that good
actions do not procure more of his favor than ill ones;
then *I conclude that, believing a Providence, we have
the foundation of all true religion; for we should love
and revere the Deity for his goodness, and thank him for
his benefits; we should adore him for his wisdom, fear
him for his power, and pray to him for his favor and
protection. And this religion will be a powerful
regulator of our actions, give us peace and tranquillity
within our own minds, and render us benevolent, useful,
and beneficial to others.*[8]

HE OUGHT TO BE WORSHIPPED

6

Although Franklin did not regularly attend Church services, he did frequently have his own private devotions, for which he prepared his own prayer book. Titled *Articles of Belief and Acts of Religion,* it contained prayers, inspirational songs, readings, and what he considered to be the first principles of belief, specifically his concept of Deity. In the following excerpt from his prayer book may be seen not only the depth of Franklin's own faith, but much that is worthy of emulation.

LET ME THEN NOT FAIL

I conceive for many Reasons that he is a good Being, and as I should be happy to have so wise, good, and powerful a Being my friend, let me consider in what manner I shall make myself most acceptable to him.

Next to the Praise resulting from and due to his Wisdom, *I believe he is pleased and delights in the Happiness of those he has created; and since without Virtue Man can have no Happiness in this world, I firmly believe he delights to see me Virtuous because he is pleased when he sees Me Happy.*

And since he has created many Things which seem purely designed for the Delight of Man, I believe he is not offended when he sees his Children solace

themselves in any manner of pleasant exercises and
Innocent Delights, and *I think no Pleasure innocent that
is to Man hurtful.*

I love him therefore for his Goodness and I adore him
for his Wisdom.

Let me then not fail to praise my God continually, for
it is his Due, and it is all I can return for his many
Favors and great Goodness to me; and let me resolve to
be virtuous, that I may be happy, that I may please Him,
who is delighted to see me happy. Amen.

1. ADORATION   2. PETITION   3. THANKS

Being mindful that before I address the Deity my soul
ought to be calm and serene, free from Passion and
Perturbation, or otherwise elevated with rational Joy and
Pleasure, I ought to use a Countenance that expresses a
filial Respect, mixed with a kind of Smiling, that
Signifies inward Joy and Satisfaction and Admiration.

O wise God,
My good Father,
Thou beholdest the sincerity of my Heart,
and of my Devotion
Grant me a Continuance of thy Favor!

(1)
O Creator, O Father, I believe that thou art Good, and
that thou art *pleased with the Pleasure* of thy children.

Praised be thy name for Ever.

(2)
By thy Power hast thou made the glorious Sun; with
his attending Worlds; from the energy of thy mighty
Will they first received [their prodigious] motion, and
by thy Wisdom hast thou prescribed the wondrous Laws
by which they move.

Praised be thy name for Ever.

(3)

By thy Wisdom hast thou formed all Things. Thou
hast created Man, bestowing Life and Reason, and
placed him in Dignity superior to thy other earthly
creatures.

Praised be thy name for Ever.

(4)

Thy Wisdom, thy Power, and thy Goodness are every
where clearly seen; in the air and in the water, in the
Heaven and on the Earth; Thou providest for the various
winged Fowl, and the innumerable Inhabitants of the
Water; Thou givest Cold and Heat, Rain and Sunshine in
their Season, and to the Fruits of the Earth Increase.

Praised be thy name for Ever.

(5)

Thou abhorrest in thy Creatures Treachery and Deceit,
Malice, Revenge, *Intemperance*, and every other hurtful
Vice; but Thou art a Lover of Justice and Sincerity, of
Friendship, Benevolence, and every Virtue. Thou art my
Friend, my Father, and my Benefactor.

Praised be thy name, O God, for Ever.
Amen.

After this, it will not be improper to read part of some such
Book as Ray's *Wisdom of God in the Creation*,
or Blackmore *On the Creation*, or the
Archbishop of Cambray's *Demonstration of the
Being of a God*, etc., or else spend some
Minutes in a serious Silence, contemplating on
those subjects.

Then sing

MILTON'S HYMN TO THE CREATOR

Here follows the Reading of some Book or part of a Book
Discoursing on and exciting to Moral Virtue.

PETITION

*Inasmuch as by Reason of our Ignorance We cannot
be certain that many Things Which we often hear mentioned in the Petitions of Men to the Deity, would prove
real Goods if they were in our Possession, and as I have
reason to hope and believe that the Goodness of my
Heavenly Father will not withhold from me a suitable
share of Temporal Blessings, if by a Virtuous and holy
Life I conciliate his Favor and Kindness, Therefore I
presume not to ask such things, but rather humbly and
with a Sincere Heart express my earnest desires that he
would graciously assist my Continual Endeavors and
Resolutions of eschewing Vice and embracing Virtue;
which Kind of Supplications will at least be thus far
beneficial, as they remind me in a solemn manner of my
Extensive*

DUTY

That I may be preserved from Atheism & Infidelity,
Impiety and Profaneness, and in my Addresses to Thee
carefully avoid Irreverence and ostentation, Formality
and odious Hypocrisy,
                       Help me, O Father.

That I may be loyal to my Prince and faithful to my
country, careful for its good, valiant in its defense, and
obedient to its Laws, abhorring Treason as much as
Tyranny,
                       Help me, O Father.

That I may to those above me, be dutiful, humble, and
submissive, avoiding Pride, Disrespect, and Contumacy,
                       Help me, O Father.

That I may to those below me, be gracious,
Condescending, & Forgiving, using Clemency,
protecting innocent Distress, avoiding Cruelty,

Harshness, and Oppression, Insolence and unreasonable
Severity,
> Help me, O Father.

That I may refrain from Censure, Calumny, and
Detraction; that I may avoid and abhor Deceit and Envy,
Fraud, Flattery, and Hatred, Malice, Lying and
Ingratitude,
> Help me, O Father.

That I may be sincere in Friendship, faithful in Trust
and impartial in Judgment, watchful against Pride and
against Anger (that momentary Madness),
> Help me, O Father.

That I may be just in all my Dealings and temperate in
my Pleasures, full of Candor and Ingenuity, Humanity
and Benevolence,
> Help me, O Father.

That I may be grateful to my Benefactors and generous
to my Friends, exerting Charity and Liberality to the
Poor and Pity to the Miserable,
> Help me, O Father.

That I may avoid Avarice and Ambition, Jealousy and
Intemperance, Falsehood, Luxury, and Lasciviousness,
> Help me, O Father.

That I may possess Integrity and Evenness of Mind,
Resolution in Difficulties, and Fortitude under
affliction; that I may be punctual in performing my
promises, Peaceable and prudent in my Behavior,
> Help me, O Father.

That I may have tenderness for the weak and a
Reverent respect for the Ancient; that I may be Kind to
my Neighbors, Goodnatured to my Companions and
Hospitable to Strangers,
> Help me, O Father.

That I may be averse to Tale bearing, Backbiting,
Detraction, Slander, and Craft, and Overreaching, abhor
Extortion and Perjury and every Kind of Wickedness,
                        Help me, O Father.

That I may be honest and open hearted, gentle,
merciful, and good, cheerful in spirit, rejoicing in the
Good of others,
                        Help me, O Father.

That I may have a constant Regard to Honor and
Probity; That I may possess a perfect innocence and a
good Conscience, and at length become Truly Virtuous
and Magnanimous,
                        Help me, Good God.
                        Help me, O Father.[1]

It is interesting to observe that Franklin's book of devotions
was prepared for his own use in the privacy of his own room and
can therefore be acknowledged as an expression of his innermost
desires. Unquestionably, religion was a powerful regulator of
Franklin's thoughts and actions. As things are, not all religions,
nor all who profess religion, admire the same virtues or abhor
the same vices that Franklin did. It should not be difficult,
however, to appreciate the benefits of his faith. Who, believing
they will be held accountable before a just God for their actions
in this life, would be anxious to offend him? Who, believing
their happiness an object of concern to a loving God, would not
be encouraged to please him? Who, praying in humility and in
the sincerity of his heart, could even utter the above expressions
of devotion and solicitude and not be improved by the process?
And, if a person were to add to such a prayer a consistent and
conscientious effort to so live, what God would refuse to grant
such a request? Surely this is an important part of the formula
for living a rich and fulfilling life.

The refining influence of Franklin's private devotions and its
influence for good in his life is exemplified in a speech he made
to the Constitutional Convention in Philadelphia. Now, eighty-
one years of age, and looking back on an eventful life in which

he had greater occasion than most to observe the affairs of men, he fully acknowledged the inadequacy of human wisdom and the need for divine guidance in laying the foundations for a free republic.

MOTION FOR PRAYERS IN THE CONVENTION

The infant republic, in 1787, was at a point of crisis. The Articles of Confederation, which had bound the colonies together during the war, had proven inadequate to govern a growing nation. Something more was needed. In May of that year representatives of the respective colonies gathered in Philadelphia to draft a new constitution. It was an ominous task, given the different interests of each of the colonies and the different views of each of the representatives. By the end of June, the convention was floundering and on the verge of breaking up. The weather was hot and the assembly room was small. Many of the delegates had only wool suits to wear. Disagreements were frequent, irritations were many, and tempers flared. With the nation on the brink of anarchy, the stakes were high. At that time of crisis, Franklin made perhaps the most eloquent and influential speech of his life, and although his recommendation was not implemented, it is acknowledged as a turning point in the convention.

> MR PRESIDENT: The small progress we have made, after four or five weeks' close attendance, and continual reasonings with each other, our different sentiments producing as many noes as ayes, is, methinks, a melancholy proof of the imperfection of the human understanding. We indeed seem to feel our own want of political wisdom, since we have been running around in search of it. We have gone back to ancient history for models of government, and examined the different forms of those republics which, having been originally formed with the seeds of their own dissolution, now no longer exist, and we have viewed modern States all round Europe, but find none of their constitutions suitable to our circumstances.

In this situation of this assembly, groping, as it were, in the dark, to find political truth, and scarce able to distinguish it when presented to us, how has it happened, sir, that we have not hitherto once thought of humbly applying to the Father of Lights to illuminate our understandings? In the beginning of the contest with Britain, when we were sensible of danger, we had daily prayers in this room for the Divine protection. Our prayers, sir, were heard, and they were graciously answered. All of us who were engaged in the struggle must have observed frequent instances of a superintending Providence in our favor. To that kind Providence we owe this happy opportunity of consulting in peace on the means of establishing our future national felicity. And have we now forgotten that powerful Friend? or do we imagine we no longer need its assistance? *I have lived, sir, a long time, and the longer I live the more convincing proofs I see of this truth, that God governs in the affairs of men. And if a sparrow cannot fall to the ground without his notice, is it probable that an empire can rise without his aid?* We have been assured, sir, in the sacred writings that "except the Lord build the house, they labor in vain that build it." I firmly believe this, and I also believe that without his concurring aid we shall succeed in this political building no better than the builders of Babel; we shall be divided by our little, partial, local interests, our projects will be confounded, and we ourselves shall become a reproach and a byword down to future ages. And, what is worse, mankind may hereafter, from this unfortunate instance, despair of establishing government by human wisdom, and leave it to chance, war, and conquest.

I therefore beg leave to move—

That henceforth prayers, imploring the assistance of Heaven and its blessings on our deliberations, be held in this assembly every morning before we proceed to business; and that one or more of the clergy of this city be requested to officiate in that service.[2]

THE MOST ACCEPTABLE
SERVICE OF GOD

7

Pure religion may be perceived in noble thoughts as expressed in the written and spoken word, but it is experienced most directly in things that people do. Benjamin once wrote to his father:

> My mother grieves that one of her sons is an Arian, another an Arminian. What an Arminian or an Arian is, I cannot say that I very well know. The truth is I make such distinctions very little my study. I think vital religion has always suffered when orthodoxy is more regarded than virtue; and *the Scriptures assure me that at the last day we shall not be examined for what we thought, but what we did*; and our recommendation will not be that we said, Lord! Lord! but that we did good to our fellow creatures.[1]

A NARRATIVE OF THE LATE MASSACRES IN LANCASTER COUNTY

Not everyone is influenced by religion in the same manner. To Franklin, unkindness to others under the guise of religion or the supposed service of God was reprehensible. Yet it is a problem both ancient and modern.

In recent times, terrorism has become a serious concern to all well-meaning people. The cowardice and cruelty of those who would murder innocent and unarmed people without regard to age, sex, or condition, cannot be excused under any code of conduct known to civilized people. That such conduct should ever be undertaken in the name of religion is wholly incomprehensible to the rational mind. Unfortunately, that kind of distorted thinking is not limited to the late 1900s nor to non-Christian peoples.

On December 14, 1763, fifty-seven armed men from frontier townships gathered before dawn on the edge of a small Indian village in Lancaster, Pennsylvania. The Indians, twenty in number (seven men, five women, and eight children), were the remnants of the Conestogo Indian tribe. The Conestogos were a peaceful people living on friendly terms with their neighbors and completely uninvolved with the Indian wars then taking place on the frontier. Franklin knew them all by name and age, and appears to have been intimately acquainted with each of them.

On a signal, the men attacked the village, and finding only three old men, two women, and one boy, murdered and scalped them. Returning to the village later in the day, the remaining Indians were terrified by the scene which greeted them and sought asylum from the Governor of Pennsylvania. They were, accordingly, placed in a work house for safety. Two days after Christmas, on the 27th of December, fifty of the men returned, broke into the workhouse, and murdered the remaining defenseless Indians—men, women and children. They then "mounted horses, huzzaed in triumph, as if they had gained a great victory, and rode off unmolested." Incensed, Franklin wrote a piece calling for the apprehension and punishment of the murderers. Among other things, he wrote:

> There are some (I am ashamed to hear it) who would extenuate the enormous wickedness of these actions by saying: "The inhabitants of the frontiers are exasperated with the murder of their relations by the enemy Indians in the present war." It is possible; but though this might justify their going out into the woods to seek for those enemies and avenge upon them those murders, it can

never justify their turning into the heart of the country to murder their friends.

If an Indian injures me, does it follow that I may revenge that injury on all Indians? It is well known that Indians are of different tribes, nations, and languages as well as the white people. In Europe, if the French, who are white people, should injure the Dutch, are they to revenge it on the English, because they too are white people? The only crime of these poor wretches seems to have been that they had a reddish-brown skin and black hair, and some people of that sort, it seems, had murdered some of our relations. If it be right to kill men for such a reason, then should any man with a freckled face and red hair kill a wife or child of mine, it would be right for me to revenge it by killing all the freckled, red-haired men, women, and children I could afterwards anywhere meet with.

But it seems these people think they have a better justification; nothing less than the Word of God. With the scriptures in their hand and mouths they can set at nought that express demand, Thou shalt do no murder, and justify their wickedness by the command given Joshua to destroy the heathen. Horrid perversion of Scripture and of religion! To father the worst of crimes on the God of peace and love! Even the Jews, to whom that particular commission was directed, spared the Gibeonites on account of their faith once given. The faith of this government has been frequently given to those Indians; but that did not avail them with people who despise government.

We pretend to be Christians, and from the superior light we enjoy we ought to exceed heathens, Turks, Sacarens, Moors, Negroes, and Indians in the knowledge and practice of what is right. I will endeavor to show, by a few examples from books and history, the sense those people had of such actions.[2]

After then relating several examples of protection afforded to strangers, to guests, to the helpless, and to prisoners by non-

Christian peoples, including barbarians at war, Franklin concluded:

> O, ye unhappy perpetrators of this horrid wickedness! reflect a moment on the mischief ye have done, the disgrace ye have brought on your country, on your religion and your Bible, on your families and children. Think on the destruction of your captivated countryfolks (now among the wild Indians) which probably may follow, in resentment of your barbarity! Think on the wrath of the United Five Nations, hitherto our friends, but now, provoked by your murdering one of their tribes, in danger of becoming our bitter enemies. Think of the mild and good government you have so audaciously insulted; the laws of your king, your country, and your God, that you have broken; the infamous death that hangs over your heads; for justice, though slow, will come at last. All good people everywhere detest your actions. You have imbrued your hands in innocent blood; how will you make them clean? The dying shrieks and groans of the murdered will often sound in your ears. Their specters will sometimes attend you, and affright even your innocent children. Fly where you will, your conscience will go with you. Talking in your sleep shall betray you; in the delirium of a fever you yourselves shall make your own wickedness known.[3]

It is easy to understand how repugnant these acts must have been to a person who believed, "the most acceptable service of God, is doing good to man."

In Franklin's letters to family and friends over the years may be found a delightful and inspiring exposition of ways in which we might serve God by doing good to man.

IT IS RIGHT TO BE SOWING GOOD SEED

Near the end of his life, Benjamin wrote to a friend in England:

When we can sow good seed we should, however, do it, and wait, when we can do no better, with patience, nature's time for their sprouting. Some lie many years in the ground, and at length certain favorable seasons or circumstances bring them forth with vigorous shoots and plentiful productions.[4]

Franklin wrote the following words of encouragement to a friend who had fallen under criticism for his scientific experiments:

One would think that a man so laboring disinterestedly for the good of his fellow creatures, could not possibly by such means make himself enemies; but there are minds who cannot bear that another should distinguish himself even by greater usefulness; and, though he demands no profit, nor any thing in return but the good will of those he is serving, they will endeavor to deprive him of that, first, by disputing the truth of his experiments, then their utility; and, being defeated there, they finally dispute his right to them, and would give the credit of them to a man that lived three thousand years ago, or at three thousand leagues' distance, rather than to a neighbor, or even a friend. *Go on, however, and never be discouraged.* Others have met with the same treatment before you, and will after you. *And, whatever some may think and say, it is worth while to do men good, for the self-satisfaction one has in the reflection.*[5]

In a letter to his wife, Franklin expressed his philosophy of doing good in such a noble vein as to render the mere reading of it an inspiring experience.

God is very good to us both in many respects. Let us enjoy his favors with a thankful and cheerful heart; and, as we can make no direct return to him, show our sense of his goodness to us by continuing to do good to our fellow creatures, without regarding the returns they make us, whether good or bad. For they are all his

*children, though they sometimes be our enemies. The
friendships of this world are changeable, uncertain,
transitory things; but his favor, if we can secure it, is an
inheritance for ever. I am, my dear Debby, your ever
loving husband.*[6]

A specific application of this philosophy is contained in a
letter to a gentleman who had applied to him for assistance:

Dear Sir: I received yours of the 15th instant, and the
memorial it enclosed. The account they give of your
situation grieves me. I send you herewith a bill for ten
louis d'ors. I do not pretend to give such a sum; I only
lend it to you. When you shall return to your country
with a good character, you cannot fail of getting into
some business that will in time enable you to pay all
your debts. *In that case, when you meet with another
honest man in similar distress, you must pay me by
lending this sum to him; enjoining him to discharge the
debt by a like operation when he shall be able, and shall
meet with another opportunity.* I hope it may thus go
through many hands before it meets with a knave that
will stop its progress. This is a trick of mine for doing a
deal of good with a little money. I am not rich enough to
afford much in good works, and so am obliged to be
cunning and make the most of a little.[7]

REPAYING DEBTS NOT CONFERRING FAVORS:

While there are those who might debate theologically the
relative importance of faith and works to one's salvation, from a
practical point of view, the benefits of Franklin's perspective
should be self-evident. He did not suppose we could merit
heaven by good works. Rather, by good works he hoped to
express his appreciation for God's many blessings to him. He
felt that would be a more useful and beneficial expression of his
love for God than mere words alone. In other words, his wish
was not to get something, but to give something.

To his sister, Jane Mecom, Benjamin wrote:

Dearest Sister Jenny:

I took your admonition very kindly, and was far from being offended at you for it. If I say any thing about it to you, it is only to rectify some wrong opinions you seem to have entertained of me; and this I do only because they give you some uneasiness, which I am unwilling to be the cause of. You express yourself as if you thought I was against the worshipping of God, and doubt that good works would merit heaven; which are both fancies of your own, I think, without foundation. *I am so far from thinking that God is not to be worshipped, that I have composed and wrote a whole book of devotions for my own use; and I imagine there are few if any in the world so weak as to imagine that the little good we can do here can merit so vast a reward hereafter.*

There are some things in your New England doctrine and worship, which I do not agree with; but I do not therefore condemn them, or desire to shake your belief or practice of them. We may dislike things that are nevertheless right in themselves. I would only have you make me the same allowance and have a better opinion both of morality and your brother. Read the pages of Mr. Edward's late book, entitled *Some Thoughts concerning the Present Revival of Religion in New England*, from 367 to 375, *and when you judge of others, if you can perceive the fruit to be good, don't terrify yourself that the tree may be evil*; but be assured it is not so, for you know who has said, "Men do not gather grapes of thorns and figs of thistles."[8]

In 1758, from London, he wrote to her again on the same subject:

Our cousin Jane Franklin, daughter of our uncle John, died about a year ago. We saw her husband, Robert Page, who gave us some old letters to his wife from uncle Benjamin. In one of them, dated Boston, July 4,

1723, he writes that your uncle Josiah has a daughter
Jane, about twelve years old, a good-humored child. So
keep up your character, and don't be angry when you
have no letters. In a little book he sent her, called *None
but Christ*, he wrote an acrostic on her name, which for
namesake's sake, as well as the good advice it contains,
I transcribe and send you, viz.:

> Illuminating from on high,
> And shining brightly in your sphere,
> Ne'er faint, but keep a steady eye,
> Expecting endless pleasures there.
>
> Flee vice as you'd a serpent flee;
> Raise *faith* and *hope* three stories higher,
> And let Christ's endless love to thee
> Ne'er cease to make thy love aspire.
>
> Kindness of heart by words express,
> Let your obedience be sincere,
> In prayer and praise your God address,
> Nor cease, till he can cease to hear.

After professing truly that I had a great esteem and
veneration for the pious author, permit me a little to play
the commentator and critic on these lines. The meaning
of three stories higher seems somewhat obscure. You are
to understand, then, that faith, hope, and charity have
been called the three steps of Jacob's ladder, reaching
from earth to heaven; our author calls them stories,
likening religion to a building, and these are the stories
of the Christian edifice. Thus improvement in religion is
called building up and edification. Faith is, then, the
ground floor; hope is up one pair of stairs. My dear
beloved Jenny, don't delight so much to dwell, in those
lower rooms, but get as fast as you can into the garret,
for in truth the best room in the house is charity. For my
part, I wish the house was turned upside down; it is so
difficult (when one is fat) to go up stairs; and not only

so, but I imagine hope and faith may be more firmly
built upon charity, than charity upon faith and hope.
However that may be, I think it the better reading to
say—

Raise faith and hope one story higher

Correct it boldly, and I'll support the alteration; for,
when you are up two stories already, if you raise your
building three stories higher you will make five in all,
which is two more than there should be, you expose
your upper rooms more to the winds and storms; and,
besides, I am afraid the foundation will hardly bear
them, unless indeed you build with such light stuff as
straw and stubble, and that, you know, won't stand fire.
Again, where the author says—

Kindness of heart by words express,

strike out words, and put in deeds. The world is too full
of compliments already. They are the rank growth of
every soil, and choke the good plants of benevolence
and beneficence; nor do I pretend to be the first in this
comparison of words and actions to plants; you may
remember an ancient poet, whose works we have all
studied and copied at school long ago:

A man full of words and not deeds
Is like a garden full of weeds.

It is a pity that good works, among some sorts of
people, are so little valued, and good words admired in
their stead; I mean seemingly pious discourses, instead
of humane, benevolent actions. Those they almost put
out of countenance, by calling morality rotten morality,
righteousness ragged righteousness, and even filthy rags.
So much by way of commentary.[9]

Probably nowhere does Franklin express his philosophy of doing good to others more eloquently and completely than in this letter to a friend:

As to the kindness you mention, I wish it could have been of more service to you. But if it had, the only thanks I should desire is, that you would always be equally ready to serve any other person that may need your assistance, and so let good offices go around, for mankind are all of a family.
For my own part, when I am employed in serving others, I do not look upon myself as conferring favors, but as paying debts. In my travels and since my settlement I have received much kindness from men, to whom I shall never have any opportunity of making the least direct return, and numberless mercies from God, who is infinitely above being benefited by our services. *These kindnesses from men I can therefore only return on their fellowmen; and I can only show my gratitude for those mercies from God, by a readiness to help his other children and my brethren.* For I do not think that thanks and compliments though repeated weekly, can discharge our real obligations to each other, and much less those to our Creator.
You will see in this my notion of good works, that I am far from expecting (as you suppose) that I shall ever merit heaven by them. By heaven we understand a state of happiness, infinite in degree and eternal in duration. I can do nothing to deserve such a reward. He that for giving a draught of water to a thirsty person should expect to be paid with a good plantation, would be modest in his demands, compared with those who think they deserve heaven for the little good they do on earth. Even the mixed, imperfect pleasures we enjoy in this world are rather from God's goodness than our merit; how much more such happiness of heaven. For my own part, I have not the vanity to think I deserve it, the folly to expect it, nor the ambition to desire it; but content myself in submitting to the will and disposal of that God

who made me, who hitherto preserved and blessed me, and in whose fatherly goodness I may well confide, that he will never make me miserable, and that even the afflictions I may at any time suffer shall tend to my benefit.

The faith you mention has doubtless its use in the world; I do not desire it to be diminished, nor would I endeavor to lessen it in any man. But I wish it were more productive of good works than I have generally seen it. I mean real good works, works of kindness, charity, mercy, and public spirit; not holiday-keeping, sermon reading or hearing, performing church ceremonies, or making long prayers, filled with flatteries and compliments, despised even by wise men, and much less capable of pleasing the Deity. The worship of God is a duty, the hearing and reading of sermons may be useful; but if men rest in hearing and praying, as too many do, it is as if a tree should value itself in being watered and putting forth leaves, though it never produced any fruit.

Your great Master thought much less of these outward appearances and professions than many of the modern disciples. He preferred the doers of the word to the mere hearers; the Son that seemingly refused to obey his father and yet performed his command, to him that professed his readiness but neglected the work; the heretical but charitable Samaritan, to the uncharitable though orthodox priest and sanctified Levite; and those who gave food to the hungry, drink to the thirsty, raiment to the naked, entertainment to the stranger, and relief to the sick, etc., though they never heard of his name, he declares shall in the last day be accepted, when those who cry Lord, Lord, who value themselves on their faith, though great enough to perform miracles, but have neglected good works, shall be rejected. He professed that he came not to call the righteous but sinners to repentance; which implied his modest opinion that there were some in His time so good that they need not hear even him for improvement.[10]

THE SOUL IS IMMORTAL 8

Hope is a virtue of inestimable worth. With it, all things are possible; without it, all is lost. Hope is the mainspring of action in all intelligent beings. It is hope that gives us the courage to venture something new and the patience to persist in something difficult. It is hope that makes another day worth living, another problem worth solving, another opportunity worth taking. To hope may be attributed the perpetuation of the species, for it is in hope that we bring forth our own, nurture them through youth, and send them forth into a hostile and dangerous world to do the same. From a child learning to walk to the olympic sprinter, from slave to master, from midwife to surgeon, from male to female, from young to old, from one culture to another, hope is the magnet that pulls us forward, giving focus to thought, purpose to action, and meaning to existence.

To those who observe with concern the inequities and injustices of this world; to those who are burdened with sorrows; and to those who see larger purpose to life than the mortal experience alone; the hope of a future state is a "powerful regulator" of both thought and action. Promising relief to the oppressed, justice to the oppressor, and ample reward to all who do good, the expectation of a better world is an immense source of courage and strength to all who embrace it. This very hope, was to Franklin, an important source of encouragement in his darkest hours.

Through his private correspondence with family and friends, we can learn Franklin's views on immortality and how the expectation of a better world yet to come provided him comfort in times of trial and gave added purpose to his earthly endeavors.

A COMFORTABLE BELIEF

At the age of 29, Franklin published his essay "On True Happiness", of which this insight was a part:

> Nothing but an indifference to the things of this world, and entire submission to the will of Providence here, and a well-grounded expectation of happiness hereafter, can give us a true satisfactory enjoyment of ourselves.[1]

Seventeen years later he wrote to his sister and her husband:

> After all, having taken care to do what appears to be for the best, we must submit to God's providence, which orders all things really for the best.[2]

At the time of John Franklin's death, Benjamin wrote the following letter of consolation to the daughter of his brother's second wife:

> I condole with you. We have lost a most dear and valuable relation. *But it is the will of God and nature that these mortal bodies be laid aside when the soul is to enter into real life.* This is rather an embryo state, a preparation for living. A man is not completely born until he be dead. Why then should we grieve that a new child is born among the immortals, a new member added to their happy society?
> We are spirits. That bodies should be lent us, while they can afford us pleasure, assist us in acquiring knowledge, or in doing good to our fellow creatures, is a kind and benevolent act of God. When they become unfit for these purposes, and afford us pain instead of pleasure, instead of an aid become an incumberance, and

answer none of the intentions for which they were given,
it is equally kind and benevolent that a way is provided
by which we may get rid of them. Death is that way. We
ourselves, in some cases, prudently choose a partial
death. A mangled painful limb which cannot be restored
we willingly cut off. He who plucks out a tooth parts
with it freely, since the pain goes with it; and he who
quits the whole body, parts at once with all pains and
possibilities of pains and diseases which it was liable to
or capable of making him suffer.

Our friend and we were invited abroad on a party of
pleasure, which is to last for ever. His chair was ready
first, and he is gone before us. We could not all
conveniently start together; and why should you and I be
grieved at this, since we are soon to follow, and know
where to find him? Adieu.[3]

In 1782, during the height of the revolutionary war and nearly
twenty years after the massacre of the Conestogo Indians,
Franklin was again to grieve over another massacre of innocent
Indians by frontiersmen, this time the Moravians. He wrote to a
friend:

My Old and Dear Friend: A letter written by you to M.
Bertin, *Ministre d Etat*, containing an account of the
abominable murders committed by some of the frontier
people on the poor Moravian Indians, has given me
infinite pain and vexation. *The dispensations of
Providence in this world puzzle my weak reason; I
cannot comprehend why cruel men should have been
permitted thus to destroy their fellow creatures.* Some of
the Indians may be supposed to have committed sins, but
one cannot think the little children had committed any
worthy of death. Why has a single man in England,
[King George] who happens to love blood and to hate
Americans, been permitted to gratify that bad temper by
hiring German murderers, and, joining them with his
own, to destroy in a continued course of bloody years
near one hundred thousand human creatures, many of

them possessed of useful talents, virtues, and abilities, to which he has no pretension? It is he who has furnished the savages with hatchets and scalping-knives, and engages them to fall upon our defenseless farmers and murder them with their wives and children, paying for their scalps, of which the account kept in America already amounts, as I have heard, to near *two thousand*!

Perhaps the people of the frontiers, exasperated by the cruelties of the Indians, have been induced to kill all Indians that fall into their hands without distinction; so that even these horrid murders of our poor Moravians may be laid to his charge. And yet this man lives, enjoys all the good things this world can afford, and is surrounded by flatterers, who keep even his conscience quiet by telling him he is the best of princes! *I wonder at this, but I cannot therefore part with the comfortable belief of a Divine Providence; and the more I see the impossibility, from the number and extent of his crimes, of giving equivalent punishment to a wicked man in this life, the more I am convinced of a future state, in which all that here appears to be wrong shall be set right, all that is crooked made straight.* In this faith let you and me, my dear friend, comfort ourselves; it is the only comfort, in the present dark scene of things that is allowed us.

I shall not fail to write to the government of America, urging that effectual care may be taken to protect and save the remainder of those unhappy people.

Since writing the above, I have received a Philadelphia paper, containing some account of the same horrid transaction, a little different, and some circumstances alleged as excuses or palliations, but extremely weak and insufficient. I send it to you enclosed. With great and sincere esteem, I am ever, my dear friend, yours most affectionately.[4]

To a friend who lost her mother he wrote:

> I condole with you on the death of the good old lady,
> your mother. Separations of this kind from those we
> love are grievous; but it is the will of God that such
> should be the nature of things in this world. All that ever
> were born are either dead or must die. It becomes us to
> submit and to comfort ourselves with the hope of a
> better life and more happy meeting hereafter.[5]

At the age of seventy-nine, Franklin expressed the following
sublime sentiments in a letter to a close friend:

> You see I have some reason to wish that, in a future
> state, I may not only be as well as I was, but a little
> better. And I hope it; for I, too, with your poet, trust in
> God. And when I observe that there is great frugality as
> well as wisdom in his works, since he has been evidently
> sparing both of labor and materials, for by the various
> inventions of propagation he has provided for the
> continual peopling his world with plants and animals,
> without being at the trouble of new creations; and by the
> natural reduction of compound substances to their
> original elements, capable of being employed in new
> compositions, he has prevented the necessity of creating
> new matter; so that the earth, water, air, and perhaps
> fire, which, being compounded from wood do when the
> wood is dissolved, return, and again become air, earth,
> fire, and water, —I say that *when I see nothing an-
> nihilated, and not even a drop of water wasted, I cannot
> suspect the annihilation of souls, or believe that he will
> suffer the daily waste of millions of minds ready made
> that now exist, and put himself to the continual trouble
> of making new ones.* Thus finding myself to exist in the
> world, I believe I shall, in some shape or other, always
> exist; and, with all the inconveniences human life is
> liable to, I shall not object to a new edition of mine;
> hoping, however, that the *eratta* of the last may be
> corrected.[6]

Then in 1787, just three years before his death, Franklin expressed this hope to a friend in England:

I often think with great pleasure on the happy days I passed in England with my and your learned and ingenious friends, who have left us to join the majority in the world of spirits. Every one of them now knows more than all of us they have left behind. *It is to me a comfortable reflection, that, since we must live forever in a future state, there is a sufficient stock of amusement in reserve for us, to be found in constantly learning something new to eternity, the present quantity of human ignorance infinitely exceeding that of human knowledge.* Adieu, my dear friend, and believe me, in whatever world, yours most affectionately.[7]

FRANKLIN'S FORMULA FOR SUCCESSFUL LIVING
NUMBER THREE

We stand at the crossroads,
each minute,
each hour,
each day,
making choices.

We choose
the thoughts
we allow ourselves to think,
the passions
we allow ourselves to feel,
and the actions
we allow ourselves to perform.

Each choice
is made in the context
of whatever value system
we've selected
to govern our lives.

In selecting that value system,
we are,
in a very real way,
making the most important choice
we will ever make.

Those who believe there is one God
who made all things
and who governs the world by his Providence
will make many choices different
from those who do not.

Those who hold in reverence
that being who gave them life
and worship Him through
adoration,
prayer,
and thanksgiving
will make many choices different
from those who do not.

Those who believe
that mankind are all of a family
and that the most acceptable
service of God
is doing good to man
will make many choices different
from those who do not.

Those who believe
in a future state
in which
all that is wrong here
will be made right
will make many choices different
from those who do not.

Those who subscribe
to the morals of Jesus
will make many choices different
from those who do not.

Since the foundation of all happiness
is thinking rightly,
and since correct action
is dependent on correct opinion,
we cannot be too careful
in choosing the value system
we allow to govern
our thoughts and actions.

And to know that God governs
in the affairs of men,
that he hears and answers prayers,
and that he is a rewarder of them that
diligently seek Him,
is indeed,
a powerful regulator
of human conduct.

GUIDING PRINCIPLE
NUMBER FOUR

CORRECT ACTION IS DEPENDENT
UPON CORRECT OPINION

Though the problem is more pronounced in some than in others, and while not all will admit to it, no one is exempt from that old bugbear, poor judgment. Invariably and inevitably, all of us sometimes do things we later think foolish and wonder why on earth we ever did them. If this problem were limited to trivial matters, it would be easy to laugh about or, at least, to ignore. Unfortunately, such is not the case. A large share of the serious problems we face in life are the result of poor decisions, either made by ourselves or by others. There are few difficulties we experience in life that were not, in the first instance, avoidable, or for which there are now no remedies.

Fortunately, the problem of poor judgment is amenable to correction, though not without effort. In solving it, there is a useful perspective that may be employed to advantage. It is the recognition that while truth is "things as they really were, as they really are, and as they really will be," we as individuals seldom see things as they really are. Frequently, the lack of adequate information impairs our perceptions. Sometimes we may even resist the knowledge necessary to see a subject in its proper light. It may not square with our preconceptions. It may run counter to our views of self-interest. Often, we simply fail to make the investment necessary to arrive at a correct understanding. Whatever the case, we may be certain that a large share of human difficulties are the result of poor decisions influenced by deficient judgment. Just as a ship may not be effectively be steered with a faulty rudder, so also human behavior can not be properly guided by faulty opinions. It is an unyielding fact of life that correct action is largely impossible without correct opinion.

The process of arriving at a proper understanding of the "nature of things", as Franklin referred to it, is not particularly a mystery. Supposedly, it is the basis of science, though we frequently find men of science ignoring it. First, it begins with a desire and willingness to know the truth about a particular subject. Next, it involves an examination of known information about the subject in which we are interested. Once we have a sufficient base of information, we may then form an hypothesis or opinion about the subject. This hypothesis must then be tested. Appropriate experiments must be conducted and the results measured against our own experience and the experience of others. It is only in this manner that we can arrive at an understanding of truth that we may have any reliance on.

While normally thought of as a process for discovering knowledge in the physical sciences, as we can learn from Franklin, it is an equally valid approach for other aspects of life as well. Scientist in all that he did, Franklin took great pains to make sure that his opinions were "according to the nature of things." Not to do so, he believed, would render him culpable, or blameworthy, for any wrongful acts he might commit.

In his quest for knowledge, Franklin was cautious in trusting the powers of human reason. He had experienced too many situations where reason was made a tool for justification as opposed to one for discovery. To be thought right, he discovered, was sometimes a more compelling ambition than to actually think right. Reason, he discovered, was as easily led by pride and passion as it was by a hunger for truth. Consequently, feeling a need to protect himself from these all too common problems, he developed several techniques and methods designed to help him "think rightly."

HUMAN REASON
AN UNRELIABLE GUIDE

9

Notwithstanding his was one of the most brilliant minds of all time, and his achievements are hardly exceeded by any other person in history, Franklin discovered, through his own experience, that human reason is often an unreliable guide in making choices and decisions. Poor Richard commented from time to time on this human weakness. In the almanac for 1744 he included this little verse:

Of all the Causes which conspire to blind
Man's erring Judgment, and misguide the Mind,
What the weak Head with strongest Biass rules,
Is Pride, *that never-failing Vice of Fools. . . .*

And, as Poor Richard warns in 1754, "*You may sometimes be much in the wrong, in owning your being in the right.*"

The following experiences from Franklin's life provide entertaining reading and useful insight into a problem from which, perhaps, none of us are completely immune.

SO CONVENIENT TO BE A REASONABLE CREATURE!

While still an apprentice for his brother, Benjamin read a book that recommended a vegetable diet. Greatly impressed with the reasons given for recommending the diet, he decided to become a vegetarian. After being a strict vegetarian for about a year, he was rescued when reason again intervened:

> In my first voyage from Boston, being becalmed off Block Island, our people set about catching cod, and hauled up a great many. Hitherto I had stuck to my resolution of not eating animal food, and on this occasion I considered, with my master Tryon, the taking [of] every fish as a kind of unprovoked murder, since none of them had, or ever could do us any injury that might justify the slaughter. All this seemed very reasonable. But I had formerly been a great lover of fish, and, when this came hot out of the frying-pan, it smelt admirably well. I balanced some time between principle and inclination, till I recollected that, when the fish were opened, I saw smaller fish taken out of their stomachs; then thought I, "If you eat one another, I don't see why we mayn't eat you." So I dined upon cod very heartily, and continued to eat with other people, returning only now and then occasionally to a vegetable diet. *So convenient a thing it is to be a reasonable creature, since it enables one to find or make a reason for every thing one has a mind to do.* [1]

LET THIS BE FOR THE INDIANS TO GET DRUNK WITH

The ability to find or make a reason for things we want to do often leads to serious problems. Not uncommonly, what we want to do is opposite of what we ought to do and contrary to our true self-interest. For example, to their way of thinking, some Indians of Benjamin Franklin's day had a very good reason for drinking rum. He learned their reason when, as a member of the Pennsylvania Assembly, he was appointed a commissioner to negotiate a treaty with them.

> A treaty being held with the Indians at Carlisle, the governor sent a message to the House, proposing that they should nominate some of their members, to be

joined with some members of council, as commissioners for that purpose. The House named the speaker (Mr. Norris) and myself; and, being commissioned, we went to Carlisle, and met the Indians accordingly.

As those people are extremely apt to get drunk and, when so, are very quarrelsome and disorderly, we strictly forbade the selling any liquor to them; and when they complained of this restriction, we told them that if they would continue sober during the treaty we would give them plenty of rum when business was over. They promised this and they kept their promise because they could get no liquor, and the treaty was conducted very orderly and concluded to mutual satisfaction. They claimed and received the rum; this was in the afternoon; they were near one hundred men, women, and children, and were lodged in temporary cabins built in the form of a square, just without the town. In the evening, hearing a great noise among them, the commissioners walked out to see what was the matter. We found they had made a great bonfire in the middle of the square; they were all drunk, men and women, quarreling and fighting. Their dark-colored bodies half naked, seen only by the gloomy light of the bonfire, running after and beating one another with firebrands, accompanied by their horrid yellings, formed a scene the most resembling our ideas of hell that could well be imagined; there was no appeasing the tumult, and we retired to our lodging. At midnight a number of them came thundering at our door, demanding more rum, of which we took no notice.

The next day, sensible they had misbehaved in giving us that disturbance, they sent three of their old counselors to make their apology. Their orator acknowledged the fault, but laid it upon the rum; and then endeavored to excuse the rum by saying: "*The Great Spirit, who made all things, made everything for some use, and whatever use he designed anything for, that use it should always be put to. Now, when he made rum, he said 'Let this be for the Indians to get drunk with,' and it must be so.*" And, indeed, if it be the design

of Providence to extirpate these savages in order to
make room for cultivators of the earth, it seems not
improbable that rum may be the appointed means. It has
already annihilated all the tribes who formerly inhabited
the sea-coast.[2]

REASONS THAT WERE NO REASONS AT ALL

In 1764, Franklin was appointed for a second time to go to
England as a representative of Pennsylvania, to attempt to
resolve problems the colony was experiencing with the Penn
family and with Parliament. About once a year, during the
eleven years he was there, he made excursions into the country
for health purposes. The following is an account of one
particularly frustrating trip:

> Soon after I left you in that agreeable society at
> Bromley, I took the resolution of making a trip with Sir
> John Pringle into France. We set out on the 28th past.
> All the way to Dover we were furnished with post-
> chaises, hung so as to lean forward, the top coming
> down over one's eyes, like a hood, as if to prevent one's
> seeing the country, which being one my great pleasures,
> I was engaged in perpetual disputes with the
> innkeepers, ostlers, and postilions, about getting the
> straps taken up a hole or two before, and let down as
> much behind, they insisting that the chaise leaning
> forward was an ease to the horses, and that the contrary
> would kill them. I suppose the chaise leaning forward
> looks to them like a willingness to go forward, and that
> its hanging back shows reluctance. *They added other*
> *reasons, that were no reasons at all, and made me, as*
> *upon a hundred other occasions, almost wish that*
> *mankind had never been endowed with a reasoning*
> *faculty, since they know so little how to make use of it,*
> *and so often mislead themselves by it, and that they had*
> *been furnished with a good sensible instinct instead of*
> *it.*[3]

HOW LONG A TRUTH MAY BE KNOWN

The human ego is a funny thing. Many times it behaves in a manner so as to destroy the very thing it seeks to preserve. For example, no one likes to be wrong, but sometimes the fear of being wrong can actually prevent our ever being right. As the following experiences from Franklin's life demonstrate, even the most learned sometimes still have a lot to learn about being teachable.

As early as 1750, Franklin had conducted experiments and written about the benefits of lightning rods in protecting dwellings from the effects of lightning. By 1767, when the following was written, hundreds of homes and public buildings in both America and Europe had benefited from lightning rods. Both Franklin's experiments and those of others had been broadly reported in scientific publications. Yet, notwithstanding all that was known about lightning rods, he had occasion to write these telling observations to a close friend:

> It is perhaps not so extraordinary that unlearned men, such as commonly compose our church vestries, should not yet be acquainted with, and sensible of the benefits of metal conductors in averting the stroke of lightning, and preserving our houses from its violent effects, or that they should be still prejudiced against the use of such conductors, *when we see how long even philosophers, men of extensive science and great ingenuity, can hold out against the evidence of new knowledge that does not square with their pre-conceptions*; and how long men can retain a practice that is conformable to their prejudices, and expect a benefit from such practice though constant experience shows its inutility.[4]

Nineteen years later, at the conclusion of a letter discussing the effects of lead poisoning, Franklin wrote the following melancholy observation:

This my dear friend, is all I can recollect on the
subject. *You will see by it, that the opinion of this
mischievous effect from lead is at least above sixty years
old; and you will observe with concern how long a
useful truth may be known and exist, before it is
generally received and practiced on.*[5]

Known as the NIH factor (Not Invented Here), this phenom-
enon is still prevalent in many technological environments to-
day. Not limited to scientific matters, however, we find that even
those who have been entrusted with great public responsibility
are sometimes not receptive to information that runs counter to
their opinions. In 1774, Franklin reported to the Speaker of the
Massachusetts Assembly, Thomas Cushing:

*When I see that all petitions and complaints of
grievances are so odious to government, that even the
mere pipe which conveys them becomes obnoxious, I am
at a loss to know how peace and union are to be
maintained or restored between the different parts of the
empire.* Grievances cannot be redressed unless they are
known; and they cannot be known but through
complaints and petitions. If these are deemed affronts,
and the messengers punished as offenders, who will
henceforth send petitions? And who will deliver them?
It has been thought a dangerous thing in any state to stop
up the vents of griefs. Wise governments have therefore
generally received petitions with some indulgence, even
when but slightly founded. Those who think themselves
injured by their rulers are sometimes, by a mild and
prudent answer, convinced of their error. But where
complaining is a crime, hope becomes despair.[6]

It is probably safe to assume that there is no person capable of
thought and action who has not experienced the problems of
unsound thinking, at one time or another, both in personal
misjudgments and in the mistakes of others. Fortunately, if the
desire exists, there are ways to make corrections for this all too
human deficiency.

HOW TO THINK RIGHTLY 10

Accepting the possibility that we may be prone to err in our thinking and that unimproved reason is a blind guide to human behavior, we are compelled to ask; "What can can be done to assure that we do think rightly?"

In his famous "War Inevitable" speech, Patrick Henry said, ". . . .whatever anguish of spirit it may cost, I am willing to know the whole truth." Franklin realized that the only remedy to faulty reasoning was to seek out and be receptive to truth, no matter how painful it might be. He knew, as should we all, that without correct information, correct opinion is impossible. Throughout his life, Franklin did everything he could to assure that his opinions were based on correct information. Specifically, Franklin realized that the inability to recognize truth and acknowledge error was more often an emotional deficiency than an intellectual one. He therefore cultivated the ability to deal with the problem emotionally as well as intellectually. He also recognized that human ignorance is infinitely greater than human wisdom and that the only way to reduce the difference is by asking questions. He therefore consciously developed an active curiosity, obtained all the information he could in forming his opinions, and devised a process to help him sort out the pros and cons of various alternatives in making important decisions.

RECOGNIZING TRUTH - ACKNOWLEDGING ERROR

If we were to have an enemy who wanted to destroy us, and if it were within his power to implant within us a device designed to so confuse our thinking and overexcite our emotions as to render us incapable of coherent and intelligent action, he could hardly do better than to implant a device akin to that part of our self-esteem that insists on being right, even when we are wrong. For the most part, this problem is probably one of misplaced values. Franklin's solution to it was a frontal attack.

First, he placed more value on understanding the truth than he did on what people thought of him. As one of the conditions for membership in the Junto, he required an affirmative answer to the following question:

> Do you love truth for truth's sake, and will you
> endeavor impartially to find and receive it yourself, and
> communicate it to others?[1]

That he observed this practice himself is evident in the following extract from a detailed letter to a philosophic correspondent, concerning the sea and lightning:

> These thoughts, my dear friend, are many of them
> crude and hasty; and if I were merely ambitious of
> acquiring some reputation in philosophy, I ought to keep
> them by me till corrected and improved by time and
> farther experience. But since even short hints and
> imperfect experiments in any new branch of science,
> being communicated, have oftentimes a good effect in
> exciting the attention of the ingenious to the subject, and
> so become the occasion of more exact disquisition and
> more complete discoveries, you are at liberty to
> communicate this paper to whom you please; *it being of*
> *more importance that knowledge should increase than*
> *that your friend should be thought an accurate*
> *philosopher.*[2]

Second, Franklin avoided investing so much of himself into an idea that he could not give it up. An example is contained in this sage observation to a friend in England:

> *By calmly discussing rather than warmly disputing, the truth is most easily obtained.* I shall give my opinion freely, as it is asked, hoping it may prove the true one; and promising myself, if otherwise, the honor at least of acknowledging frankly my error, and of being thankful to him who kindly showed it to me.[3]

Third, Franklin recognized the benefits of a straightforward admission of error when called for. Thus he wrote concerning a theory of his own:

> The questions you ask about the pores of glass, I cannot answer otherwise than that I know nothing of their nature; and *suppositions, however ingenious, are often mere mistakes. My hypothesis*, that they were smaller near the middle of the glass, —too small to admit the passage of electricity, which could pass through the surface till it came near the middle, *was certainly wrong.* For soon after I had written that letter, I did, in order to confirm the hypothesis (which indeed I ought to have done before I wrote it), make an experiment. I ground away five sixths of the thickness of the glass from the side of one of my phials, expecting that, the supposed denser part being so removed, the electric fluid might come through the remainder of the glass, which I had imagined more open; *but I found myself mistaken.* The bottle charged as well after the grinding as before. I am now as much as ever at a loss to know how or where the quantity of electric fluid on the positive side of the glass is disposed of.[4]

Fourth, as so well expressed in another portion of the letter just quoted, Franklin was not too proud to acknowledge there were things he simply didn't know. Concerning the results of an experiment he did not understand he wrote:

The fact is singular. *You require the reason; I do not know it.* Perhaps you may discover it, and then you will be so good as to communicate it to me. *I find a frank acknowledgment of one's ignorance is, not only the easiest way to get rid of a difficulty, but the likeliest way to obtain information, and therefore I practise it; I think it an honest policy. Those who affect to be thought to know every thing, and so undertake to explain every thing, often long remain ignorant of many things that others could and would instruct them in, if they appeared less conceited.*[5]

DEVELOPING AN ACTIVE CURIOSITY

Given the amount of knowledge available, it is amazing the lack of curiosity most of us have about the world in which we live. Yet, if one wishes to possess opinions that are more nearly "according to the nature of things," there are few things of greater value than an active curiosity. Although some individuals seem to be more naturally endowed with this gift than others, it is one that can be acquired and, in the process, provide a great deal of enjoyment and entertainment.

An example of how curiosity increased both Franklin's fund of knowledge and his enjoyment of life is contained in this delightful account of a whirlwind:

Being in Maryland, riding with Colonel Tasker, and some other gentlemen, to his country-seat, where I and my son were entertained by that amiable and worthy man with great hospitality and kindness, we saw, in the vale below us, a small whirlwind beginning in the road, and showing itself by the dust it raised and contained. . . . When it passed by us, its smaller part near the ground appeared no bigger than a common barrel; but, widening upwards, it seemed, at forty or fifty feet high, to be twenty or thirty feet in diameter. The rest of the company stood looking after it; *but, my curiosity being stronger*, I followed it, riding close by its side, and observed its licking up, in its progress, all the dust that was under its smaller part. As it is a common opinion that a shot, fired through a water-spout, will break it, I tried to break this little whirlwind by striking my whip frequently through, but without any effect. Soon after, it quitted the road and took into the woods, growing every moment larger and stronger, raising, instead of dust, the old dry leaves with which the ground was thick covered, and making a great noise with them and the branches of the trees, bending some tall trees round in a circle swiftly and very surprisingly, though the progressive motion of the whirl was not so swift but that a man on foot might have kept pace with it; but the circular motion was amazingly rapid. By the leaves it was now filled with, I could plainly perceive that the current of air they were driven by moved upwards in a spiral line; and when I saw the passing whirl continue entire, after leaving the trunks and bodies of large trees which it had enveloped, I no longer wondered that my whip had no effect on it in its smaller state. I accompanied it about three quarters of a mile, till some limbs of dead trees, broken off by the whirl, flying about and falling near me, made me more apprehensive of danger; and then I stopped, looking at the top of it as it went on, which was visible, by means of the leaves contained in it, for a very great height above the trees. Many of the leaves, as they got loose from the upper and widest part, were scattered in the wind; but so great was their height in the air, that they appeared no bigger than flies. . . . Upon my asking Colonel Tasker if such whirlwinds were common in Maryland, he answered pleasantly: "No, not at all common; but we got this on purpose to treat Mr. Franklin." And a very high treat it was.[6]

FORMING OPINIONS

In forming his opinions, Franklin was careful to do his homework.

Getting The Facts

As exemplified in this letter to a young friend who had asked him a question, he made sure he had the facts before attempting to answer a question:

> Your first question, "What is the reason water at this place, though cold at the spring, becomes warm by pumping? it will be most prudent in me to forbear attempting to answer, till, by a more circumstantial account, you assure me of the fact. I own I should expect that operation to warm, not so much the water pumped as the person pumping. The rubbing of dry solids together has been long observed to produce heat; but the like effect has never yet, that I have heard, been produced by the mere agitation of fluids, or friction of fluids with solids. . . .
>
> The prudence of not attempting to give reasons before one is sure of the facts, I learned from one of your sex, who, as Selden tells us, being in company with some gentlemen that were viewing and considering something which they called a Chinese shoe, and disputing earnestly about the manner of wearing it, and how it could possibly be put on, put in her word, and said modestly, Gentlemen, are you sure it is a shoe? Should not that be settled first?"[7]

Acquiring Knowledge

As a young man, Benjamin sought knowledge out of the best books he could obtain. Given the fact that he had little opportunity for a formal education, only two years in a grammar school, and that he was later to be considered, "the first man of letters in America", this aspect of his life is not only a tribute to his own resourcefulness, but an example of what can be done if a person has the desire and is willing to make the effort. In the following brief excerpts from his autobiography, he shares with us his experience:

From a child, I was fond of reading, and all the money that ever came into my hands was ever laid out in books. Pleased with the *Pilgrim's Progress*, my first collection was of John Bunyan's works in separate little volumes. .... *Plutarch's Lives*. .... I read abundantly, and I still think that time spent to great advantage. There was also a book of De Foe's, called an *Essay on Projects*, and another of Dr. Mather's, called *Essays to do Good*, which perhaps gave me a turn of thinking that had an influence on some of the principle future events of my life.[8]

At age 12, Benjamin was apprenticed as a printer to his brother James which opened new opportunities for learning to him:

I now had access to better books. An acquaintance with the apprentices of booksellers enabled me sometimes to borrow a small one, which I was careful to return soon and clean. I often sat up in my room reading the greatest part of the night, when the book was borrowed and to be returned in the morning, lest it should be missed or wanted.[9]

Later in life, after being instrumental in helping to establish a lending library in Philadelphia, he was to derive great personal benefit from it:

This library afforded me the means of improvement by constant study, for which I set apart an hour or two each day, and thus repaired in some degree the loss of the learned education my father once intended for me. Reading was the only amusement I allowed myself. I spent no time in taverns, games or frolicks of any kind. . . .[10]

Seeking Out The Opinions of Others

In addition to seeking knowledge from books, Benjamin sought out the ideas of those whose opinions he respected. The most conspicuous method he used for amplifying his own knowledge was to organize some of his most ingenious friends into the mutual-improvement club they called the Junto. At each meeting, among other questions, they were to ask:

> Have you read over these queries this morning, in order to consider what you might have to offer the Junto touching any one of them? viz:
> 1. Have you met with any thing in the author you last read, remarkable or suitable to be communicated to the Junto, particularly in history, morality, poetry, physic, travels, mechanic arts, or other parts of knowledge?
> 2. What new story have you lately heard agreeable for telling in conversation?
> 3. Hath any citizen in your knowledge failed in his business lately, and what have you heard of the cause?
> 4. Have you heard lately of any citizen's thriving well, and by what means?[11]

There were twenty-four such questions.

Additionally, throughout his adult life, Benjamin carried on an active correspondence with a wide range of people. This correspondence was a continual source of useful information to him, as well as a way of testing his own ideas on others. The following is but one brief example:

> Sir: I shall be very willing and ready, when you think proper to publish your piece on gravitation, to print it at my own expense and risk. If I can be the means of communicating anything valuable to the world, I do not always think of gaining, nor even of saving, by my business; but a piece of that kind, as it must excite the curiosity of all the learned, can hardly fail of bearing its own expense.
>   . . . .As to your pieces on Fluxions and the different species of matter, it is not owing to reservedness that I have not yet sent you my thoughts; but because I cannot please myself with them, having had no leisure yet to digest them. If I was clear that you are anywhere

mistaken, I would tell you so, and give you my reasons with all freedom, as believing nothing I could do would be more obliging to you. *I am persuaded you think, as I do, that he who removes a prejudice or an error from our minds contributes to their beauty, as he would do that of our faces who should clear them of a wart or a wen.* [12]

Evaluating Information

The popularity or unpopularity of an idea may have nothing at all to do with its merit. Furthermore, it is entirely possible, on occasion, for wise people to be wrong and for foolish people to be right. Franklin recognized, for example, that it is important to evaluate information independent from the source because even from foolish people it is possible to learn worth-while things. Although probably not of his own authorship, the following instructive poem was printed in Poor Richard:

Altho' thy teacher act not as he preaches,
Yet ne'ertheless, if good, do what he teaches;
Good counsel, failing men may give, for why?
He that's aground knows where the shoal doth lie.
My old friend Berryman oft, when alive,
Taught others thrift, himself could never thrive.
Thus like the whetstone, many men are wont
To sharpen others while themselves are blunt. [13]

As an aid to learning, Benjamin suggested to his young friend, Mary Stevenson, that she keep a pen and dictionary handy when reading for understanding:

I would advise you to read with a pen in your hand,
and enter in a little book short hints of what you find
that is curious, or that may be useful; for this will be the
best method of imprinting such particulars in your
memory, where they will be ready, either for practice on
some future occasion, if they are matters of utility, or at
least to adorn and improve your conversation, if they are

rather points of curiosity. And as many of the terms of
science are such, as you cannot have met with in your
common reading, and may therefore be unacquainted
with, I think it would be well for you to have a good
dictionary at hand, to consult immediately when you
meet with a word you do not comprehend the precise
meaning of. This may at first seem troublesome and
interrupting; but it is a trouble that will daily diminish,
as you will daily find less and less occasion for your
dictionary, as you become more acquainted with the
terms; and in the mean time you will read with more
satisfaction, because with more understanding.[14]

As shown by this example of notes, written in the margins of a
report on impressing seamen by a Judge Foster, Franklin was
one who followed his own advice. Obviously he did not agree
with the Judge's sophistry:

JUDGE FOSTER: "The only question at present is,
whether mariners, persons who have freely chosen a sea-
faring life, persons whose education and employment
have fitted them for the service, and inured them to it,
whether such persons may not be legally pressed into the
service of the crown, whenever the public safety
requireth it; *ne quid detrimenti respublica capiat.*
"For my part, I think they may. I think the crown hath
a right to command the service of these people whenever
the public safety calleth for it. The same right that it
hath to require the personal service of every man able to
bear arms in case of a sudden invasion or formidable
insurrection. The right in both cases is founded on one
and the same principle, the necessity of the case in order
to the preservation of the whole."
FRANKLIN'S NOTE: "The conclusion here, from the
whole to a part, does not seem to be good logic. When
the personal service of every man is called for, there the
burthen is equal. Not so, when the service of part is
called for, and others excused. If the alphabet should
say, Let us all fight for the defense of the whole; that is

equal, and may therefore be just. But if they should say,
Let A, B, C, and D go and fight for us, while we stay at
home and sleep in whole skins; that is not equal, and
therefore cannot be just.[15]

Throughout the article, Franklin challenged the Judge's position by writing notes in the margin:

JUDGE FOSTER: "And as for the mariner himself, he,
when taken into the service of the crown, only changeth
masters for a time; his service and employment continue
the very same, with this advantage, that the dangers of
the sea and enemy are not so great in the service of the
crown as in that of the merchant.
FRANKLIN'S NOTE: "These are false facts. His
service and employment are not the same. Under the
merchant, he goes in an unarmed vessel not obliged to
fight, but only to transport merchandise. In the king's
service, he is obliged to fight, and to hazard all the
dangers of battle. Sickness on board the king's ships is
also more common and more mortal. The merchant's
service too he can quit at the end of a voyage, not the
king's. Also the merchant's wages are much higher.[16]

At the conclusion of the article, the Judge justified the length
of his paper by the importance of the topic. Franklin felt there
were other reasons:

The author could not well have made his argument
shorter. *It required a long discourse to throw dust in the
eyes of common sense, confound all our ideas of right
and wrong, make black seem white, and the worse
appear the better opinion.*[17]

Moral Algebra

In making difficult decisions, Dr. Franklin employed a technique he called moral algebra. He explained this technique in a letter to a close friend:

In the affair of so much importance to you, wherein you ask my advice, I cannot, for want of sufficient premises, advise you what to determine; but, if you please, I will tell you how. When these difficult cases occur, they are difficult, chiefly because, while we have them under consideration, all the reasons *pro* and *con* are not present to the mind at the same time; but sometimes one set present themselves, and at other times another, the first being out of sight. Hence the various purposes or inclinations that alternately prevail, and the uncertainty that perplexes us.

To get over this, my way is, to divide half a sheet of paper by a line into two columns; writing over the one *pro,* and over the other *con*; then during three or four days' consideration, I put down under the different heads short hints of the different motives, that at different times occur to me, *for* or *against* the measure. When I have thus got them all together, in one view, I endeavor to estimate their respective weights; and, where I find two (one on each side) that seem equal, I strike them both out. If I find a reason *pro* equal to some two reasons *con*, I strike out the three. If I judge some two reasons, *con* equal to three reasons *pro*, I strike out the five; and thus proceeding I find at length where the balance lies; and if, after a day or two of farther consideration, nothing new that is of importance occurs on either side, I come to a determination accordingly. And though the weight of reasons cannot be taken with the precision of algebraic quantities, yet, when each is thus considered separately and comparatively, and the whole lies before me, I think I can judge better, and am less likely to make a rash step; and in fact I have found great advantage from this kind of equation, in what may be called *moral* or *prudential algebra*.[18]

In summary, Benjamin Franklin utilized a number of methods to help him acquire accurate information, properly evaluate it, and arrive at a correct understanding of "the nature of things."

FRANKLIN'S FORMULA FOR SUCCESSFUL LIVING
NUMBER FOUR

Like a giant jigsaw puzzle,
the truths of human existence
are assembled together,
piece by piece.

It is not given to any one person
to see the whole picture
or to hold all of the pieces.

Only by actively searching
and freely sharing
are we able to piece together
some understanding
of the meaning of life
and the world in which we live

To aid us
in piecing together this puzzle
we have been given the gift of reason;
the ability to gather, organize, and evaluate
each piece of information and
to see where, and how, it fits
in the overall picture.

Reason, of itself, however,
is insufficient
for piecing together
the puzzle.

Sometimes, reason may join forces
with passion or appetite
to create designs of our own choosing,
but which do not fit well
in the larger picture.

Sometimes, we may enlist
reason to support
preconceptions of our own,
but which make it more difficult
to see the true picture.

Unfortunately, reason may be used
to fabricate as well as find
pieces to the puzzle—
pieces that will not stand the
tests of reality
or close inspection.

Since all of us are subject
to the tendency to make or create
reasons for things we want to do
and to reject new knowledge
that does not agree
with our preconceptions,
Benjamin Franklin developed
several safeguards
to protect him
against these tendencies.

First,
he cultivated
the ability to recognize truth
and acknowledge error
by placing more value on truth
than on personal feelings or ambitions,
by never investing so much in an idea
that he could not give it up if wrong,
by being willing to admit to error, and
by being willing to acknowledge ignorance
of things unknown.

Second,
he consciously developed
an active curiosity.

Third,
he made sure he was on solid
ground in forming his opinions
by getting the facts necessary
to form those opinions,
by continuously seeking to
acquire new knowledge through study,
by seeking out the opinions of others,
even those whose opinions
might differ from his,
by evaluating all information
on the basis of its merits, and
by being as objective as possible
in making important decisions.

With this approach
Franklin was able to see
a larger share of the picture,
and therefore,
able to act out his part
with greater clarity and capability
than most who travel
the paths of mortal life.

GUIDING PRINCIPLE NUMBER FIVE

MOTIVES OF PERSONAL GAIN TEND TO BE OPPOSITE OF ONE'S TRUE SELF-INTEREST

There is a bias that tends to infect human thinking in a similar manner to the way in which a virus infects the body. Just as a virus attacks the body and beats down all resistance, this bias can also be all consuming and overcome all our natural mental restraints and protections. It is called the "I Want Bias." The "I Want Bias" predisposes us to look favorably on any argument in support of what we want and, at the same time, to discount every argument that runs contrary to what we want. The problem is that sometimes we may want things that would not be good for us if we got them, and other times, we may not want things that would really be in our best interest if we did have them.

The effects of this bias, which so often are misguided perceptions of self-interest, may be observed almost daily, in the news and in our own associations. Examples include, a highly successful attorney being disbarred from his profession for misappropriation of a clients funds, a senior government official on trial for misuse of his office, a mother leaving her young and their father to follow the lure of temporary pleasure, a teenager risking years of mental and physical incapacitation by injecting his arm with a drug that can, at best, provide moments of pleasure and will most likely be followed by hours of depression and anguish. The examples are so prevalent it is hard to understand why so many, so often, repeat the same mistakes. The only answer can be that judgment becomes clouded and reason becomes dysfunctional when self-gratification becomes a primary motivation in choosing and pursuing one's goals. Whenever we begin to feel ourselves strongly pulled by perceptions of self-interest or personal gain, it may be recognized as a warning sign of approaching danger and of the need to exercise caution in our judgments.

If we were to list the causes of human suffering in the world, we would find that most are either self-inflicted or imposed by others of our own kind. It would seem that many people so little understand the true source of happiness that, notwithstanding their constant search for it, they are never able to find it. Is it not true that virtually all misery and unhappiness resulting from oppression, war, crime, licentiousness, chemical dependency, abusiveness, domestic discord and every other form of human misconduct are the direct offspring of misguided perceptions of self-interest on the part of someone somewhere?

To avoid or overcome the perpetual problems caused by miscalculations of self-interest, Benjamin Franklin chose the course of modesty and disinterestedness as a means for progressing. True, Franklin wanted to succeed in his business and he worked hard to do so. True, he wanted to make contributions to science and politics, and he worked hard to do so. But in all his endeavors, his objectives were to *do* good and to *be* useful as opposed to getting rich or gathering honors. His emphasis was on contributing rather than obtaining; on giving, rather than receiving. Strange as it may seem, it was Franklin's "indifference to the things of this world" that unleashed his full creative powers. Unencumbered by warped perspectives of private ambition, Franklin was free to be his own man. He was able to focus his full energies on those things he perceived to be truly useful and worthwhile. In doing so, he left behind a legacy of discoveries, inventions, and contributions that have blessed millions of lives. Just as important, however, this approach also enabled him to live a personally satisfying life; productive, because he always had something interesting to do, and enjoyable, because he was never troubled by those ambitions and jealousies so disturbing to the human mind.

HOW LITTLE
WE KNOW OUR OWN GOOD

11

I PREVAILED WITH THE CAPTAIN TO PUT ME ASHORE

In his youth, Franklin had several experiences that taught him to be careful in the things he wanted, for when he got them, they weren't always what he expected. The following, as contained in a letter to a close friend, was one of those experiences:

> *All human situations have their inconveniences; we feel those that we find in the present, and we neither feel nor see those that exist in another. Hence we make frequent and troublesome changes without amendment, and often for the worse.*
> In my youth I was passenger in a little sloop descending the river Delaware. There being no wind, we were obliged, when the ebb was spent, to cast anchor and wait for the next. The heat of the sun on the vessel was excessive, the company strangers to me and not very agreeable. Near the river-side I saw what I took to be a pleasant green meadow, in the middle of which was a large shady tree, where, it struck my fancy, I could sit and read (having a book in my pocket) and pass time agreeably till the tide turned. I therefore prevailed with the captain to put me ashore. Being landed, I found the

greatest part of my meadow was really a marsh, in crossing which, to come to my tree, I was up to my knees in mire; and I had not placed myself under its shade five minutes before the mosquitoes, in swarms, found me out, attacked my legs, hands, and face, and made my reading and my rest impossible, so that I returned to the beach and called for the boat to come and take me on board again, where I was obliged to bear the heat I had strove to quit, and also the laugh of the company. Similar cases in the affairs of life have since frequently fallen under my observation.[1]

MUNGO'S EPITAPH

In this delightful letter to a young friend of his, Franklin gives us the opportunity to learn from a squirrel's experience:

To Miss Georgiana Shipley

On the loss of her American squirrel, who, escaping from his cage was killed by a shepherd's dog

London, 26 September, 1772

DEAR MISS: I lament with you most sincerely the unfortunate end of poor MUNGO. Few squirrels were better accomplished; for he had had a good education, had travelled far, and seen much of the world. As he had the honor of being, for his virtues, your favorite, he should not go like common skuggs, without an elegy or epitaph. Let us give him one in the monumental style and measure, which, being neither prose nor verse, is perhaps the properest for grief; since to use common language would look as if we were not affected, and to make rhymes would seem trifling in sorrow.

epitaph

Alas! poor MUNGO!
Happy wert thou hadst thou known
Thy own felicity.
Remote from the fierce bald eagle,
Tyrant of thy native woods,
Thou hadst nought to fear from his piercing talons,
Nor from the murdering gun
Of the thoughtless sportsman.
Safe in thy wired castle
Grimalkin never could annoy thee.
Daily wert thou fed with the choicest viands,
By the fair hand of an indulgent mistress;
But, discontented,
Thou wouldst have more freedom,
Too soon, alas! didst thou obtain it;
And wandering,
Thou art fallen by the fangs of wanton, cruel RANGER!
Learn hence,
Ye who blindly seek more liberty,
Whether subjects, sons, squirrels, or daughters,
That apparent restraint may be real protection,
Yielding peace and plenty
With security.

You see, my dear Miss, how much more decent and
proper this broken style is, than if we were to say, by
way of epitaph:

Here SKUGG
Lies snug
As a bug
In a rug.

And yet perhaps there are people in the world of so little
feeling as to think this would be a good enough epitaph
for poor MUNGO.

If you wish, I shall procure another to succeed him; but perhaps you will now choose some other amusement.

Remember me affectionately to all the good family and believe me ever your affectionate friend,[2]

HE AIMS AT GLORY

In an essay on government, published in the Pennsylvania Gazette in 1736, Franklin illustrated how the path to presumed glory is often, instead, the path to dishonor and contempt.

A wicked prince imagines that the crown receives a new lustre from absolute power, whereas every step he takes to obtain it is a forfeiture of the crown.

His conduct is as foolish as it is detestable; he aims at glory and power and treads the path that leads to dishonor and contempt; he is a plague to his country, and deceives himself.

During the inglorious reigns of the Stuarts (excepting a part of Queen Anne's), it was a perpetual struggle between them and the people. . . . What were the consequences? One lost his life on the scaffold, another was banished. The memory of all of them stinks in the nostrils of every true lover of his country; and their history stains with indelible blots the English annals.

The reign of Queen Elizabeth furnishes a beautiful contrast. All her views centered in one object, which was the public good. She made it her study to gain the love of her subjects, not by flattery or little soothing arts, but by rendering them substantial favors. It was far from her policy to encroach on their privileges; she augmented and secured them.[3]

GOD GRANT THEY MAY BE AS BLIND

During the French and Indian war, many members of the New York Assembly became so embroiled in party politics they were seriously hindered in their ability to prosecute the war. Franklin wrote to a friend:

SIR: The violent party spirit that appears in all the
votes, etc., of your Assembly seems to me to be
extremely unseasonable as well as unjust, and to
threaten mischief not only to yourselves but to your
neighbors. It begins to be plain that the French may reap
great advantages from your divisions. *God grant they
may be as blind to their own interest and as negligent of
it as the English are of theirs.*[4]

On November 20, 1772, the inhabitants of Boston approved a
report expressing their grievances with the British government.
Franklin published that report in England, prefacing it with a
clear and concise description of the adverse effects of the stamp
act. It provides an excellent example of the natural results of
misguided self-interest. In their perverse attempt to tax tea, over
which they had a monopoly, Britain not only lost their entire
trade in tea with the colonies, but spent enormous sums in an
ineffectual attempt to enforce the tax, for which they received
only a pittance in return. Ultimately, their persistence cost them
all participation in American commerce. In part, he wrote:

The colonies had from their first settlement been
governed with more ease than perhaps can be equaled by
any instance in history; of dominions so distant. Their
affection and respect for this country, while they were
treated with kindness, produced an almost implicit
obedience to the instructions of the Prince, and even to
acts of the British Parliament; though the right of
binding them by a legislature in which they were
unrepresented, was never clearly understood. That
respect and affection produced a partiality in favor of
everything that was English; whence their preference of
English modes and manufactures; their submission to
restraints on the importation of foreign goods, which
they had but little desire to use; and the monopoly we so
long enjoyed of their commerce, to the great enriching
of our merchants and artificers.
The mistaken policy of the Stamp Act first disturbed
this happy situation. . . . and combinations were entered

into throughout the continent to stop trading with Britain till those duties should be repealed. All were accordingly repealed but one, *the duty on tea.* This was reserved (professedly so) as a standing claim and exercise of the right assumed by Parliament of laying such duties. . . .

The Dutch, the Danes, and French took this opportunity thus offered them by our imprudence, and began to smuggle their teas into the plantations. At first this was something difficult; but at length, as all business is improved by practice, it became easy. . . .

It is supposed that at least a million of Americans drink tea twice a day, which, at the first cost here, can scarce be reckoned at less than half a guinea a head per annum. *This market, that in the five years which have run on since the act passed, would have paid two million five hundred thousand guineas for tea alone, into the coffers for the Company, we have wantonly lost to foreigners.*

Meanwhile, it is said the duties have so diminished, that the whole remittance of the last year amounted to no more than the pitiful sum of eighty-five pounds, for the expense of some hundred thousands, in armed ships and soldiers, to support the officers. Hence the tea, and the other India goods, which might have been sold in America, remain rotting in the Company's warehouses; while those of foreign ports are known to be cleared by the American demand. Hence, in some degree, the Company's inability to pay their bills; the sinking of their stock, by which millions of property have been annihilated; the lowering of their dividend, whereby so many must be distressed; the loss to government of the stipulated four hundred thousand pounds a year, which must make a proportionable reduction in our savings towards the discharge of our enormous debt; and hence, in part, the severe blow suffered by credit in general, to the ruin of many families; the stagnation of business in Spitalfields and Manchester, through want of vent for their goods; with other future evils, which, as they cannot, from the numerous and secret connections in general commerce, easily be foreseen, can hardly be avoided.[5]

Franklin wrote much about the folly of war. In addition to the inhumanity of war, he thought it:

> . . . .wrong in point of human prudence, for whatever advantage one nation would obtain from another, whether it be part of their territory, the liberty of commerce with them, free passage on their river, etc., it would be much cheaper to purchase such advantage with ready money, than to pay the expense of acquiring it by war. . . . It seems to me that if statesmen had a little more arithmetic, or were more accustomed to calculation, wars would be much less frequent.[6]

As a case in point, here is an excerpt from a letter he wrote to a friend in England during the war:

> *Britain at the expense of three millions, has killed one hundred and fifty yankees this campaign, which is twenty thousand pounds a head*; and at Bunker's Hill she gained a mile of ground, half of which she lost again by our taking post on Ploughed Hill. *During the same time sixty thousand children have been born in America.* From these data his mathematical head will easily calculate the time and expense necessary to kill us all, and to conquer our whole territory.[7]

To Lord Howe, commander of the british fleet in America, Franklin wrote about the foolishness of Britain's excesses:

> By punishing those American governors who have created and fomented the discord; rebuilding our burnt towns, and repairing as far as possible the mischiefs done us, [Great Britain] might yet recover a great share of our regard, and the greatest part of our growing commerce, with all the advantage of that additional strength to be derived from a friendship with us; but I

know too well her abounding pride and deficient
wisdom, to believe she will ever take such salutary
measures. *Her fondness for conquest, as a warlike
nation, her lust of dominion as an ambitious one, and
her thirst for a gainful monopoly as a commercial one
(none of them legitimate causes of war), will all join to
hide from her eyes every view of her true interests, and
continually goad her on in those ruinous distant expedi-
tions, so destructive both of lives and treasure, that must
prove as pernicious to her in the end, as the crusades
formerly were to most of the nations of Europe.*[8]

WHATEVER IS PRUDENT THEY WILL OMIT

During the war, France planned an attack on England that was
never executed. In its planning stages, Franklin wrote Lafayette:

You ask my opinion what conduct the English will
probably hold on this occasion, and whether they will
not rather propose a negotiation for a peace. *I have but
one rule to go by in judging of those people, which is,
that whatever is prudent for them to do they will omit,
and what is most imprudent to be done they will do it.*
This like other general rules, may sometimes have its ex-
ceptions; but I think it will hold good for the most part,
at least while the present ministry continues, or, rather,
while the present madman has the choice of ministers.[9]

That Franklin was unpressed with Benedict Arnold's perceptions of self-interest is evident in another letter to Lafayette:

Your friends have heard of your being gone against
the traitor Arnold, and are anxious to hear of your
success, and that you have brought him to punishment.
Enclosed is a copy of a letter from his agent in England,
captured by one of our cruisers, and by which the price
or reward he received for his treachery may be guessed
at. *Judas sold only one man, Arnold three millions.
Judas got for his one man thirty pieces of silver, Arnold*

*not a halfpenny a head. A miserable bargain! especially
when one considers the quantity of infamy he has
acquired to himself and entailed on his family.*

To which he added:

The English are in a fair way of gaining still more
enemies; they play a desperate game. Fortune may favor
them, as it sometimes does a drunken dicer; but by their
tyranny in the East, they have at length roused the
powers there against them, and I do not know that they
have in the West a single friend. If they lose their India
commerce (which is one of their present great supports),
and one battle at sea, their credit is gone, and their
power follows. *Thus empires, by pride, folly, and
extravagance, ruin themselves like individuals.*[10]

Near the end of the war, Franklin wrote to John Adams:

SIR: I received yours of the 10th instant, and am of
opinion, with you, that the English will evacuate New
York and Charleston; as the troops there, after the late
resolutions of Parliament, must be useless, and are
necessary to defend their remaining islands, where they
have not at present more than three thousand men. *The
prudence of this operation is so obvious, that I think
they can hardly miss it; otherwise, I own that, considering their conduct for several years past, it is not reasoning consequentially to conclude they will do a thing
because the doing of it is required by common-sense.*[11]

If we are capable of learning from the lessons of history, these
classic examples of misguided self-interest may teach us much.
The misguided self-interest of a young man led him into a marsh
full of mosquitoes. The misguided self-interest of a king and his
ministers led to the shedding of much blood and the breaking
apart of the British empire. One inconsequential, the other
monumental. Both incompatible with success and happiness.

THE POWER
OF SELFLESSNESS

12

MODESTY AND DISINTERESTEDNESS:
A MEANS FOR PROGRESSING

In Business

Benjamin Franklin had larger objectives in his business than simply making money or acquiring reputation. In his autobiography, Franklin revealed some of his motives for publishing *Poor Richard's Almanac*, and his newspaper, *The Pennsylvania Gazette*. As can be seen, profit was not his sole objective and there were things he was not willing to do for money.

In 1732 I first published my Almanack, under the name of Richard Saunder; it was continued by me about twenty-five years, commonly called Poor Richard's Almanack. *I endeavored to make it both entertaining and useful*, and it accordingly came to be in such demand, that I reaped considerable profit from it, vending annually near ten thousand. And observing that it was generally read, scarce any neighborhood in the province being without it, *I considered it as a proper vehicle for conveying instruction among the common people, who bought scarcely any other books*; I therefore filled all the little spaces that occurred between the remarkable days in the calendar with proverbial sentences, chiefly such as inculcated industry and frugality, as the means of procuring wealth, and thereby securing virtue; it being more difficult for a man in want, to act always honestly, as, to use here one of those proverbs, *it is hard for an empty sack to stand upright.* . . .

I considered my newspaper, also, as another means of communicating instruction, and in that view frequently reprinted in it extracts from the Spectator and other moral writers; and sometimes published little pieces of my own, which had been first composed for reading in our Junto. Of these are a Socratic dialogue, tending to prove that, whatever might be his parts and abilities, a vicious man could not properly be called a man of sense; and a discourse on self-denial, showing that virtue was not secure till its practice became a habitude, and was free from the opposition of contrary inclinations. These may be found in the papers about the beginning of 1735.

In the conduct of my newspaper, I carefully excluded all libeling and personal abuse which is of late years become so disgraceful to our country. Whenever I was solicited to insert any thing of that kind, and the writers pleaded, as they generally did, the liberty of the press, and that a newspaper was like a stage-coach in which anyone who would pay had a right to a place, my answer was, that I would print the piece separately if desired and the author might have as many copies as he pleased to distribute himself, but that *I would not take upon me to spread his detraction; and that, having contracted with my subscribers to furnish them with what might be either useful or entertaining, I could not fill their papers with private altercation,* in which they had no concern, without doing them manifest injustice.[1]

In Science

During the years Franklin was engaged in electrical experiments and writing papers on the benefits of pointed lightning rods, a scientist in France, Abbe Nollet, personally attacked Franklin and his ideas in several publications. Franklin never publicly answered these attacks or attempted to defend his ideas. Some years later, he had the satisfaction of writing his son:

> Last night I received a letter from Paris, of which the enclosed is an extract, acquainting me that I am chosen [a foreign member] of the Royal Academy there. . . . *This mark of respect* from the first academy in the world, which Abbe Nollet, one of its members, took so much pains to prejudice against my doctrines, *I consider as a kind of victory without ink shed, since I never answered him.* I am told he has but one of his sect now remaining in the Academy. All the rest, who have in any degree acquainted themselves with electricity, are, as he call them, *Franklinists.*[2]

Franklin expressed his guiding philosophy to a friend:

> I have never entered into any controversy in defense of my philosophical opinions; I leave them to take their chance in the world. If they are *right*, truth and experience will support them; if *wrong,* they ought to be refuted and rejected. Disputes are apt to sour one's temper, and disturb one's quiet. *I have no private interest in the reception of my inventions by the world, having never made, nor proposed to make, the least profit by any of them.*[3]

In Politics

Prior to the outbreak of the Revolutionary War, Franklin was in England as a representative of Pennsylvania and several other colonies. At the time, he also jointly held the position of Deputy Postmaster General for North America with William Hunter. It was a position to which he had risen over the course of nearly forty years. When Franklin and Hunter first took the position the service was not profitable, but through considerable effort and even some personal loans, they were eventually able to turn it around. Hunter was ill during much of this period and most of the responsibility fell on Franklin. Notwithstanding the important contributions he had made to the postal service, however, the British ministers, displeased with Franklin's efforts as a representative of the Colonies to repeal the stamp act and other measures unpopular with the colonists, threatened to deprive him of his postmaster's position. By way of assurance to his sister, Franklin wrote of his unwillingness to compromise his beliefs to retain his position:

> Possibly they may still change their minds, and remove me; but no apprehension of that sort will, I trust, make the least alteration in my political conduct. *My rule, in which I have always found satisfaction, is, never to turn aside in public affairs through views of private interest; but to go straight forward in doing what appears to me right at the time, leaving the consequences with Providence.* What in my younger days enabled me more easily to walk upright was, that I had a trade, and that I knew I could live upon little; and thence (never having had views of making a fortune) I was free from avarice, and contented with the plentiful supplies my business afforded me. And now it is still more easy for me to preserve my freedom and integrity, when I consider that I am almost at the end of my journey, and therefore need less to complete the expense of it; and that what I now possess, through the blessing of God, may, with tolerable economy, be sufficient for me (great misfortunes excepted), though I should add nothing more to it by any office or employment whatsoever.[4]

Near the end of the war with England, giving in for a time to failing health and the criticism of some of his enemies in America, Franklin submitted his resignation to Congress. When his resignation was refused, he wrote the following to a colleague in Holland:

> The Congress have done me the honor to refuse accepting my resignation, and insist on my continuing in

their service till the peace. I must therefore buckle again to business, and thank God that my health and spirits are of late improved. I fancy it may have been a double mortification to those enemies you have mentioned to me, that I should ask as a favor what they hoped to vex me by taking from me; and that I should nevertheless be continued. But this sort of consideration should never influence our conduct. *We ought always to do what appears best to be done, without much regarding what others may think of it.* I call this continuance an honor, and I really esteem it to be a greater than my first appointment, when I consider that all the interest of my enemies, united with my own request were not sufficient to prevent it.[5]

In Personal Affairs

Benjamin's willingness to ignore the provocations of others extended beyond mere words. To those of us who live in a litigious society, it is refreshing to learn of a great man who, during the course of his entire life, refrained from initiating a single lawsuit against any other person.

Rev'd Sir: I am favored with yours of the 27th instant,. . . . It will be a pleasure to me to find it so, that I may have no occasion to have recourse to the law, which is so disagreeable a thing to me, that *through the whole course of my life I have never entered an action against any man. . . .* I think with you that they are a weak and foolish people; but there seems no small mixture of knavery with their folly.[6]

On another occasion, Benjamin wrote to a friend who was still smarting from some criticism of a piece he had written:

For my part, I know not when I have read a piece that has more affected me; so noble and just are the sentiments, so warm and animated the language, yet, *as censure from your friends may be of more use, as well*

as more agreeable, to you than praise, I ought to
mention that I wish you had omitted, not only the
quotation from the *Review*, which you are now justly
dissatisfied with, but those expressions of resentment
against your adversaries, in pages 65 and 79. *In such
cases, the noblest victory is obtained by neglect and by
shining on.*[7]

MODESTY OF EXPRESSION

There may be some to whom modesty of expression is not an
important thing. However, to those who wish to have influence
with people of wisdom and judgment and who have ambitions of
larger consequence than their own self-interests, modesty of
expression is a more effective means of communication than any
other. Franklin tells us why in his autobiography.

While I was intent on improving my language, I met
with an English grammar. . . . at the end of which there
were two little sketches of the arts of rhetoric and logic,
the latter finishing with a specimen of a dispute in the
Socratic method, and soon after I procured Xenophon's
Memorable Things of Socrates, wherein there are many
instances of the same method. I was charmed with it,
adopted it, dropt my abrupt contradiction and positive
argumentation, and put on the humble inquirer and
doubter. . . . I continued this method some few years, but
gradually left it, retaining only the habit of expressing
myself in terms of modest diffidence, never using, when
I advanced any thing that may possibly be disputed, the
words *certainly, undoubtedly*, or any others that give an
air of positiveness to an opinion, but rather say, *I
conceive or apprehend a thing to be so and so; it
appears to me, or I imagine it to be so; or it is so, if I am
not mistaken*. This habit, I believe, has been of great
advantage to me when I have had occasion to inculcate
my opinions, and persuade men into measures that I
have from time to time engaged in promoting; and, as
the chief ends of conversation are to *inform* or to be

informed, to *please* or to *persuade*, I wish well-meaning, sensible men would not lessen their power of doing good by a positive, assuming manner, that seldom fails to disgust, tends to create opposition, and to defeat every one of those purposes for which speech was given to us, —to wit, giving or receiving information or pleasure. For, if you would inform, a positive and dogmatical manner in advancing your sentiments may provoke contradiction and prevent a candid attention. If you wish information and improvement from the knowledge of others, and yet at the same time express yourself as firmly fixed in your present opinions, modest, sensible men, who do not love disputation, will probably leave you undisturbed in the possession of your error. And by such a manner, you can seldom hope to recommend yourself in pleasing your hearers, or to persuade those whose concurrence you desire. [8]

IMPROPRIETY OF PUTTING ONESELF FORTH

It is said that there is no limit to the things a person may accomplish if he is not concerned about who gets the credit. If the objective is of considerable benefit to those who may be in need, the sacrifice of one's vanity may be a small thing when compared to the internal satisfaction of having accomplished something of significant worth.

At the time I established myself in Pennsylvania, there was not a good bookseller's shop in any of the colonies to the southward of Boston. . . . Those who loved reading were obliged to send for their books from England; the members of the Junto had each a few. We had left the alehouse, where we first met, and hired a room to hold our club in. I proposed that we should all of us bring our books to that room, where they would not only be ready to consult in our conferences, but become a common benefit, each of us being at liberty to borrow such as he wished to read at home. This was accordingly done, and for some time contented us.

Finding the advantage of this little collection, I proposed to render the benefit from books more common, by commencing a public subscription library. I drew a sketch of the plan and rules that would be necessary, and got a skillful conveyancer, Mr. Charles Brockden, to put the whole in form of articles of agreement to be subscribed, by which each subscriber engaged to pay a certain sum down for the first purchase of books, and an annual contribution for increasing them. So few were the readers at that time in Philadelphia, and the majority of us so poor, that I was not able, with great industry, to find more than fifty persons, mostly young tradesmen, willing to pay down for this purpose forty shillings each, and ten shillings per annum. . . .

The objections and reluctances I met with in soliciting the subscriptions, made me soon feel the impropriety of presenting one's self as the proposer of any useful project, that might be supposed to raise one's reputation in the smallest degree above that of one's neighbors, when one has need of their assistance to accomplish the project. I therefore put myself as much as I could out of sight, and stated it as a scheme of a number of friends, who had requested me to go about and propose it to such as they thought lovers of reading. In this way my affair went on more smoothly, and I ever after practiced it on such occasions; and, from my frequent successes, can heartily recommend it. The present little sacrifice of your vanity will afterwards be amply repaid. If it remains a while uncertain to whom the merit belongs, some one more vain than yourself will be encouraged to claim it, and then even envy will be disposed to do you justice by plucking those assumed feathers, and restoring them to their right owner.[9]

Perhaps few of us think of selflessness, moderation, and modesty as qualities of power. But Franklin's life provides much insight as to how these qualities can unleash a person's full potential and increase his influence for good.

FRANKLIN'S FORMULA FOR SUCCESSFUL LIVING
NUMBER FIVE

Only dimly perceiving their own good
and failing to consider the good of others,
there are many who,
in the pursuit of happiness,
rush headlong down
the path to self-destruction.

History records
the stories of Kings
who aimed at power and glory,
but tread paths that led to
dishonor and contempt.

Current news media records
the stories of talented and gifted people
who aimed at wealth and fame,
but tread paths that led to
shame and imprisonment.

Personal experience records
the stories of friends and loved ones
who aimed at pleasure,
but tread paths that led to
inconstancy and dissipation.

All human experience unites to demonstrate
that if, to obtain something we want,
we become involved in
foolish, unworthy, or harmful activities,
we forfeit all claim to
the clearness of mind,
and the freedom of action,
necessary to significant accomplishment.

To overcome the all-too-natural
tendencies toward misguided self-interest,
Benjamin Franklin chose
to live usefully rather than die rich,
to contribute more than he gained,
to do what he believed right,
rather than what he thought popular,
to put the public good ahead
of his private interests, and
to never engage in activities
harmful to others, even
at the cost of income
or position.

In working with other people
he also chose
to avoid personal disputes,
to be modest in expressing his ideas,
to avoid putting himself forward,
and to give maximum credit to others
even at the sacrifice of his own vanity.

By thus choosing a course
of modesty and indifference
Franklin was able to free himself
from those passions, and
self-serving ambitions
that so often
distract the mind,
distort the vision,
and distress the soul.

With that freedom
he was able
to concentrate
the full force
of his talents and energies
on useful and worthwhile endeavors
of immense value to the whole human race.

GUIDING PRINCIPLE
NUMBER SIX

WHERE TRUTH AND HONESTY ARE WANTING, EVERYTHING IS WANTING

> This above all: to thine own self be true,
> And it must follow, as the night the day,
> Thou canst not then be false to any man.
> William Shakespeare

Benjamin Franklin's own insight into the above thought was, "We can never choose evil, as evil, but under the appearance of an imaginary good." The very nature of dishonesty is that we must first practice it on ourselves before we can ever practice it on anyone else. If we do not discover some "good reasons" to justify our wicked deeds, we will be overcome by pangs of conscience. Being reasonable creatures and unwilling to suffer the discomforts of guilt, we often find it easier to lie to ourselves than to be honest with others.

To be honest means to be worthy of trust, to be credible and reliable. One who is honest is said to possess integrity or to possess sound moral principles. Integrity is the quality of being whole or complete. Thus those who are dishonest are, by definition, unsound. They are neither whole nor complete. The process of rejecting or repressing truth so undermines the foundation of human relationships and weakens the mortar of intelligent action as to render those who engage in it extremely vulnerable. Being unworthy of trust themselves, they are unable to trust others and are thereby deprived of the joy and comfort of trustworthy friends. There is no place nor any persons among whom the dishonest are wholly safe. Required to live by their wits, they must always be on the defensive and are constantly subject to exposure and ruin. Well did Poor Richard write: *"Vice knows she's ugly, so puts on her Mask."* (1746) and "Craft *must be at charge for clothes, but* Truth *can go naked."* (1747) So, *"Do not do that which you would not have known."* (1736) For, if you would live with ease, then you must, *"Do what you ought and not what you please."* (1734) To Poor Richard, the reason was simple, *"He that doth what he should not, shall feel what he would not."* (1754)

Benjamin Franklin concluded early in life that "truth, sincerity and integrity in dealings between man and man were of the utmost importance to the felicity of life."[1] In planning to write *The Art of Virtue,* it was Franklin's design to show:

> *that vicious acts are not hurtful because they are forbidden, but forbidden because they are hurtful,* the nature of man alone considered; *that it was,* therefore, *everyone's interest to be virtuous who wished to be happy even in this world;* and I should, from this circumstance (there being always in the world a number of rich merchants, nobility, states, and princes, who have need of honest instruments for the management of their affairs, and such being rare), have endeavored to convince young persons that no qualities were so likely to make a poor man's fortune as of probity and integrity.[2]

WHERE TRUTH
IS NOT

13

I PLEADED THE USEFULNESS

Benjamin learned early from his father the importance of being honest:

> There was a salt-marsh that bounded part of the mill-pond, on the edge of which, at high water, we used to stand to fish for minnows. By much trampling, we had made it a mere quagmire. My proposal was to build a wharf there fit for us to stand upon, and I showed my comrades a large heap of stones, which were intended for a new house near the marsh, and which would very well suit our purpose. Accordingly, in the evening, when the workmen were gone, I assembled a number of my play-fellows, and working with them diligently like so many emmets, sometimes two or three to a stone, we brought them all away and built our little wharf. The next morning the workmen were surprised at missing the stones, which were found in our wharf. Inquiry was made after the removers; we were discovered and complained of; several of us were corrected by our fathers; and, though I pleaded the usefulness of the work, *mine convinced me that nothing was useful which was not honest.*[1]

ON SMUGGLING AND ITS VARIOUS SPECIES

While living in England, Benjamin observed how easy it is for
honorable people to slip into unworthy practices. The following
piece is instructive in reminding us how insidiously little indiscretions erode the foundations of society; for, while large crimes
seldom enjoy broad approval, small crimes may sometimes
become the common practice.

> *Sir: There are many people that would be thought, and
> even think themselves, honest men, who fail nevertheless
> in particular points of honesty; deviating from that
> character sometimes by the prevalence of mode or
> custom, and sometimes through mere inattention; so
> that their honesty is partial only, and not general or
> universal.* Thus one, who would scorn to overreach you
> in a bargain, shall make no scruple of tricking you a
> little now and then at cards; another, that plays with the
> utmost fairness, shall with great freedom cheat you in
> the sale of a horse. *But there is no kind of dishonesty,
> into which otherwise good people more easily and
> frequently fall, than that of defrauding government of its
> revenues* by smuggling when they have an opportunity,
> or encouraging smugglers by buying their goods.
>   I fell into these reflections the other day, on hearing
> two gentlemen of reputation discoursing about a small
> estate, which one of them was inclined to sell and the
> other to buy; when the seller, in recommending the
> place, remarked, that its situation was very advantageous
> on this account, that, being on the seacoast in a
> smuggling country, one had frequent opportunities of
> buying many of the expensive articles used in a family
> (such as tea, coffee, chocolate, brandy, wines, cambrics,
> Brussels laces, French silks, and all kinds of India
> goods), twenty, thirty, and in some articles fifty per cent
> cheaper than they could be had in the more interior
> parts, of traders that paid duty. The other *honest*
> gentleman allowed this to be an advantage, but insisted
> that the seller, in the advanced price he demanded on

that account, rated the advantage much above its value. And neither of them seemed to think dealing with smugglers a practice that an *honest* man (provided he got his goods cheap) had the least reason to be ashamed of.

At a time when the load of our public debt, and the heavy expense of maintaining our fleets and armies to be ready for defense on occasion, make it necessary, not only to continue old taxes, but often to look out for new ones, perhaps it may not be unuseful to state this matter in a light that few seem to have considered it in. . . .

What should we think of a companion who, having supped with his friends at a tavern, and partaken equally of the joys of the evening with the rest of us, would nevertheless contrive by some artifice to shift his share of the reckoning upon others, in order to go off scot-free? If a man who practiced this would, when detected, be deemed and called a scoundrel, what ought he to be called who can enjoy all the inestimable benefits of public society, and yet by smuggling, or dealing with smugglers, contrive to evade paying his just share of the expense, as settled by his own representatives in Parliament, and wrongfully throw it upon his honester and perhaps much poorer neighbors?. . . .

Mean as this practice is, do we not daily see people of character and fortune engaged in it for trifling advantages to themselves? Is any lady ashamed to request of a gentleman of her acquaintance, that when he returns from abroad he would smuggle her home a piece of silk or lace from France or Flanders? Is any gentleman ashamed to undertake and execute the commission? Not in the least. They will talk of it freely, even before others whose pockets they are thus contriving to pick by this piece of knavery.

Among other branches of the revenue, that of the post-office is, by the late law, appropriated to the discharge of our public debt, to defray the expense of the state. None but members of Parliament, and a few public officers, have now a right to avoid, by a frank, the payment of postage. When any letter not written by them

or on their business, is franked by any of them, it is a
hurt to the revenue, an injury which they must now take
the pains to conceal by writing the whole superscription
themselves. And yet such is our insensibility to justice
in this particular, that nothing is more common than to
see, even in reputable company, a *very honest* gentleman
or lady declare his or her intention to cheat the nation of
three pence by a frank, and without blushing apply to
one of the very legislators themselves, with a modest
request, that he would be pleased to become an
accomplice in the crime, and assist in the perpetration.

There are those who by these practices take a great
deal in a year out of the public purse, and put the money
into their own private pockets. If, passing through a
room where public treasure is deposited, a man takes the
opportunity of clandestinely pocketing and carrying off
a guinea, is he not truly and properly a thief? And if
another evades paying into the treasury a guinea he
ought to pay in, and applies it to his own use, when he
knows it belongs to the public as much as that which has
been paid in, what difference is there in the nature of the
crime, or the baseness of committing it?

Some laws make the receiving of stolen goods equally
penal with stealing, and upon this principle, that if there
were no receivers there would be few thieves. Our
proverb too says truly, that *the receiver is as bad as the
thief.* By the same reasoning there would be few
smugglers if there were none who knowingly
encouraged them by buying their goods, we may say that
the encouragers of smuggling are as bad as the
smugglers; and that, as smugglers are a kind of thieves,
both equally deserve the punishment of thievery.[2]

WHAT NAME THE IMPARTIAL READER WILL GIVE

The primary force that drew Benjamin Franklin to the fore-
front of public affairs was his opposition to what he considered
to be oppressive and unjust government. As in most instances of
this kind, those in positions of power, through misguided views

of self-interest, began to abuse the power entrusted to them. Although reluctant to enter into public altercations to defend himself personally, Franklin never hesitated to speak out when he felt the public interest was at stake. Virtually all of the enmity he incurred in public affairs arose because of his opposition to the corruption of others and his unwillingness to become corrupted himself.

The descendants of William Penn, the founder of Pennsylvania, did not share their father's larger views of the colonies and governed the province with self-serving policies. In those days, as the proprietors of Pennsylvania, the Penn family appointed their own governors to oversee the province. Laws in the colony were made by an assembly elected by the people; but, to become effective, they had to be approved by the governor. Being thus placed in a position of considerable power over the colony, successive governors began "to consider any laws they approved as so many jobs for which they ought to be particularly paid."[3] In order to get laws passed, the assembly had to resort to giving the existent governor "presents" at the end of each session. The tensions arising from this form of government led Pennsylvania to submit a petition to the King of England asking the king to revoke the Penn's charter and bring the province directly under his own control. Franklin's contributions to the debate leading to this petition were incisive:

> What name the impartial reader will give this kind of commerce, I cannot say. *To me it appears an extortion of more money from the people*, for that to which they had before an undoubted right, both by the constitution and by purchase; but there was no other shop they could go to for the commodity they wanted, and they were obliged to comply. Time established the custom and made it seem honest; so that our governors, even those of the most undoubted honor, have practiced it.[4]

Referencing minutes from previous sessions of the assembly, Franklin described some transactions in which negotiations of this type had taken place, and presented several instances where governors had required advance assurances of such payments before passing any bills of importance. He then described a secret bond which required Governor Denny to share with the Penn family monies he obtained from the people through this form of extortion. Of this arrangement, Franklin wrote:

> This reservation of the properties they were at that time a little ashamed of, and therefore such bonds were then to be secrets. *But as in every kind of sinning frequent repetition lessens shame and increases boldness*, we find the proprietaries [the Penn family] ten years afterwards openly insisting on these advantages to themselves, *over and above* what was paid to their deputy.[5]

These practices put the assemblies in an awkward position on several occasions. Franklin continued:

> Thus we see the practice of purchasing and paying for laws is interwoven with our proprietary constitution, used in the best of times, and under the best governors. And yet, alas, poor assembly! how will you steer your brittle bark between these rocks? If you pay ready money for your laws, and those laws are not liked by the proprietaries, you are charged with bribery and corruption; if you wait a while before you pay, you are accused of detaining the governor's customary right, and dunned as a negligent or dishonest debtor, that refuses to discharge a just debt.
>
> But Governor Denny's case, I shall be told, differs from all these; for the acts he was induced to pass were, as the Prefacer tells us, "contrary to his duty, and to every tie of honor and justice." *Such is the imperfection of our language, and perhaps of all other languages, that, notwithstanding we are furnished with dictionaries innumerable, we cannot precisely know the import of words, unless we know of what party the man is that uses them.* In the mouth of an assemblyman, or true Pennsylvanian, "contrary to his duty and to every tie of honor and justice," would mean, the governor's long

refusal to pass laws, however just and necessary, for taxing the proprietary estate; a refusal contrary to the trust reposed in the lieutenant-governor by the royal charter; to the rights of the people, whose welfare it was his duty to promote; and to the nature of the contract made between the governor and the governed, when the quick-rents and license fees were established, which confirmed what the proprietaries call our "undoubted right" to necessary laws. But, in the mouth of the proprietaries, or their creatures, "contrary to his duty, and to every tie of justice and honor," means, his passing laws contrary to proprietary instructions and contrary to the bonds he had previously given to observe those instructions, however, that were unjust and unconstitutional; and bonds, that were illegal and void from the beginning.[6]

A PARLIAMENT THAT MUST BE BRIBED

In Franklin's day, it was common practice for members of Parliament in England to bribe voters to vote for them. The investment was generally quite profitable, as it put them in a position where the King, on occasion, would need to bribe them to assure passage of his favorite measures. Such practices were a significant factor leading to the War for Independence and many other problems the British empire experienced at that time.

When Franklin was in London seeking a solution to the growing crisis with England, he had occasion to write to a friend in America:

Mr Beckford has brought in a bill for preventing bribery and corruption in elections, wherein was a clause to oblige every member to swear, on his admission into the House, that he had not directly or indirectly given any bribe to any elector; but this was so universally exclaimed against, as answering no end but perjuring the members, that he has been obliged to withdraw that clause. It was indeed a cruel contrivance of his, worse than the gunpowder plot; for that was only to blow the Parliament up to heaven, this to sink them all down to ____. Mr Thurlow opposed his bill by a long speech. Beckford, in reply, gave a dry hit to the House, that is repeated everywhere. "The honorable gentleman," says he, "in his learned discourse, gave us first one definition of corruption, then he gave us another definition of corruption, and I think he was about to give us a third. *Pray does that gentleman imagine there is any member of this House that does not know what corruption is?"* which occasioned only a roar of laughter, for they are so hardened in the practice, that they are very little ashamed of it.[7]

Three weeks later he elaborated further to this same friend:

The first instance of bribery to be chosen a member, taken notice of on the journals, is no longer ago than Queen Elizabeth's time, when being sent to Parliament was looked upon as a troublesome service, and therefore not sought after. *It is said that such a one, "being a simple man and conceiving it might be of some advantage to him, had given four pounds to the mayor and corporation that they might choose him to serve them in Parliament."*
The price is monstrously risen since that time, for it is now no less than four thousand pounds! It is thought that near two millions will be spent this election; but those who understand figures and act by computation say *the crown has two millions a year in places and pensions to dispose of, and it is well worth while to engage in such a seven years' lottery, though all that have tickets should not get prizes.*[8]

Twelve years later, during the war with England, Franklin wrote from France to a friend in England:

I do not expect that your new Parliament will be either wiser or honester than the last. All projects to procure an honest one, by place bills, etc., appear to me vain and impracticable. *The true cure, I imagine, is to be found only in rendering all places unprofitable, and the king too poor to give bribes and pensions.* Till this is done, which can only be by a revolution (and I think you have not virtue enough left to procure one), your nation will always be plundered and obliged to pay by taxes the plunderers for plundering and ruining.[9]

Four years later, he wrote the same friend on the same subject:

When I think of your present crazy constitution and its diseases, I imagine the enormous emoluments of place [appointments to highly paid positions in government] *to be among the greatest; and while they exist, I doubt whether even the reform of your representation will cure the evils arising from your perpetual factions.* As it seems to be a settled point at present that the minister must govern the Parliament, who are to do everything he would have done, and he is to bribe them to do this, and the people are to furnish the money to pay these bribes, the Parliament appears to me a very expensive machine for government; and I apprehend the people will find out in time that they may as well be governed, and that it will be much cheaper to be governed, by the minister alone, no Parliament being preferable to the present.[10]

During the Constitutional Convention, Franklin gave a speech upon the subject of salaries for federal officers, in which he clearly articulated the harmful effects of large salaries for public officials. The following is a brief excerpt:

Sir, there are two passions which have a powerful influence in the affairs of men. These are *ambition* and *avarice*; the love of power and the love of money. *Separately, each of these has great force in prompting men to action; but when united in view of the same object, they have in many minds the most violent effects. Place before the eyes of such men a post of honor, that shall at the same time be a place of profit, and they will move heaven and earth to obtain it.* The vast number of such places it is that renders the British government so tempestuous. The struggles for them are the true source of all those factions which are perpetually dividing the nation, distracting its councils, hurrying it sometimes into fruitless and mischievous wars, and often compelling a submission to dishonorable terms of peace.

And of what kind are the men that will strive for this profitable preeminence through all the bustle of cabal, the heat of contention, the infinite mutual abuse of parties, tearing to pieces the best of characters? It will not be the wise and moderate, the lovers of peace and good order, the men fittest for the trust. It will be the bold and the violent, the men of strong passion and indefatigable activity in their selfish pursuits. These will thrust themselves into your government, and be your rulers. And these, too, will be mistaken in the expected happiness of their situation; for their vanquished competitors, of the same spirit, and from the same motives, will perpetually be endeavoring to distress their administration, thwart their measures, and render them odious to the people.[11]

Needless to say, Benjamin Franklin could see grave consequences flowing from the wells of dishonest conduct, none of which had the slightest tendency toward human happiness or well being. When those in power engaged in it, oppressive government was the result. When the people engaged in it, a weakened and innervated society was the result.

THE POWER
OF A GOOD CONSCIENCE

14

ATTEMPTS TO BRIBE FRANKLIN

Over the years, Franklin recorded several attempts by English agents to bribe him. His responses were consistent and are priceless in the example they provide.

As a member of the Pennsylvania Assembly, Franklin was active in resisting the policies of Thomas Penn. Shortly after Captain Denny was appointed Governor of Pennsylvania, a dinner was held in which Governor Denny presented Dr. Franklin with a medal from the Royal Society for his work with electricity. After the dinner, Governor Denny took Franklin into a separate room to talk with him privately. Among other things, he said much to Franklin:

> . . . .of the proprietor's good disposition towards the province *and of the advantage it might be to us all, and to me in particular, if the opposition that had been so long continued to his measures was dropt*, and harmony restored between him and the people; in effecting which, it was thought no one could be no more serviceable than myself; *and I might depend on adequate acknowledgments and recompense. . . .*
>
> *My answers were to this purpose; that my circumstances, thanks to God, were such as to make*

proprietary favors unnecessary to me and that, being a member of the Assembly I could not possibly accept of any; that, however, I had no personal enmity to the proprietary, and that, whenever the public measures he proposed should appear to be for the good of the people, no one should espouse and forward them more zealously than myself; my past opposition having been founded on this, that the measures which had been urged were evidently intended to serve the proprietary interest, with great prejudice to that of the people.[1]

LIKE SPITTING IN THE SOUP

In England, as a representative of several colonies, Franklin labored anxiously to avert the impending war. In this role, he was very outspoken as to what changes in English policy would be necessary to avoid the conflict. This time, it was the British ministry who attempted to influence his opinions by offers of reward. Among others, Lord Howe, later Commander of the British Fleet in America, was requested to feel Franklin out and to offer him encouragements to alter his position. The following excerpt from his account of this period shows the subtlety by which such people work:

He expatiated on the infinite service it would be to the nation, and the great merit in being instrumental in so good a work; that he should not think of influencing me by any selfish motive, but certainly I might with reason expect any reward in the power of government to bestow.

This to me was what the French vulgarly call spitting in the soup.[2]

During this tense period Franklin had been asked to stipulate what conditions the colonists might accept in coming to terms with England. Franklin prepared an unofficial response titled *HINTS* containing those items he considered essential to a peaceful settlement. Notwithstanding a total lack of interest in considering any of these proposals, the ministry continued to bait Franklin. They had no trouble finding henchmen to do their work. After attempts by several others to bribe Franklin had failed, Lord North, himself, made a personal attempt. In his record of this conversation, Franklin told Lord North that taxation by threats was no different than a highwayman putting a pistol to the coach door, and besides, there was a new dispute, the Parliament's pretending to a power to alter the charters and establish laws in the colonies, which was of even greater consequence than the taxation issue. Lord North asked what Franklin would suggest. Franklin responded that he was sure Lord North had seen the *HINTS* he had prepared on the subject. Franklin's record of this experience continues:

> He said he had; but some of my articles were such as would never be agreed to. That it was apprehended I had several instructions and powers to offer more acceptable terms, but was extremely reserved, and perhaps from a desire he did not blame, of doing better for my constituents; but my expectations might deceive me; and he did think I might be assured I should never obtain better terms than what were now offered by Lord North. That administration had a sincere desire of restoring harmony with America; and it was thought, *if I would cooperate with them, the business would be easy. . . .* that I was, as he understood, in high esteem among the Americans; that, *if I would bring about a reconciliation on terms suitable to the dignity of government, I might be honored and rewarded, perhaps, beyond my expectation.*
>
> I replied, that I thought I had given a convincing proof of my sincere desire of promoting peace, when, on being informed that all wanted for the honor of government was, to obtain payment for the tea [destroyed in the Boston Tea Party], I offered, without any instruction to warrant my so doing, or assurance that I should be reimbursed, or my conduct approved, to engage for that payment, if the Massachusetts acts were to be repealed; an engagement in which I must have risked my whole fortune, which I thought few besides me would have

done. That, in truth, private resentments had no weight with me in public business; that I was not the reserved man imagined, having really no secret instructions to act upon. That I was certainly willing to do every thing that could be reasonably expected of me. *But, if any supposed I could prevail with my countrymen to take black for white, and wrong for right, it was not knowing either them or me; they were not capable of being so imposed on, nor was I capable of attempting it.*[3]

Little did the English realize that Franklin, on his first visit to England, had made an observation which would prevent his ever being corrupted as they proposed. In the journal he kept of his voyage home, he recorded his visit to a castle on the Isle of Wight and his impressions of a former governor who had lived there:

> At his death it appeared he was a great villain, and a great politician; there was no crime so damnable which he would not stick at in the execution of his designs, and yet he had the art of covering all so thick, that with almost all men in general, while he lived, he passed for a saint. . . . *In short, I believe it is impossible for a man, though he has all the cunning of a devil, to live and die a villain, and yet conceal it so well as to carry the name of an honest fellow to the grave with him, but some one, by some accident or other, shall discover him.* Truth and sincerity have a certain distinguishing native lustre about them, which cannot be perfectly counterfeited; they are like fire and flame, that cannot be painted.[4]

THE INTERNAL SATISFACTION OF A CLEAR CONSCIENCE

Perhaps the greatest benefit to be derived from being honest is a clear conscience, without which true happiness is not possible. A clear conscience renders one immune from the censures of others and the vexations of guilt. Internally sound, the person can stand against the storms of life with tranquillity and peace.

The following extracts from some of Franklin's private letters illustrate the benefits of a clear conscience. To a friend he wrote:

> The favorable sentiments you express of my conduct, with regard to the repeal of the Stamp Act, give me real pleasure; and *I hope*, in every other matter of public concern, *to so behave myself as to stand fair in the opinion of the wise and good, and what the rest think and say of me will then give me less concern.*[5]

To Jane Mecom his sister, Benjamin wrote:

> As to the reports you mention, that are spread to my disadvantage, I give myself as little concern about them as possible. I have often met with such treatment from people that I was all the while endeavoring to serve. At other times I have been extolled extravagantly, where I had little or no merit. These are the operations of nature. It sometimes is cloudy, it rains, it hails; again it is clear and pleasant, and the sun shines on us. Take one thing with another, and the world is a pretty good sort of world, and it is our duty to make the best of it and be thankful. *One's true happiness depends more upon one's own judgment of one's own self, or a consciousness of rectitude in action and intention, and the approbation of those few who judge impartially, than upon the applause of the unthinking, undiscerning multitude, who are apt to cry Hosanna to-day, and to-morrow, Crucify him.*[6]

To a discouraged friend, Franklin wrote the following:

> We must not in the course of public life expect immediate approbation and immediate grateful acknowledgment of our services. But let us persevere through abuse and even injury. *The internal satisfaction of a good conscience is always present, and time will do us justice in the minds of the people, even those at present the most prejudiced against us.*[7]

In 1773, Benjamin Franklin came in possession of letters written by Governor Hutchinson and Lieutenant-Governor Oliver of Massachusetts, requesting the British ministry to send troops to quell a pending rebellion in that province. This was an exaggeration of the facts, deliberately made for the purpose of strengthening their own political position with the ministry. Franklin sent the letters to members of the Massachusetts assembly in the hope they would lessen resentment against England by showing how the ministry had been misled by the governor and his lieutenant. With this information, he thought the governor could be held accountable by both the ministry and by his own province. The assembly made the letters public, which caused no small stir in England. Amazingly, however, the ministry's ire was not directed against Hutchinson and Oliver for misleading them, but at the person who had sent the letters to the assembly. At first, it was suspected in England that someone else had forwarded the letters and the life of an innocent man became endangered. At this time, Franklin wrote to his son:

> Our friend Temple, as you will see by the papers, had been engaged in a duel, about an affair in which he had no concern. As the combat was interrupted, and understood to be finished, I thought it incumbent on me to do what I could for preventing further mischief, and so declared my having transmitted the letters in question. *This has drawn some censure on myself; but, as I grow old, I grow less concerned about censure, when I am satisfied that I act rightly*; and I have the pleasure of having exculpated a friend, who lay undeservedly under an imputation much to his dishonor.[8]

In Massachusetts, the reaction to the letters was a petition calling for the removal of the Governor and his Lieutenant. Franklin was requested to present the petition. A hearing for the petition was arranged but, instead of considering the petition, it proved to be a kangaroo court for Franklin. Dr. Priestly, one of Franklin's close friends, preserved this account of the hearing:

When the business was opened, it was sufficiently evident, from the speech of Mr. Wedderburn, who was counsel for the government, that the real object of the court was to insult Dr. Franklin. All this time, he stood in a corner of the room, not far from me, without the least apparent emotion.

Mr. Dunning, who was the leading counsel on the part of the colony, was so hoarse that he could hardly make himself heard; and Mr. Lee, who was the second, spoke but feebly in reply; so that Mr. Wedderburn had a complete triumph. At the sallies of his sarcastic wit, all the members of the council, the president himself (Lord Gower) not excepted, frequently laughed outright. No person belonging to the council behaved with decent gravity, except Lord North, who, coming late, took his stand behind the chair opposite to me.

When the business was over, Dr. Franklin, in going out, took me by the hand in a manner that indicated some feeling. I soon followed him, and, going through the anteroom, saw Mr. Wedderburn there, surrounded by a circle of his friends and admirers. Being known to him, he stepped forward, as if to speak to me; but I turned aside, and made what haste I could out of the place.

The next morning, I breakfasted with the Doctor, when he said he had never before been so sensible of the power of a good conscience; for that if he had not considered the thing for which he had been so much insulted, as one of the best actions of his life, and what he should certainly do again in the same circumstances, he could not have supported it.[9]

I HAVE LONG OBSERVED ONE RULE

During the war, when Franklin was in France, several friends wrote warning him of spies in his household.

P.S. If tempestuous times should come, take care of your own safety; events are uncertain, and men may be capricious.[10]

Dr. Franklin answered:

> I thank you for your kind caution, but having nearly
> finished a long life, I set but little value on what remains
> of it. Like a draper, when one chaffers with him for a
> remnant, I am ready to say: "*As it is only the fag end, I
> will not differ with you about it; take it for what you
> please.*" Perhaps the best use such an old fellow can be
> put to, is to make a martyr of him.[11]

Bigelow, in his edition of Franklin's writings, provided the
following subscript on the above exchange:

> After Mr. Hartley returned to London, a friend of Dr.
> Franklin received an anonymous letter. . . .The writer
> said: "Mr. Hartley told Lord Camden this morning that
> he was sure the Commissioners, and particularly Dr.
> Franklin, were much disconcerted at Paris; for they
> might as well live in the Bastile, as be exposed, as they
> were, to the perpetual observation of French ministerial
> spies. This must not, however, be repeated."
> In reply Dr. Franklin said: "Be so good as to answer
> our friend, that it is impossible Mr. Hartley could have
> said what is here represented, no such thing having ever
> been intimated to him; nor has the least idea of the kind
> ever been in the mind of the Commissioners, particularly
> *Dr. Franklin, who does not care how many spies are
> placed about him by the Court of France, having
> nothing to conceal from them.*"[12]

To another friend, Franklin wrote:

> MADAM: I am much obliged to you for your kind
> attention to my welfare in the information you gave me.
> I have no doubt of its being well founded, but as it is
> impossible to discover in every case the falsity of
> pretended friends who would know our affairs, and more
> so to prevent being watched by spies when interested
> people may think proper to place them for that purpose.

I have long observed one rule which prevents any inconvenience from such practices. *It is* simply this—*to be concerned in no affairs that I would blush to have made public,* and to do nothing but what spies may see and welcome. When a man's actions are just and honorable, the more they are known, the more his reputation is increased and established. If I was sure, therefore, that my *valet de place* was a spy, as probably he is, I think I should not discharge him for that, if in other respects I liked him. . . .[13]

THIS IS, IN OLD AGE, A COMFORTABLE REFLECTION

To John Jay, Franklin wrote this marvelous affirmation of the advantages of being an honest man.

I have, as you observe, some enemies in England, but they are my enemies as an American; I have also two or three in America, who are my enemies as a minister; but *I thank God there are not in the whole world any who are my enemies as a man; for by his grace, through a long life, I have been enabled so to conduct myself that there does not exist a human being who can justly say, "Ben. Franklin has wronged me." This, my friend, is in old age a comfortable reflection.* You too have, or may have, your enemies; but let not that render you unhappy. If you make a right use of them, they will do you more good than harm. They point out to us our faults; they put us upon our guard, and help us to live more correctly.[14]

It should not be difficult to see in Franklin's life the benefits he derived from a life of "probity and integrity." It gave him enormous influence in protecting the freedom of an infant nation from the capricious ambitions of a few powerful and self-serving men. It also gave him the courage and moral fortitude to resist both temptation and threat, and allowed him to glide through turbulent waters of grave human conflicts with cheerfulness and serenity.

FRANKLIN'S FORMULA FOR SUCCESSFUL LIVING
NUMBER SIX

Experience and observation
will quickly teach us
that no form of dishonesty
is compatible with human happiness,
and that neither lasting fortune
nor personal honor
can be firmly established
on its shaky foundation.

Driven by misguided motives
of self-interest and ever willing
to injure others for their own gain,
the dishonest must always have
their enemies and can only have
knaves or fools for friends.

Capable of neither trusting
nor of being trusted,
constantly subject
to betrayal and exposure,
and deprived of
the power and comfort
of a good conscience,
the dishonest may never enjoy
the sweet fruits
of peace and contentment.

Unfortunately, many
have failed to learn
that "vicious acts are not
hurtful because they are forbidden,
but forbidden because they are hurtful"
and consequently there is
"nothing useful which is not honest."

Even otherwise honorable people,
by living beyond their means,
sometimes make commitments
they cannot keep
by honest endeavor, while
others who think themselves honest,
often for the most trifling of reasons,
will cheat their government,
their employer,
or someone else.

Franklin determined,
early in life,
to do better.
He formulated a model
of the man he wanted to be,
a man who, knowing he means well,
could always speak
the thing he means
without shame or fear;
a man whose consciousness
of his own innate worth and
unshaken integrity
could render him
calm and undaunted
in the presence
of the great
and most powerful.

So, early in life,
Franklin made a rule
to which he faithfully adhered.
It was,
to be concerned in no affairs
that he would blush
to have made public.

GUIDING PRINCIPLE NUMBER SEVEN

THE PROPER ACQUISITION OF MONEY
MAY BE A BLESSING
BUT ITS OPPOSITE IS ALWAYS A CURSE

The acquisition of wealth is one of those whistles for which many people pay too much. Convinced its possession will bring them happiness, there are those who are willing to sacrifice family, friends, health, reputation, independence and even their lives on the altar to this golden calf. All too many, entranced by the spellbinding glitter of easy riches, plunge themselves into adventures that ultimately lead to their own ruin and often that of others as well. Few seem to realize that everything has its price and the price of wealth may be very high indeed.

Throughout history, the rise and fall of nations, along with the consequent suffering of millions, is closely tied to the reign of those whose passions have been governed by ambitions of avarice and greed. Many nations have been enfeebled by wealthy classes that feed like parasites off the labors of the poor, while other nations have been weakened by the other extreme of feeding the poor off the labors of the rich. Throughout the world, the offspring of many families, both rich and poor, have been taught to despise the rigors of labor by removing from them the need to provide for themselves.

Benjamin Franklin was one of those rare individuals who had it within his power to become immensely wealthy, but who declined the opportunity to do so. To his mother he had written that he would rather have it said of him that he had lived usefully than that he had died rich. When his business attained a level to assure him financial independence he turned his interests to science and government. Believing "That, as we enjoy great advantages from the inventions of others, we should be glad of an opportunity to serve others by any invention of ours; and this we should do freely and generously,"[1] he made no effort to patent or profit from any of his inventions. The Franklin stove alone could have made him a fortune, but he chose not to patent it, and printed the plans for it in his own newspaper.

To Franklin, the process by which one accumulates and uses wealth was more important than wealth itself. He believed that when a person possessed the virtues of industry and frugality, he was assured of wealth if he wanted it. In fact, to him, the possession of these virtues was a form of wealth in itself, rendering those who possess them free from both want and envy.

PINCHED OFF THE BACKS AND OUT OF THE BELLIES

Franklin saw many evils in the exploitation of one class of people by another to achieve wealth. When he saw the rich exploiting the poor, his comments were scathing.

While in England on public business, he had an occasion to tour Ireland and reported his impressions to Thomas Cushing, the speaker of the Massachusetts Assembly:

> Ireland is itself a poor country, and Dublin a
> magnificent city; but the appearances of general extreme
> poverty among the lower people are amazing. They live
> in wretched hovels of mud and straw, are clothed in
> rags, and subsist chiefly on potatoes. Our New England
> farmers, of the poorest sort, in regard to the enjoyment
> of all the comforts of life, are princes when compared to
> them. Such is the effect of the discouragements of
> industry, the nonresidence not only of pensioners, but of
> many original landlords, who lease their lands in gross
> to undertakers that rack the tenants and fleece them skin
> and all to make estates to themselves, while the first
> rents, as well as most of the pensions, are spent out of
> the country. An English gentleman there said to me, that

by what he had heard of the good grazing in North America, and by what he saw of the plenty of flaxseed imported in Ireland from thence, he could not understand why we did not rival Ireland in the beef and butter trade to the West Indies, and share with them in its linen trade. But he was satisfied when I told him that I supposed the reason might be, *our people eat beef and butter every day, and wear shirts themselves. In short, the chief exports of Ireland seem to be pinched off the backs and out of the bellies of the miserable inhabitants.*[1]

In a piece titled, "Observations Concerning the Increase of Mankind and the Peopling of Countries", Franklin hit hard at the foolishness, as well as the wickedness, of slavery:

The negroes brought into the English sugar islands have greatly diminished the whites there; the poor are by this means deprived of employment, while a few families acquire vast estates, which they spend on foreign luxuries, and in educating their children in the habit of those luxuries. The same income is needed for the support of one that might have maintained one hundred. *The whites who have slaves, not laboring are enfeebled, and therefore not so generally prolific; the slaves being worked too hard and ill fed, their constitutions are broken, and the deaths among them are more than the births; so that a continual supply is needed from Africa.* The northern colonies, having few slaves, increase in whites. Slaves also pejorate the families that use them; the white children become proud, disgusted with labor, and being educated in idleness, are rendered unfit to get a living by industry.[2]

ALL MANKIND LOVE LAZY

If Franklin was critical of the rich who abused the poor, he was no more approving of the poor who took advantage of the rich. He saw great problems in welfare schemes that simply doled out to the poor without requiring them to work for what they got. In a lengthy letter to a philosophical correspondent, Franklin expressed these views:

Sir: I thank you for the kind and judicious remarks you have often made on my little piece. I have often observed with wonder that temper of the poorer English laborers which you mention, and acknowledge it to be pretty general. When any of them happen to come here, where labor is much better paid than in England, their industry seems to diminish in equal proportion. But it is not so with the German laborers; they retain the habitual industry and frugality they bring with them, and receiving higher wages, an accumulation arises that makes them all rich. When I consider that the English are the offspring of Germans; that the climate they live in is much of the same temperature, and when I see nothing in nature that should create this difference, I am tempted to suspect it must arise from the constitution; and I have sometimes doubted whether the laws peculiar to England, which compel the rich to maintain the poor, have not given the latter a dependence that very much lessens the care of providing against the wants of old age.

I have heard it remarked that the poor in Protestant countries, on the continent of Europe, are generally more industrious than those of Popish countries. May not the more numerous foundations in the latter for the relief of the poor have some effect towards rendering them less provident? *To relieve the misfortunes of our fellow creatures is concurring with the Deity; it is godlike; but if we provide encouragement for laziness, and support for folly, may we not be found fighting against the order of God and nature, which perhaps has appointed want and misery as the proper punishments for, and cautions against, as well as necessary con-sequences of, idleness and extravagance? Whenever we attempt to amend the scheme of Providence, and to interfere with the government of the world, we had need*

to be very circumspect, lest we do more harm than good.
In New England they once thought black birds useless,
and mischievous to the corn. They made efforts to
destroy them. The consequence was, the blackbirds were
diminished; but a kind of worm, which devoured their
grass, and which the blackbirds used to feed on,
increased prodigiously; then, finding their loss in grass
much greater than their saving in corn, they wished
again for their blackbirds.

We had some years since a Transylvanian Tartar, who
had travelled much in the East, and came hither merely
to see the West, intending to go home through the
Spanish West Indies, China, etc. He asked me one day,
what I thought might be the reason that so many and
such numerous nations, as the Tartars in Europe and
Asia, the Indians in America, and the Negroes in Africa,
continued a wandering, careless life, and refused to live
in cities, and cultivate the arts they saw practiced by the
civilized part of mankind? While I was considering what
answer to make him he said, in his broken English:
"God make man for Paradise. He make him for live lazy.
Man make God angry. God turn him out of Paradise, and
bid workee. Man no love workee; he want to go to
Paradise again; he want to live lazy. So all mankind love
lazy.". . . .

*However, as matters now stand with us, care and
industry seem absolutely necessary to our well being.
They should therefore have every encouragement we
can invent, and not one motive to diligence be
subtracted; and the support of the poor should not be by
maintaining them in idleness, but by employing them in
some kind of labor suited to their abilities of body, as I
am informed begins to be of late the practice in many
parts of England, where workhouses are erected for that
purpose.* If these were general, I should think the poor
would be more careful, and work voluntarily to lay up
something for themselves against a rainy day, rather
than run the risk of being obliged to work at the pleasure
of others for a bare subsistence. . . .[3]

QUICK RICHES

In his twenty-third year, Franklin wrote a series of articles for publication in the *Weekly Mercury*, a paper in Philadelphia, under the heading, *The Busy-Body*. In the following excerpts from an entertaining exchange between Titan Pleiades and The Busy Body there is much to be learned about the acquisition, use, and preservation of wealth.

Titan Pleidaes writes:
   You cannot be ignorant, Sir, (for your intimate second-sighted correspondent knows all things,) that there are large sums of money hidden under ground in divers places about this town and in many parts of the country; but, alas, Sir, notwithstanding I have used all the means laid down in the immortal authors before mentioned, and when they failed, the ingenious Mr. P-d-l, with his mercurial wand and magnet, I have still failed in my purpose. This therefore I send, to propose and desire an acquaintance with you; and I do not doubt, notwithstanding my repeated ill fortune, but we may be exceedingly serviceable to each other in our discoveries; and that if we use our united endeavors the time will come when the Busy-Body, his second-sighted correspondent, and your very humble servant will be three of the richest men in the province. . . .

The Busy-Body answers:

   In the evening after I had received this letter I made a visit to my second-sighted friend and communicated to him the proposal. When he had read it he assured me that to his certain knowledge there is not at this time so much as one ounce of silver or gold hid under ground in any part of this province; for that the late and present scarcity of money had obliged all those who were living, and knew where they had formerly hid any, to take it up and use it in their own necessary affairs; and as to all the rest which was buried by pirates and others in old times, who were never likely to come for it, he himself had dug it all up and applied it to charitable uses: and this he desired me to publish for the public good. For, as he acquainted me, there are among us great numbers of honest artificers and laboring people who, fed with a vain hope of growing suddenly rich, neglect their business, almost to the ruining of themselves and families, and voluntarily endure abundance of fatigue in a fruitless search after imaginary hidden treasure. They wander through the woods and bushes by day to discover the marks and signs; at midnight they repair to the hopeful spots with spades and pickaxes; full of expectation, they labor violently, trembling at the same time in every joint, through fear of certain malicious demons who are said to haunt and guard such places. At length a mighty hole is dug. . . . but, alas, no keg or iron pot is found. . . .

This odd humor of digging for money, through a belief that much has been hid by pirates formerly frequenting the river, has for several years been mighty prevalent among us: insomuch that you can hardly walk half a mile out of the town on any side without observing several pits dug with that design, and perhaps some lately opened. *Men, otherwise of very good sense, have been drawn into this practice through an overweening desire of sudden wealth and an easy credulity of what they so earnestly wished might be true; while the rational and almost certain methods of acquiring riches by industry and frugality are neglected or forgotten.* There seems to be some peculiar charm in the conceit of finding money: and if the sands of Schuylkill were so mixed with small grains of gold that a man might in a day's time, with care and application, get together to the value of half a crown, I make no question but we should find several people employed there that can with ease earn five shillings a day at their proper trades.[4]

POORER FOR THE FIDDLING MAN

In a letter written to a friend, Franklin expressed the belief that
most of us tend to labor for the wrong things:

> It has been computed by some political arithmetician,
> that if every man and woman would work for four hours
> each day on something useful, that labor would produce
> sufficient to procure all the necessaries and comforts of
> life, want and misery would be banished out of the
> world, and the rest of the twenty-four hours might be
> leisure and pleasure.
>
> What occasions then so much want and misery? It is
> the employment of men and women in works that
> produce neither necessaries nor conveniences of life,
> who, with those who do nothing, consume necessaries
> raised by the laborious. To explain this.
>
> The first elements of wealth are obtained by labor,
> from the earth and waters. I have land, and raise corn.
> With this, if I feed a family that does nothing, my corn
> will be consumed, and at the end of the year I shall be
> no richer than I was at the beginning. But if, while I feed
> them, I employ them, some in spinning, others in making
> bricks, etc., for building, the value of my corn will be
> arrested and remain with me, and at the end of the year
> we may all be better clothed and better lodged. And if,
> instead of employing a man I feed in making bricks, I
> employ him in fiddling for me, the corn he eats is gone,
> and no part of his manufacture remains to augment the
> wealth and convenience of the family; I shall therefore
> be the poorer for this fiddling man, unless the rest of my
> family work more, or eat less, to make up the deficiency
> he occasions.
>
> Look around the world and see the millions employed
> in doing nothing, or in something that amounts to
> nothing, when the necessaries and conveniences of life
> are in question. What is the bulk of commerce, for
> which we fight and destroy each other, but the toil of
> millions for superfluities, to the great hazard and loss of

many lives by the constant dangers of the sea? How much labor is spent in building and fitting great ships, to go to China and Arabia for tea and coffee, to the West Indies for sugar, to America for tobacco? These things cannot be called the necessaries of life, for our ancestors lived very comfortably without them.

A question may be asked: Could all these people now employed in raising, making, or carrying superfluities be subsisted by raising necessaries? I think they might. The world is large, and a great part of it still uncultivated. Many hundred millions of acres in Asia, Africa, and America are still in a forest, and a great deal even in Europe. On a hundred acres of this forest a man might become a substantial farmer, and a hundred thousand men, employed in clearing each his hundred acres, would hardly brighten a spot big enough to be visible from the moon, unless with Herschel's telescope; so vast are the regions still in wood. . . .

One reflection more and I will end this long rambling letter. Almost all the parts of our bodies require some expense. The feet demand shoes; the legs, stockings; the rest of the body, clothing; and the belly, a good deal of victuals. Our eyes, though exceedingly useful, ask, when reasonable, only the cheap assistance of spectacles, which could not much impair our finances. *But the eyes of other people are the eyes that ruin us.* If all but myself were blind, I should want neither fine clothes, fine houses, nor fine furniture.[5]

WHAT WE HAVE ABOVE WHAT WE NEED

In a letter to another friend, Benjamin expressed the foible of mankind in the pursuit of wealth in these terms:

Your sentiments of the general foible of mankind in the pursuit of wealth to no end are expressed in a manner that gave me great pleasure in reading. They are extremely just; at least they are perfectly agreeable to mine. But London citizens, they say, are ambitious of what they call dying worth a great sum. The very notion seems to me absurd; and just the same as if a man should run in debt for 1,000 superfluities, to the the end that when he should be stripped of all, and imprisoned by his creditors, it might be said, he broke worth a great sum. *I imagine that what we have above what we can use, is not properly ours, though we possess it; and that the rich man who must die, was no more worth what he leaves, than the debtor who must pay.*[6]

As may be seen from the foregoing selections, in the misguided pursuit and use of wealth, many people have lost the very things for which they were seeking. Wealth beyond the necessaries is never essential to happiness and may often be detrimental. Or, in the words of Poor Richard:

Content and Riches seldom meet together,
Riches take thou, contentment I had rather. (1743)

A Man has no more Goods *than he gets Good by.* (1749)

If worldly Goods cannot save me from Death,
They ought not to hinder me of eternal Life. (1751)

A wise Man will desire no more than what he
may get justly, use soberly, distribute cheerfully,
and leave contentedly. (1756)

THE WAY TO WEALTH   16

Over the years Franklin published Poor Richard's Almanac, he had used it as a means of promoting the virtues of industry and frugality through various proverbs containing, as he said, "the wisdom of many ages and nations." In 1757, he assembled and formed many of them into a connected discourse and prefixed it to the almanac of that year. In reading it, the wisdom of many ages and nations will be found as relevant today as when first assembled in this form in 1757.

THE WAY TO WEALTH AS CLEARLY SHOWN
IN THE PREFACE OF AN OLD ALMANAC ENTITLED
"POOR RICHARD IMPROVED"

COURTEOUS READER:
   I have heard that nothing gives an author so great pleasure as to find his works respectfully quoted by others. Judge, then, how much I must have been gratified by an incident I am going to relate to you. I stopped my horse lately where a great number of people were collected at an auction of merchants' goods. The hour of the sale not being come, they were conversing on the badness of the times; and one of the company called to a plain, clean, old man with white locks: "Pray, Father Abraham, what do you think of the times? Will not these heavy taxes quite ruin the country? How shall we ever be able to pay them? What

would you advise us to do?" Father Abraham stood up and
replied: "If you would have my advice, I will give it you in
short; for *A word to the wise is enough,* as Poor Richard says."
They joined in desiring him to speak his mind, and gathering
round him he proceeded as follows:

"Friends," said he, "The taxes are indeed very heavy, and if
those laid on by the government were the only ones we had to
pay, we might more easily discharge them, but we have many
others and much more grievous to some of us. We are taxed
twice as much by our idleness, three times as much by our pride,
and four times as much by our folly, and from these taxes the
commissioners cannot ease or deliver us by allowing an
abatement. However, let us hearken to good advice and
something may be done for us; *God helps them that help
themselves,* as Poor Richard says.

[Industriousness]

"I. It would be thought a hard government that should
tax its people one-tenth part of their time, to be
employed in its service, but idleness taxes many of us
much more; sloth by bringing on diseases, absolutely

shortens life. *Sloth, like rust, consumes faster than labor wears, while the used key is always bright,* as Poor Richard says. *But dost thou love life, then do not squander time, for that is the stuff life is made of,* as Poor Richard says. How much more than is necessary do we spend in sleep, forgetting that *The sleeping fox catches no poultry,* and that *There will be sleeping enough in the grave,* as Poor Richard says.

"*If time be of all things the most precious, wasting time must be,* as Poor Richard says, *the greatest prodigality,* since, as he elsewhere tells us, *Lost time is never found again, and what we call time enough always proves little enough.* Let us then be up and doing, and doing to the purpose; so by diligence shall we do more with less perplexity. *Sloth makes all things difficult, but industry all things easy*; and *He that riseth late must trot all day, and shall scarce overtake his business at night*; while *Laziness travels so slowly that Poverty soon overtakes him. Drive thy business, let not that drive thee*; and *Early to bed and early to rise, makes a man healthy, wealthy, and wise,* as Poor Richard says.

"So what signifies wishing and hoping for better times? We may make these times better if we bestir ourselves. *Industry need not wish, and he that lives upon hope will die fasting. There are no gains without pains; then help, hands, for I have no lands*; or if I have they are smartly taxed. *He that hath a trade hath an estate, and he that hath a calling hath an office of profit and honor,* as Poor Richard says; but then the trade must be worked at and the calling followed, or neither the estate nor the office will enable us to pay our taxes. If we are industrious we shall never starve, for *At the working man's house hunger looks in but dares not enter.* Nor will the bailiff nor the constable enter, for *Industry pays debts, while despair increaseth them.* What though you have found no treasure, nor has any rich relative left you a legacy, *Diligence is the mother of good luck, and God gives all things to industry. Then plough deep while sluggards sleep, and you shall have corn to sell and to keep.* Work while it is called to-day, for you know how much you may be hindered to-morrow. *One to-day is worth two to-morrows*, as Poor Richard says; and further, *Never leave that till to-morrow which you can do to-day.* If you were a good servant would not you be ashamed that a good master should catch you idle? Are you then your own master? Be ashamed to catch yourself idle when there is much to be done for yourself, your family, your country, and your king. Handle your tools without mittens; remember that *The cat in gloves catches no mice*, as Poor Richard says. It is true there is much to be done, and perhaps you are weak-handed, but stick to it steadily and you will see great effects; for *Constant dropping wears away stones*; and *By diligence and patience the mouse ate in two the cable*; and *Little strokes fell great oaks.*

"Methinks I hear some of you say, 'Must a man afford himself no leisure?' I will tell thee my friend, what Poor Richard says: *Employ thy time well, if thou meanest to gain leisure; and, since thou art not sure of a minute, throw not away an hour.* Leisure is time for doing something useful; this leisure the diligent man will obtain, but the lazy man never; for *A life of leisure and a life of laziness are two things. Many, without labor, would live by their wits only, but they break for want of stock*; whereas industry gives comfort and plenty of respect. *Fly pleasures, and they will follow you. The diligent spinner has a large shift; and now I have a sheep and a cow, everybody bids me good morrow.*

[Prudence]

"II. But with our industry we must likewise be steady, settled, and careful, and oversee our own affairs with our own eyes, and not trust too much to others; for, as Poor Richard says:

> *I never saw an oft removed tree,*
> *Nor yet an oft-removed family,*
> *That throve so well as those that settled be.*

And again, *Three removes are as bad as a fire*; and
again, *Keep thy shop, and thy shop will keep thee*; and
again: *If you would have your business done, go; if not,
send.* And again:

> *He that by the plough would thrive,*
> *Himself must either hold or drive.*

And again, *The eye of a master will do more work than
both his hands*; and again, *Want of care does us more
damage than want of knowledge*; and again, *Not to
oversee workmen is to leave them your purse open.*
Trusting too much to others' care is the ruin of many;
for, *In the affairs of this world men are saved, not by
faith, but by the want of it*; but a man's own care is
profitable; for, *If you would have a faithful servant, and
one that you like, serve yourself. A little neglect may
breed great mischief; for want of a nail the shoe was
lost; for want of a shoe the horse was lost; and for want
of a horse the rider was lost, being overtaken and slain
by the enemy; all for the want of a little care about a
horse-shoe nail.*

[Frugality]

"III. So much for industry, my friends, and attention to
one's own business; but to these we must add frugality,
if we would make our industry more certainly successful. A man may, if he knows not how to save as he gets,
keep his nose all his life to the grindstone and die not
worth a groat at last. *A fat kitchen makes lean will*; and

> *Many estates are spent in the getting,*
> *Since women for tea forsook spinning and knitting,*
> *And men for punch forsook hewing and splitting.*

*If you would be wealthy, think of saving as well as of
getting. The Indies have not made Spain rich, because
her outgoes are greater than her incomes.*

"Away then with your expensive follies, and you will
not then have so much cause to complain of hard times,
heavy taxes, and chargeable families; for

Women and wine, game and deceit,
Make wealth small and the want great.

And further, *What maintains one vice would bring up*
two children. You may think, perhaps, that a little tea, or
a little punch now and then, diet a little more costly,
clothes a little finer, and a little entertainment now and
then, can be no great matter; but remember, *Many a*
little makes a mickle [much]. Beware of little expenses:
A small leak will sink a great ship, as Poor Richard says;
and again, *Who dainties love, shall beggars prove*; and
moreover, *Fools make feasts, and wise men eat them.*
"Here you are all got together at this sale of fineries
and knick-knacks. You call them *goods*; but if you do
not take care they will prove *evils* to some of you. You
expect them to be sold cheap, and perhaps they may for
less than they cost; but if you have no occasion for them
they must be dear to you. Remember what Poor Richard
says: *Buy what thou hast no need of, and ere long thou*
shalt sell thy necessaries. And again, *At a great*
pennyworth pause a while. He means, that perhaps the
cheapness is apparent only, and not real; or the bargain,
by straitening thee in thy business, may do thee more
harm than good. For in another place he says, *Many*
have been ruined by buying good pennyworths. Again, *It*
is foolish to lay out money in a purchase of repentance;
and yet this folly is practiced every day at auctions for
want of minding the Almanac. Many a one, for the sake
of finery on the back, have gone with a hungry belly and
half-starved their families. *Silks and satins, scarlet and*
velvets, put out the kitchen fire, as Poor Richard says.
"These are not the necessaries of life; they can
scarcely be called the conveniences; and yet, only
because they look pretty, how many want to have them!
By these and other extravangances the genteel are

reduced to poverty and forced to borrow of those whom they formerly despised, but who, through industry and frugality, have maintained their standing; in which case it appears plainly that *A ploughman on his legs is higher than a gentleman on his knees*, as Poor Richard says. Perhaps they have had a small estate left them, which they knew not the getting of: they think, *It is a day, and will never be night*; and that a little to be spent out of so much is not worth minding; but *Always taking out of the meal-tub, and never putting in, soon comes to the bottom*, as Poor Richard says; and then, *When the well is dry, they know the worth of water*. But this they might have known before, if they had taken his advice. *If you would know the value of money, go and try to borrow some; for he that goes a borrowing goes a sorrowing*, as Poor Richard says; and indeed so does he that lends to such people, when he goes to get it again. Poor Dick further advises and says,

> *Fond pride of dress is sure a very curse;*
> *Ere fancy you consult, consult your purse.*

And again, *Pride is as loud a beggar as Want, and a great deal more saucy*. When you have bought one fine thing you must buy ten more, that your appearance may be all of a piece; but Poor Dick says, *It is easier to suppress the first desire than to satisfy all that follow it*. And it is as truly folly for the poor to ape the rich, as for the frog to swell in order to equal the ox.

> *Vessels large may venture more,*
> *But little boats should keep near shore.*

It is, however, a folly soon punished; for, as Poor Richard says, *Pride that dines on vanity sups on contempt, Pride breakfasted with Plenty, dined with Poverty, and supped with Infamy*. And after all, of what use is this pride of appearance, for which so much is risked, so much is suffered? It cannot promote health,

nor ease pain; it makes no increase of merit in the
person; it creates envy; it hastens misfortune.

"But what madness must it be to *run in debt* for these
superfluities! We are offered by the terms of this sale six
months' credit; and that, perhaps, has induced some of
us to attend it, because we cannot spare the ready
money, and hope now to be fine without it. But ah! think
what you do when you run in debt; you give to another
power over your liberty. If you cannot pay at the time,
you will be ashamed to see your creditor; you will be in
fear when you speak to him; you will make poor, pitiful,
sneaking excuses, and by degrees come to lose your
veracity, and sink into base, downright lying; for, *The
second vice is lying, the first is running in debt*, as Poor
Richard says; and again, to the same purpose, *Lying lies
upon Debt's back*; whereas a free-born Englishman
ought not to be ashamed nor afraid to see or speak to
any man living. But poverty often deprives a man of all
spirit and virtue. *It is hard for an empty bag to stand
upright*.

"What would you think of that prince or of that
government who should issue an edict forbidding you to
dress like a gentleman or gentlewoman, on pain of
imprisonment or servitude? Would you not say that you
were free, have a right to dress as you please, and that
such an edict would be a breach of your privileges, and
such a government tyrannical? And yet you are about to
put yourself under such tyranny when you run in debt
for such dress! Your creditor has authority, at his
pleasure, to deprive you of your liberty by confining you
in gaol [jail] till you shall be able to pay him. When you
have got your bargain you may perhaps think little of
payment, but, as Poor Richard says, *Creditors have
better memories than debtors; creditors are a
superstitious sect, great observers of set days and times*.
The day comes round before you are aware, and the
demand is made before you are prepared to satisfy it; or,
if you bear your debt in mind, the term, which at first
seemed so long, will, as it lessens, appear extremely

short. Time will seem to have added wings to his heels as well as his shoulders. *Those have a short Lent who owe money to be paid at Easter.* At present, perhaps, you may think yourselves in thriving circumstances, and that you can bear a little extravagance without injury, but—

> *For age and want save while you may;*
> *No morning sun lasts a whole day.*

Gain may be temporary and uncertain, but ever, while you live, expense is constant and certain; and *It is easier to build two chimneys than to keep one in fuel,* as Poor Richard says; so, *Rather go to bed supperless than rise in debt.*

> *Get what you can, and what you get hold;*
> *T'is the stone that will turn all your lead into gold.*

And, when you have got the Philosopher's stone, sure you will no longer complain of bad times or the difficulty of paying taxes.

"IV. *This doctrine, my friends, is reason and wisdom; but, after all, do not depend too much on your own industry and frugality and prudence, though excellent things, for they may be blasted, without the blessings of Heaven; and therefore ask that blessing humbly, and be not uncharitable to those that at present seem to want it, but comfort and help them.* Remember Job suffered and was afterwards prosperous.

"And now, to conclude, *Experience keeps a dear school, but fools will learn in no other,* as Poor Richard says, and scarce in that, for it is true *We may give advice, but we cannot give conduct.* However, remember this, *They that will not be counselled cannot be helped;* and further, that *If you will not hear Reason, she will surely rap your knuckles'* as Poor Richard says."

Thus the old gentleman ended his harangue. The people heard it and approved the doctrine, and immediately practiced the contrary, just as if it had been a common sermon; for the auction opened, and they began to buy extravagantly. I found the good man had thoroughly studied my Almanacs, and digested all I had dropped on these topics during the course of twenty-five years. The frequent mention he made of me must have tired any one else, but my vanity was wonderfully delighted with it, though I was conscious that not a tenth part of the wisdom was my own which he ascribed to me, but rather the gleanings that I had made of the sense of all ages and nations. However, I resolved to be the better for the echo of it, and though I had at first determined to buy stuff for a new coat, I went away resolved to wear my old one a little longer. Reader, if thou wilt do the same thy profit will be as great as mine. I am, as ever, thine to serve thee,

RICHARD SAUNDERS[1]

ADVICE TO A YOUNG TRADESMAN

In "Advice to a Young Tradesman", originally prepared as a letter to a young friend, Franklin concluded with this brief and sage summary of the only safe and sure way to wealth.

In short, the way to wealth, if you desire it, is as plain as the way to market. It depends chiefly on two words, *industry* and *frugality*—that is, waste neither *time* nor *money*, but make the best use of both. Without industry and frugality nothing will do, and with them every thing. He that gets all he can honestly, and saves all he gets (necessary expenses excepted), will certainly become rich, if that Being who governs the world, to whom all should look for a blessing on their honest endeavors, doth not, in his wise providence, otherwise determine.

An Old Tradesman[2]

FRANKLIN'S FORMULA FOR SUCCESSFUL LIVING
NUMBER SEVEN

In the world may be seen many people,
past and present,
whose lives and reputations have been ruined
because of the improper acquisition
and the unwise use
of wealth.

Many rich have pinched their wealth
off the backs of the poor.

Many poor have picked their substance
out of the pockets of the rich.

Others have given themselves over
to schemes by which they hoped to get rich quickly
and lost all they had in the process.

Still others have stooped
to immoral and criminal acts
to obtain the illusive blessings of money.

All these, and more,
in their misguided pursuit of wealth
have forsaken
all hope for happiness.

Surrounded by beautiful things without,
they can find no beauty within,
and are left destitute
of the things that really count.

Benjamin Franklin believed that,
the only sure and safe way to wealth
is through industry, frugality and prudence.

Formula Seven

Dost thou love life?
Then do not squander time,
for that is the stuff life is made of,
               says Poor Richard

Industry need not wish,
and he that lives on hope will die fasting,
               says Poor Richard

At the working man's house
hunger looks in but dares not enter,
               says Poor Richard

Buy what thou hast no need of
and ere long thou shalt sell thy necessaries,
               says Poor Richard

For age and want save while you may;
No morning sun lasts a whole day,
               says Poor Richard

Rather to go to bed supperless than rise in debt,
               says Poor Richard

Keep thy shop and thy shop will keep thee,
               says Poor Richard

Want of care does us more damage
than want of knowledge,
               says Poor Richard

If you would have a faithful servant,
and one that you like, serve yourself,
               says Poor Richard

GUIDING PRINCIPLE
NUMBER EIGHT

IT IS, BY FAR, MUCH EASIER
TO PRESERVE HEALTH THAN TO REGAIN IT

There are few things which are appreciated more in their absence and less in their presence than health. When we have it, we take it for granted, giving little care to its preservation. When we do not have it, there is precious little we would not do to get it back. Since, in most cases, health is much easier to retain than it is to regain, a prudent person will give some attention to the preservation of this most precious commodity. As Franklin noted in his essay on happiness, health may not be sufficient in itself to make us happy, but, neither can we be perfectly happy without it.

In his life, there were few things of importance that escaped Benjamin Franklin's attention, and the preservation of health was not one of them. He practiced and taught that proper nutrition, adequate exercise, and sufficient rest would do more to secure the blessings of good health, barring the misfortunes of accident, than perhaps anything else.

In any modern bookstore or library may be found a multitude of excellent books and articles on nutrition and exercise. Since the late 1960s when Americans started to become increasingly health conscious, science and research have combined with common sense to provide a wealth of information on health preservation. It is interesting to observe, however, that boiled down to their essentials, they all resemble those principles understood and practiced by Franklin. While Americans discovered the principles of aerobic exercising in the 1970s, Franklin preached and practiced them in the 1770s. He recognized the disadvantages of overeating and of heavy meat diets. He recognized the advantages of eating vegetables and lighter meats, such as poultry and mutton. He recognized the problems of heavy alcohol consumption. He also well understood the need for the body to get adequate rest and the importance of fresh air to health. He especially understood the importance of such virtues as temperance, moderation, and self-discipline to the preservation of health.

Although the thoughts contained in this section may not be as complete as those found in many modern writings, one may read and "observe with concern how long a useful truth may be known and exist, before it is generally received and practiced on."[1] Notwithstanding the tremendous advances in medicine in the last two hundred years, the idea of preventative health care as understood by Franklin has only become generally accepted in recent years.

PRESERVING HEALTH THROUGH
NUTRITION AND EXERCISE

17

I MADE GREATER PROGRESS

Of the virtues Franklin selected to work on, Temperance was first, "as it tends to procure that coolness and clearness of head, which is so necessary where constant vigilance was to be kept up, and guard maintained against the unremitting attraction of ancient habits, and the force of perpetual temptations."[1] By the time Franklin prepared his plan for achieving moral perfection, he had already learned from experience some of the benefits of a temperate diet.

Franklin's dietary interests began when he was still a young man. At the age of 16, he met with a book recommending a vegetable diet and determined to follow its plan. During the period he observed that diet, he realized some useful benefits:

> When about 16 years of age I happened to meet with a book, written by one Tryon, recommending a vegetable diet. I determined to go into it. My brother, being yet unmarried, did not keep house, but boarded himself and his apprentices in another family. My refusing to eat flesh occasioned an inconveniency, and I was frequently chid [chided] for my singularity. I made myself acquainted with Tryon's manner of preparing some of his dishes, such as boiling potatoes or rice, making hasty

pudding, and a few others, and then proposed to my
brother, that if he would give me, weekly, half the
money he paid for my board, I would board myself. He
instantly agreed to it, and I presently found that I could
save half what he paid me. This was an additional fund
for buying books. But I had another advantage in it. My
brother and the rest going from the printinghouse to
their meals, I remained there alone, and, dispatching
presently my light repast, which often was no more than
a bisket or a slice of bread, a handful of raisins, or a tart
from the pastry-cook's, and a glass of water, had the rest
of the time, till their return, for study, *in which I made
the greater progress, from that greater clearness of
head and quicker apprehension which usually attend
temperance in eating and drinking.*[2]

The discipline Franklin learned from his dietary practices
served him well during his first stay in England. He had gone to
England to get printing equipment at the encouragement of
Governor Sir William Keith, who had promised to help him set
up a printing business. Upon arriving there, he discovered the
Governor to be more liberal im making promises than dutiful in
in keeping them, and did not receive the needed money with
which to purchase his printing equipment and return home. Thus
stranded, Benjamin took work, first in one printing house, then
in another. The following is a partial account of his experiences
at Watt's, the second printing house in which he worked:

At my first admission into this printing-house I took to
working at press, imagining I felt a want of the bodily
exercise I had been used to in America, where press
work is mixed with composing. I drank only water; the
other workmen, near fifty in number, were great
guzzlers of beer. On occasion, I carried up and down
stairs a large form of types in each hand, when others
carried but one in both hands. They wondered to see,
from this and several instances, that the "Water-
American", as they called me, was stronger than
themselves, who drank strong beer! We had an alehouse

boy who attended in the house to supply the workmen.
My companion at the press drank every day a pint before
breakfast, a pint at breakfast with his bread and cheese,
a pint between breakfast and dinner, a pint in the
afternoon about six o'clock, and another when he had
done his day's work. I thought it a detestable custom;
but it was necessary, he supposed, to drink strong beer,
that he might be strong to labor. I endeavored to
convince him that the bodily strength afforded by beer
could only be in proportion to the grain or flour of the
barley dissolved in the water of which it was made; that
there was more flour in a pennyworth of bread; and
therefore, if he would eat that with a pint of water, it
would give him more strength than a quart of beer. He
drank on, however, and had four or five shillings to pay
out of his wages every Saturday night for that muddling
liquor; an expense I was free from.[3]

Although unsuccessful with his companion at the press,
Franklin's example did influence many:

From my example, a great part of them left their muddling breakfast of beer, and bread, and cheese, finding
they could with me be supplied from a neighboring
house with a large porringer of hot water-gruel,
sprinkled with pepper, crumbed with bread, and a bit of
butter in it, for the price of a pint of beer, viz., a three
half-pence. This was a more comfortable as well as
cheaper breakfast, and kept their heads clearer.[4]

Several years later, while in London as a representative of
Pennsylvania, Franklin wrote the following advice to his wife:

I am glad to hear you continue so well, and that the
pain in your side and head have left you. Eat light foods,
such as fowls, mutton, etc., and but little beef or bacon,
avoid strong tea, and use what exercise you can; by
these means you will preserve your health better, and be
less subject to lowness of spirits.[5]

I CANNOT WALK AN HOUR, BRISKLY, WITHOUT GLOWING

At a time when his son, William, then Governor of New Jersey, was ill, Benjamin wrote him from London to encourage him to take more exercise. In his letter, Benjamin discussed the benefits of several methods of exercising in a manner that showed his understanding of the need for what we now call aerobic exercise:

Dear Son,

In yours of May 14th, you acquaint me with your indisposition, which gave me great concern. The resolution you have taken to use more exercise is extremely proper; and I hope you will steadily perform it. It is of the greatest importance to prevent diseases, since the cure of them by physic is so very precarious.

In considering the different kinds of exercise, I have thought that the *quantum* of each is to be judged of, not by time or distance, but by the degree of warmth it produces in the body. Thus, when I observe it, if I am cold when I get into a carriage in a morning, I may ride all day without being warmed by it; that, if on horseback my feet are cold, I may ride some hours before they become warm, but if I am ever so cold on foot, I cannot walk an hour briskly, without glowing from head to foot by the quickened circulation, I have been ready to say (using round numbers without regard to exactness, but merely to make a great difference) that there is more exercise in *one* mile's riding on horseback, than in *five* in a coach; and more in one mile's walking on foot, than in five on horseback; to which I may add that there is more in walking one mile up and down stairs, than in five on a level floor. The two latter exercises may be had within doors, when the weather discourages going abroad; and the last may be had when one is pinched for time, as containing a great quantity of exercise in a handful of minutes. The dumb-bell is another exercise of the latter compendious kind. By the use of it I have in

forty swings quickened my pulse from sixty to one
hundred beats in a minute, counted by a second watch;
and I suppose the warmth generally increases with
quickness of pulse.[6]

To a colleague in Holland, during the war for independence,
Franklin wrote:

Be of good courage, and keep up your spirits. Your
last letter has a melancholy turn. Do you take sufficient
bodily exercise? Walking is an excellent thing for those
whose employment is chiefly sedentary.[7]

THE EXERCISE OF SWIMMING

Franklin was a very good swimmer and highly recommended
the exercise to others. In the following two letters, Benjamin
provided some sound counsel on learning how to swim, discussed the benefits of swimming, and described some entertaining things one might do in water.

Dear Sir,
I cannot be of opinion with you that it is too late in life
for you to learn to swim. The river near the bottom of
your garden affords a most convenient place for the
purpose. And as your new employment requires your
being often on the water, of which you have such a
dread, I think you would do well to make the trial;
nothing being so likely to remove those apprehensions
as the consciousness of an ability to swim to the shore,
in case of an accident, or of supporting yourself in the
water till a boat should come to take you up.
I do not know how far corks or bladders may be useful
in learning to swim, having never seen much trial of
them. Possibly they may be of service in supporting the
body while you are learning what is called the stroke, or
that manner of drawing in and striking out the hands and
feet that is necessary to produce progressive motion. But
you will be no swimmer till you can place some

confidence in the power of the water to support you; I would therefore advise the acquiring of that confidence in the first place; especially as I have known several who, by a little of the practice necessary for that purpose, have insensibility acquired the stroke, taught as it were by nature.

The practice I mean is this: Choosing a place where the water deepens gradually, walk coolly into it till it is up to your breast, then turn around, your face to the shore, and throw an egg into the water between you and the shore. It will sink to the bottom, and be easily seen there, as your water is clear. It must lie in water so deep that you cannot reach it to take it up but by diving for it. To encourage yourself in order to do this, reflect that your progress will be from deeper to shallower water, and that at any time you may, by bringing your legs under you and standing on the bottom, raise your head far above the water. Then plunge under it with your eyes open, throwing yourself towards the egg, and endeavoring by the action of your hands and feet against the water to get forward till within reach of it. In this attempt you will find that the water buoys you up against your inclination; that it is not so easy a thing to sink as you imagined; that you cannot but by active force get down to the egg. Thus you feel the power of the water to support you, and learn to confide in that power; while your endeavors to overcome it, and to reach the egg, teach you the manner of acting on the water with your feet and hands, which action is afterwards used in swimming to support your head higher above water, or to go forward through it.

I would the more earnestly press you to the trial of this method, because, though I think I satisfied you that your body is lighter than water, and that you might float in it a long time with your mouth free for breathing, if you would put yourself in a proper posture, and would be still and forbear struggling; yet till you have obtained this experimental confidence in the water, I cannot depend on your having the necessary presence of mind to recollect that posture and the directions I gave you relating to it. The surprise may put all out of your mind. For though we value ourselves on being reasonable, knowing creatures, reason and knowledge seem on such occasions to be of little use to us; and the brutes, to whom we allow scarce a glimmering of either, appear to have the advantage of us.

I will, however, take this opportunity of repeating those particulars to you which I mentioned in our last conversation, as, by perusing them at your leisure, you may possibly imprint them so in your memory as on occasion to be of some use to you.

1. That though the legs, arms,and head of a human body, being solid parts, are specifically something heavier than fresh water, yet the trunk, particularly the upper part, from its hollowness, is so much lighter than water, as that the whole of the body taken together is too light to sink wholly under water, but some part will remain above, until the lungs become filled with water, which happens from drawing water into them instead of air, when a person in the fright attempts breathing while the mouth and nostrils are under water.

2. That the legs and arms are specifically lighter than salt water, and will be supported by it, so that a human body would not sink in salt water, though the lungs were filled as above, but from the greater specific gravity of the head.

3. That therefore a person throwing himself on his back in salt water, and extending his arms, may easily lie so as to keep his mouth and nostrils free for breathing; and by a small motion of his hands may prevent turning, if he should perceive any tendency to do it.

4. That in fresh water, if a man throws himself on his back, near the surface, he cannot long continue in that situation but by proper action of his hands on the water. If he uses no such action, the legs and lower part of the body will gradually sink till he comes into an upright position, in which he will continue suspended, the hollow of the breast keeping the head uppermost.

5. But if, in this erect position, the head is kept upright above the shoulders, as when we stand on the ground, the immersion will, by the weight of that part of the head that is out of water, reach above the mouth and nostrils, perhaps a little above the eyes, so that a man cannot long remain suspended in water with his head in that position.

6. The body continuing suspended as before, and upright, if the head be leaned quite back, so that the face looks upwards, all the back part of the head being then under water, and its weight consequently in a great measure supported by it, the face will remain above water quite free for breathing, will rise an inch higher every inspiration, and sink as much every expiration, but never so low as that the water may come over the mouth.

7. If therefore a person unacquainted with swimming and falling accidentally into the water, could have presence of mind sufficient to avoid struggling and plunging, and to let the body take this natural position, he might continue long safe from drowning till perhaps help would come. For as to the clothes, their additional weight while immersed is very inconsiderable, the water supporting it, though when he comes out of the water he would find them very heavy indeed.

But, as I said before, I would not advise you or any one to depend on having this presence of mind on such an occasion, but learn firmly to swim; as I wish all men were taught to do in their youth. They would, on many occurrences, be the safer for having that skill, and on many more the happier, as freer from painful apprehensions of danger, to say nothing of the enjoyment in so delightful and wholesome an exercise. Soldiers particularly should, methinks, all be taught to swim; it might be of frequent use either in surprising an enemy, or saving themselves. And if I had now boys to educate, I should prefer those schools (other things being equal) where an opportunity was offered for acquiring so advantageous an art, which, once learned, is never forgotten.[8]

In responding to another friend's philosophical inquiries, Franklin included these comments:

When I was a boy I made two oval palettes, each about ten inches long and six broad, with a hole for the thumb, in order to retain it fast in the palm of my hand. They much resembled a painter's palettes. In swimming I pushed the edges of these forward and I struck the water with their flat surfaces as I drew them back. I remember I swam faster by means of these palettes, but they fatigued my wrists. I also fitted to the soles of my feet a kind of sandals; but I was not satisfied with them, because I observed that the stroke is partly given by the inside of the feet and the ankles, and not entirely with the soles of the feet. . . .

I know by experience that it is a great comfort to a swimmer who has a considerable distance to go, to turn himself sometimes on his back, and to vary in other respect the means of procuring a progressive motion.

When he is seized with the cramp in the leg, the method of driving it away is, to give to the parts affected a sudden, vigorous, and violent shock; which he may do in the air as he swims on his back. . . .

The exercise of swimming is one of the most healthy and agreeable in the world. After having swam for an hour or two in the evening, one sleeps coolly the whole night, even during the most ardent heat of summer. Perhaps, the pores being cleansed, the insensible perspiration increases and occasions this coolness. It is certain that much swimming is the means of stopping a diarrhoea, and even of producing a constipation. With respect to those who do not know how to swim, or who are affected with a diarrhoea at a season which does not permit them to use that exercise, a warm bath, by cleansing and purifying the skin, is found very salutary, and often effects a radical cure. I speak from my own experience, frequently repeated, and that of others, to whom I have recommended this.

You will not be displeased if I conclude these hasty remarks by informing you that as the ordinary method of swimming is reduced to the act of rowing with the arms and legs, and is consequently a laborious and fatiguing operation when the space of water to be crossed is considerable, there is a method in which a swimmer may pass to a great distance with much facility, by means of a sail. This discovery I fortunately made by accident, and in the following manner:

When I was a boy I amused myself one day with flying a paper kite; and approaching the bank of a pond, which was near a mile broad, I tied the string to a stake and the kite ascended to a very considerable height above the pond while I was swimming. In a little time, being desirous of amusing myself with my kite, and enjoying at the same time the pleasure of swimming, I returned, and loosing from the stake the string with the little stick which was fastened to it, went again into the water, where I found that lying on my back and holding the stick in my hands, I was drawn along the surface of the water in a very agreeable manner. Having then engaged another boy to carry my clothes round the pond, to a place which I pointed out to him on the other side, I began to cross the pond with my kite, which carried me quite over without the least fatigue, and with the greatest pleasure imaginable. I was only obliged occasionally to halt a little in my course and resist its progress when it appeared that, by following too quick, I lowered the kite too much; by doing which occasionally I made it rise again. I have never since that practiced this singular mode of swimming though I think it not impossible to cross in this manner from Dover to Calais. The packet-boat, however, is still preferable.[9]

From the foregoing selections may be seen the benefits of observing good dietary practices and exercising on a regular basis. A greater clearness of thinking, the warm glow of health, and many hours of enjoyable recreation are among the rewards of proper nutrition and sufficient exercise.

18

THE ART OF PROCURING PLEASANT DREAMS

Vince Lombardi, the famous coach of the Green Bay Packers, has been quoted as saying, "fatigue makes cowards of us all." Without adequate rest, life can become most oppressive; we become irritable, we tend to think less clearly, our emotions are easily inflamed, and our productivity decreases. In addition, our resistance weakens and we become more susceptible to disease and more prone to accident. In the preservation of both physical and mental health, getting adequate rest is absolutely essential. If in the process we can add pleasure to our rest, our enjoyment of life is increased and our burdens made lighter. In the following article, written to a friend on request, Franklin offered some unique and interesting thoughts on "The Art of Procuring Pleasant Dreams."

As a great part of our life is spent in sleep, during which we have sometimes pleasant and sometimes painful dreams, it becomes of some consequence to obtain the one kind and avoid the other; for, whether real or imaginary, pain is pain and pleasure is pleasure. If we can sleep without dreaming, it is well that painful dreams are avoided. *If, while we sleep, we can have any pleasing dream, it is, as the French say, autante de gagne', so much added to the pleasure of life.*

To this end it is, in the first place, necessary to be careful in preserving health, by due exercise and great temperance; for, in sickness, the imagination is disturbed, and disagreeable, sometimes terrible, ideas are apt to present themselves. Exercise should precede meals, not immediately follow them; the first promotes, the latter, unless moderate, obstructs digestion. If, after exercise, we feed sparingly, the digestion will be easy and good, the body lightsome, the temper cheerful, and all the animal functions performed agreeably. Sleep, when it follows, will be natural and undisturbed; while indolence, with full feeding, occasions nightmares and horrors inexpressible; we fall from precipices, are assaulted by wild beasts, murderers, and demons, and experience every variety of distress. Observe, however, that the quantities of food and exercise are relative things; those who move much may, and indeed ought to, eat much more; those who use little exercise should eat little. *In general, mankind, since the improvement of cookery, eat about twice as much as nature requires.* Suppers are not bad, if we have not dined; but restless nights naturally follow hearty suppers after full dinners. Indeed, as there is a difference in constitutions, some rest well after these meals; it costs them only a frightful dream and an apoplexy, after which they sleep till doomsday. Nothing is more common in the newspapers than instances of people who, after eating a hearty supper, are found dead abed in the morning.

Another means of preserving health to be attended to is the having a constant supply of fresh air in your bed chamber. It has been a great mistake the sleeping in rooms exactly closed, and in beds surrounded by curtains. No outward air that may come in to you is so unwholesome as the unchanged air, often breathed, of a close chamber. As boiling water does not grow hotter by longer boiling, if the particles that receive greater heat can escape, so living bodies do not putrefy, if the particles, so fast as they become putrid, can be thrown off. Nature expels them by the pores of the skin and the lungs, and in a free, open air they are carried off; but in a close room we receive them again and again, though they become more and more corrupt. A number of persons crowded into a small room thus spoil the air in a few minutes, and even render it mortal, as in the Black Hole at Calcutta. A single person is said to spoil only a gallon of air per minute, and therefore requires a longer time to spoil a chamberfull; but it is done, however, in proportion, and many putrid disorders hence have their origin. It is recorded of Methusalem, who, being the longest liver, may be supposed to have best preserved his health, that he slept always in the open air; for, when he had lived five hundred years, an angel said to him, "Arise Methusalem, and build thee an house, for thou shalt live yet five hundred years longer." But Methusalem answered and said, "If I am to live but five hundred years longer, it is not worth while to build me a house; I will sleep in the air, as I have been used to do." Physicians, after having for ages contended that the sick should not be indulged with fresh air, have at length discovered that it may do them good. It is therefore to be hoped that they may in time discover likewise that it is not hurtful to those who are in health, and that we may then be cured of the *aerophibia* that at present distresses weak minds, and makes them choose to be stifled and poisoned, rather than leave open the window of a bed-chamber, or put down the glass of a coach.

Confined air, when saturated with perspirable matter, will not receive more; and that matter must remain in the bodies, and occasion diseases; but it gives some previous notice of its being about to be hurtful, by producing certain uneasiness, slight indeed at first, such as with regard to the lungs is a trifling sensation, and to the pores of the skin a kind of restlessness, which is difficult to describe, and few that feel it know the cause of it. But we may recollect that sometimes, on waking in the night, we have, if warmly covered, found it difficult to get to sleep again. We turn often, without finding repose in any position. This fidgetiness (to use a vulgar expression for want of a better) is occasioned wholly by an uneasiness in the skin, owing to the retention of the perspirable matter, the bed-clothes having received their quantity, and, being saturated, refusing to take any more. To become sensible of this by an experiment, let a person keep his position in the bed, but throw off the bed-clothes, and suffer fresh air to approach the part uncovered of his body; he will then feel that part suddenly refreshed; for the air will immediately relieve the skin, by receiving, licking up, and carrying off the load of perspirable matter that incommoded it. For every portion of cool air that approaches the warm skin, in receiving its part of that vapor, receives therewith a degree of heat that rarefies and renders it lighter, when it will be pushed away with its burthern [burden], by cooler and therefore heavier fresh air, which for a moment supplies its place, and then, being likewise changed and warmed, gives way to a succeeding quantity. This is the order of nature, to prevent animals being infected by their own perspiration. He will now be sensible of the difference between the part exposed to the air and that which, remaining sunk in the bed, denies the air access; for this part now manifests its uneasiness more distinctly by the comparison, and the seat of the uneasiness is more plainly perceived than when the whole surface of the body was affected by it.

Here then is one great and general cause of unpleasing dreams. For when the body is uneasy the mind will be disturbed by it, and disagreeable ideas of various kinds will in sleep be the natural consequences. The remedies, preventative and curative, follow.

1. By eating moderately (as before advised for health's sake), less perspirable matter is produced in a given time; hence bed-clothes receive it longer before they are saturated, and we may therefore sleep longer before we are made uneasy by their refusing to receive any more.

2. By using thinner and more porous bed-clothes, which will suffer the perspirable matter more easily to

pass through them, we are less incommoded, such being longer tolerable.

3. When you are awakened by this uneasiness, and find you cannot easily sleep again, get out of bed, beat up and turn your pillow, shake the bed-clothes well with at least twenty shakes, then throw the bed open to leave it cool; in the meanwhile, continuing undressed, walk about your chamber till your skin has had time to discharge its load, which it will do sooner as the air may be drier and colder. When you begin to feel the cold air unpleasant, then return to your bed, and you will soon fall asleep and your sleep will be sweet and pleasant. All the scenes presented to your fancy will be too of the pleasing kind. I am often as agreeably entertained with them as by the scenery of an opera. If you happen to be too indolent to get out of bed, you may instead of it lift up your bed-clothes with one arm and leg, so as to draw in a good deal of fresh air, and by letting them fall force it out again. This, repeated twenty times, will so clear them of the perspirable matter they have imbibed, as to permit your sleeping well for some time afterwards. But this latter method is not equal to the former.

Those who do not love trouble and can afford to have two beds, will find great luxury in rising, when they wake in a hot bed, and going into the cool one. Such shifting of beds would also be of great service to persons ill of a fever, as it refreshes and frequently procures sleep. A very large bed that will admit a removal so distant from the first situation as to be cool and sweet, may, in a degree, answer the same end.

One or two observations more will conclude this little piece. Care must be taken when you lie down to dispose your pillow so as to suit your manner of placing your head, and to be perfectly easy; then place your limbs so as not to bear inconveniently hard upon one another, as, for instance, the joints of your ankles; for, though a bad position may at first give but little pain and be hardly noticed, yet a continuance will render it less tolerable, and the uneasiness may come on while you are asleep, and disturb your imagination. These are the rules of the art. But, though they will generally prove effectual in procuring the end intended, there is a case in which the most punctual observance of them will be totally fruitless. I need not mention the case to you, my dear friend, but my account of the art would be imperfect without it. The case is, when the person who desires to have pleasant dreams has not taken care to preserve, what is necessary above all things,

A GOOD CONSCIENCE[1]

BATHING IN AIR

In a letter to a friend in France, Franklin included the following suggestions of a practice that had been useful to him:

You know the cold bath has long been in vogue here as a tonic; but the shock of the cold water has always appeared to me, generally speaking, as too violent, and I have found it much more agreeable to my constitution to bathe in another element, I mean cold air. With this view I rise almost every morning and sit in my chamber without any clothes whatever, half an hour or an hour, according to the season, either reading or writing. This practice is not in the least painful, but, on the contrary, agreeable; and, if I return to bed afterwards, before I dress myself, as sometimes happens, I make a supplement to my night's rest of one or two hours of the most pleasing sleep that can be imagined. I find no ill consequences whatever resulting from it, and that at least it does not injure my health, if it does not in fact contribute much to its preservation. I shall therefore call it for the future a *bracing* or *tonic* bath.[2]

The novelty of Franklin's thoughts on how to sleep restfully and pleasantly should not detract from their practicality. For those who may be troubled with bad dreams or who are having difficulties getting adequate rest, they are well worth the experiment.

FRANKLIN'S FORMULA FOR SUCCESSFUL LIVING
NUMBER EIGHT

When we are young,
and sometimes when older,
we fail to appreciate
the importance of good health
and what it takes to preserve it.

To the extent a person
is careless in preserving his health,
or foolish,
in doing things injurious to himself,
he will detract so much
from his potential
for happiness.

Prudence,
temperance,
moderation,
and self discipline
are those virtues best suited
for fostering physical and mental health.

Proper nutrition,
sufficient exercise,
and adequate rest
are those activities best suited
for promoting physical and mental health.

These virtues
and activities,
when combined with a clear conscience,
are the best preservatives
of a strong body
a sound mind,
and a healthy constitution.

GUIDING PRINCIPLE
NUMBER NINE

HAPPINESS SPRINGS IMMEDIATELY FROM THE MIND

There are those people who go through life "laughing on the outside, while crying on the inside." However unhappy this situation may be, it is far superior to one where inner tears breed bitterness and hostility.

All situations have their inconveniences, and admittedly some can be terrible experiences. It is interesting to observe, however, that not all who are unhappy have had terrible experiences and that not all who have had terrible experiences are unhappy. Life is like a river, continually flowing, and any given experience only occupies a point in time and, like a tree along the bank, is soon left behind. All that remains of the experience is what we carry downstream with us. No one has complete control, and sometimes we may have very little control, over the circumstances in which we find ourselves. But, as many have learned, it is possible to control our attitudes and feelings about the experiences we do have. In fact, it is not only possible, but essential to exercise that kind of control, if we wish to be happy.

Some people seem, by nature, to be more resilient and better able to see the good in life than others. There is no question that we are born with different dispositions, but nature does not require that we limit ourselves to her initial gifts. Just as we are able, with effort, to improve our ability to think and reason about the world around us, so also we are able, with effort, to improve how we think and reason about what goes on within us. Unfortunately, since thoughts and feelings flow to us, often without conscious effort, we tend to accept them as they are, without any effort to improve them. Thus it is that many people, well educated in other respects, never obtain the emotional and mental maturity to enjoy life to its fullest potential.

Benjamin Franklin, sage in all that he did, determined not to delegate his enjoyment of life to the operations of nature or to the actions of other people. As with other aspects of his life, he accepted full responsibility for the things he thought and felt. He determined early, and in writing, to "be not disturbed at trifles, or at accidents common or unavoidable."[1] He deliberately cultivated a cheerful and pleasant disposition. He looked for the good in others and in the world around him. He knew the value of keeping busy physically and mentally. He perceived more clearly than most of us seem to, that the seat of human happiness is in the mind.

LOOKING

ON THE BRIGHT SIDE

19

PARSONS AND POTTS

There are many people, who, though good and virtuous in other respects, have not learned to gain sufficient control of their thoughts and feelings as to be able to experience a full enjoyment of themselves or of the world around them. Franklin expressed his perspective of this in a letter to a fellow Junto member:

> Two of the former members of the Junto, you tell me, are departed this life, Potts and Parsons. Odd characters both of them. Parsons a wise man, that often acted foolishly; Potts a wit, that seldom acted wisely. If enough were the means to make a man happy, one had always the means of happiness, without ever enjoying the thing; the other had always the thing, without ever possessing the means. Parsons, even in his prosperity, always fretting; Potts, in the midst of his poverty, ever laughing. *It seems, then, that happiness in this life rather depends on internals than externals; and that, besides the natural effects of wisdom and virtue, vice and folly, there is such a thing as a happy or an unhappy constitution.* They were both our friends, and loved us. So peace to their shades. They had their virtues as well

as their foibles; they were both honest men, and that alone, as the world goes, is one of the greatest of chara-cters. They were old acquaintances, in whose company I formerly enjoyed a great deal of pleasure and I cannot think of losing them without concern and regret.[1]

GOUT MORE A REMEDY THAN A DISEASE

To develop a happy constitution requires a conscious effort to see the good around us, to make the best of things, to look on the bright side. There is something good that can be derived from virtually every human situation if the will and desire is there to do so. Franklin's attitude toward the gout is characteristic of his approach to this important principle. In his classic essay, "Dialogue Between Franklin and the Gout", he not only enter-tains and instructs, but also demonstrates how to have a little fun even with difficult problems that may come our way:

FRANKLIN: Eh! oh! eh! What have I done to merit these cruel sufferings?
GOUT: Many things; you have ate and drank too freely, and too much indulged those legs of yours in their indolence.
FRANKLIN: Who is it that accuses me?
GOUT: It is I, even I, the Gout.
FRANKLIN: What! my enemy in person?
GOUT: No, not your enemy.
FRANKLIN: I repeat it, my enemy; for you would not only torment my body to death, but ruin my good name; you reproach me as a glutton and a tippler; now all the world, that knows me, will allow that I am neither the one or the other.
GOUT: The world may think as it pleases; it is always very complaisant to itself, and sometimes to its friends; but I very well know the quantity of meat and drink for a man, who takes a reasonable degree of exercise, would be too much for another, who never takes any.
FRANKLIN: I take—eh! oh!—as much exercise—eh! —as I can, Madam Gout. You know my sedentary state,

and on that account, it would seem, Madam Gout, as if
you might spare me a little, seeing it is not altogether my
fault.

GOUT: Not a jot; your rhetoric and your politeness are
thrown away; your apology avails nothing. If your
situation in life is a sedentary one, your amusements,
your recreation, at least, should be active. You ought to
walk or ride; or, if the weather prevents that, play at
billiards. But let us examine your course of life. While
the mornings are long and you have leisure to go abroad,
what do you do? Why, instead of gaining an appetite for
breakfast, by salutary exercise, you amuse yourself with
books, pamphlets, or newspapers, which commonly are
not worth the reading. Yet you eat an inordinate
breakfast, four dishes of tea, with cream, and one or two
buttered toasts, with slices of hung beef, which I fancy
are not things the most easily digested. Immediately
afterwards you sit down to write at your desk, or
converse with persons who apply to you on business.
Thus the time passes till one, without any kind of bodily
exercise. But all this I could pardon, in regard, as you
say, to your sedentary condition. But what is your
practice after dinner? Walking in the beautiful gardens
of those friends with whom you have dined would be the
choice of men of sense; yours is to be fixed down to
chess, where you are found engaged for two or three
hours! This is your perpetual recreation, which is the
least eligible of any for a sedentary man, because,
instead of accelerating the motion of the fluids, the rigid
attention to it requires helps to retard the circulation and
obstruct internal secretions. Wrapt in the speculations of
this wretched game, you destroy your constitution. What
can be expected from such a course of living, but a body
replete with stagnant humors, ready to fall a prey to all
kinds of dangerous maladies, if I, the Gout, did not
occasionally bring you relief by agitating those humors,
and so purifying or dissipating them? If it was in some
nook or alley in Paris, deprived of walks, that you
played awhile at chess after dinner this might be excus-

able; but, the same taste prevails with you in Passy, Auteuil, Montmarte, or Sanoy, places where there are the finest gardens and walks, a pure air, beautiful women, and most agreeable and instructive conversation; all which you might enjoy by frequenting the walks. But these are rejected for this abominable game of chess. Fie, then, Mr. Franklin! But amidst my instructions, I had almost forgot to administer my wholesome corrections; so take that twinge,—and that.

FRANKLIN: Oh! eh! oh! ohhh! As much instruction as you please, Madam Gout, and as many reproaches; but pray, Madam, a truce with your corrections!

GOUT: No, Sir, no,—I will not abate a particle of what is so much for your good,—therefore—

FRANKLIN: Oh! ehhh!—It is not fair to say I take no exercise, when I do very often, going out to dine and returning in my carriage.

GOUT: That, of all imaginable exercises, is the most slight and insignificant, if you allude to the motion of a carriage suspended on springs. By observing the degree of heat obtained by different kinds of motion, we may form an estimate of the quantity of exercise given by each. Thus, for example, if you turn out to walk in winter with cold feet, in an hour's time you will be in a glow all over; ride on horseback, the same effect will scarcely be perceived by four hours' round trotting; but if you loll in a carriage, such as you have mentioned, you may travel all day and gladly enter the inn to warm your feet by a fire. Flatter yourself then no longer, that half an hour's airing in your carriage deserves the name of exercise. Providence has appointed few to roll in carriages, while he has given to all a pair of legs, which are machines infinitely more commodious and serviceable. Be grateful, then, and make a proper use of yours. Would you know how they forward the circulation of your fluids, in the very action of transporting you from place to place; observe when you walk, that all your weight is alternately thrown from one leg to the other; this occasions a great pressure on the vessels of the foot, and repels their contents; when relieved, by the weight being thrown on the other foot, the vessels of the first are allowed to replenish, and, by a return of this weight, this repulsion again succeeds; thus accelerating the circulation of the blood. The heat produced in any given time depends on the degree of this acceleration; the fluids are shaken, the humors attenuated, the secretions facilitated, and all goes well; the cheeks are ruddy, and health is established. Behold your fair friend at Auteuil; a lady who received from bounteous nature more really useful science than half a dozen such pretenders to philosophy as you have been able to extract from all your books. When she honors you with a visit, it is on foot. She walks all hours of the day, and leaves indolence, and its concomitant maladies, to be endured by her horses. In this, see at once the preservative of her health and personal charms. But when you go to Auteuil, you must have your carriage, though it is no farther from Passy to Auteuil than from Auteuil to Passy.

FRANKLIN: Your reasonings grow very tiresome.

GOUT: I stand corrected. I will be silent and continue my office; take that, and that.

FRANKLIN: Oh! Ohh! Talk on I pray you.

GOUT: No, no; I have a good number of twinges for you to-night, and you may be sure of some to-morrow.

FRANKLIN: What, with such a fever! I shall go distracted. Oh! eh! Can no other bear it for me?

GOUT: Ask that of your horses; they have served you faithfully.

FRANKLIN: How can you so cruelly sport with my torments?

GOUT: Sport! I am very serious. I have here a list of offenses against your own health distinctly written, and can justify every stroke inflicted on you.

FRANKLIN: Read it then.

GOUT: It is too long a detail; but I will briefly mention some particulars.

FRANKLIN: Proceed. I am all attention.

GOUT: Do you remember how often you have promised yourself, the following morning, a walk in the grove of Boulogne, in the garden de la Muette, in your own garden, and have violated your promise, alleging, at one time, it was too cold, at another too warm, too windy, too moist, or what else you pleased; when in truth it was too nothing, but your insuperable love of ease?

FRANKLIN: That I confess may have happened occasionally, probably ten times a year.

GOUT: Your confession is very far short of the truth; the gross amount is one hundred and ninety-nine times.

FRANKLIN: Is it possible?

GOUT: So possible, that it is fact; you may rely on the accuracy of my statement. You know M. Brillon's gardens, and what fine walks they contain; you know the handsome flight of an hundred steps, which lead from the terrace above to the lawn below. You have been in the practice of visiting this amiable family twice a week, after dinner, and it is a maxim of your own, that "a man may take as much exercise in walking a mile, up and down stairs, as in ten on level ground." What an opportunity was here for you to have had exercise in both these ways! Did you embrace it, and how often?

FRANKLIN: I cannot immediately answer that question.

GOUT: I will do it for you; not once.

FRANKLIN: Not once?

GOUT: Even so. During the summer you went there at six o'clock. You found the charming lady with her lovely children and friends, eager to walk with you, and entertain you with their agreeable conversation; and what has been your choice? Why, to sit on the terrace, satisfying yourself with the fine prospect, and passing your eye over the beauties of the garden below, without taking one step to descend and walk about in them. On the contrary, you call for tea and the chess-board; and lo! you are occupied in your seat till nine o'clock, and that besides two hours' play after dinner; and then,

instead of walking home, which would have bestirred
you a little, you step into your carriage. How absurd to
suppose that all this carelessness can be reconcilable
with health, without my interposition!

FRANKLIN: I am convinced now of the justness of
Poor Richard's remark, that "Our debts and our sins are
always greater than what we think for."

GOUT: So it is. You philosophers are sages in your
maxims, and fools in your conduct.

FRANKLIN: But do you charge among my crimes, that
I return in a carriage from M. Brillon's?

GOUT: Certainly; for, having been seated all the while,
you cannot object to the fatigue of the day, and cannot
want therefore the relief of a carriage.

FRANKLIN: What then would you have me do with
my carriage?

GOUT: Burn it if you choose; you would at least get
heat out of it once in this way; or, if you dislike that
proposal, here's another for you; observe the poor
peasants, who work in the vineyards and grounds about
the villages of Passy, Auteuil, Chaillot, etc.; you may
find every day among these deserving creatures, four or
five old men and women, bent and perhaps crippled by
weight of years, and too long and too great labor. After a
most fatiguing day, these people have to trudge a mile or
two to their smoky huts. Order your coachman to set
them down. This is an act that will be good for your
soul; and, at the same time, after your visit to the
Brillons, if you return on foot, that will be good for your
body.

FRANKLIN: Ah! how tiresome you are!

GOUT: Well, then, to my office; it should not be
forgotten that I am your physician. There.

FRANKLIN: Ohhh! what a devil of a physician!

GOUT: How ungrateful you are to say so! Is it not I
who, in the character of your physician, have saved you
from the palsy, dropsy, and apoplexy? one or other of
which would have done for you long ago, but for me.

FRANKLIN: I submit, and thank you for the past, but entreat the discontinuance of your visits for the future; for, in my mind, one had better die than be cured so dolefully. Permit me just to hint, that I have also not been unfriendly to you. I never feed physician or quack of any kind, to enter the list against you; if then you do not leave me to my repose, it may be said you are ungrateful too.

GOUT: I can scarcely acknowledge that as any objection. As to quacks, I despise them; they may kill you indeed, but cannot injure me. And, as to regular physicians, they are at last convinced the gout, in such a subject as you are, is no disease but a remedy; and wherefore cure a remedy?—but to our business,—there.

FRANKLIN: Oh! oh!—for Heaven's sake leave me! and I promise faithfully never more to play chess, but to take exercise daily, and live temperately.

GOUT: I know you too well. You promise fair; but, after a few months of good health, you will return to your old habits; your fine promises will be forgotten like the forms of the last year's clouds. Let us then finish the account, and I will go. But I leave you with an assurance of visiting you again at a proper time and place; for my object is your good and you are sensible now that I am your *real friend*.[2]

THE BLESSING OF ENEMIES

In the course of his public responsibilities, there were those who opposed Franklin, and some whose enmity was sufficient to qualify them as his enemies. As with his philosophical views, he took "no pains to retaliate" against personal attacks, and for the most part, he was even able to avoid taking offense. Rarely did he respond directly to personal attacks, and only occasionally, in private letters did he even acknowledge them. In this aspect of his life as in others, he demonstrated the absolutely wonderful ability he had to "look at the bright side" and see the good that could be derived from otherwise unpleasant situations.

Respecting his enemies, Franklin wrote to one friend:

> As to the friends and enemies you just mention, I have
> hitherto, thanks to God, had plenty of the former kind;
> they have been my treasure, and it has perhaps been of
> no disadvantage to me that I have had a few of the latter.
> They serve to put us upon correcting the faults we have,
> and avoiding those we are in danger of having. They
> counteract the mischief flattery might do us, and the
> malicious attacks make our friends more zealous in
> serving us and promoting our interest.[3]

To another, he wrote:

> By this ship I hear that my enemies (for God has
> blessed me with two or three, to keep me in order) are
> now representing me at home as an opposer and
> obstructor of his Majesty's service here.[4]

And to another:

> At present I am here as much the butt of party rage and
> malice, expressed in pamphlets and prints, and have as
> many pelted at my head in proportion, as if I had the
> misfortune of being your prime minister. . . . You can
> scarcely conceive how acceptable and satisfactory your
> letters always are on public affairs to me and my friends.
> For my part I rely entirely on your accounts and
> sentiments—only making a small abatement when you
> forbode any misfortune. *But that is mere temper in me,*
> *who always love to view the bright side of things. . . .*[5]

Certainly Franklin practiced what Poor Richard preached:

> *The wise Man draws more Advantage from his Enemies,*
> *[and his Problems] than a Fool from his Friends [and*
> *his Opportunities.]* (1749)

KEEPING BUSY
PHYSICALLY AND MENTALLY 20

Under the virtue of Industry, Franklin stated his objective as follows, "Lose no time; be always employed in something useful." In addition to whatever temporal benefits this approach may provide, it is also a very important key to mental and emotional health.

THE DEVIL HIMSELF MAY MAKE A GREAT DEAL OF THAT

Someone has offered this perceptive insight, "Through God's distribution of talents, he has ordained that we should serve one another." In all of us are dispositions with which we are born, that go beyond those of attitude and may be more appropriately described as aptitude, or natural ability. Since, it is "swimming upstream" to attempt to develop talents for which we have no natural ability, there is great satisfaction in discovering our natural talents, and finding constructive ways to develop and use them for the benefit of ourselves and others. While there may be times when it is necessary to "swim upstream" to acquire abilities not naturally ours, one of the easiest and quickest ways to gain control of our thoughts is to occupy them with natural interests; and, being most likely to succeed in those things in which we have some ability and interest, we tend to feel much better about ourselves. To a fellow printer, Franklin wrote:

You cannot conceive the satisfaction and pleasure you give your friends here by your political letters. Your accounts are so clear, circumstantial, and complete, that though there is nothing too much, nothing is wanting to give us, as I imagine, a more perfect knowledge of your public affairs than most people have that live among you. The characters of your speakers and actors are so admirably sketched, and their views so plainly opened, that we see and know everybody; they all become of our acquaintance. So excellent a manner of writing seems to me a superfluous gift to a mere printer. *If you do not commence author for the benefit of mankind, you will certainly be found guilty hereafter of burying your talent. It is true that it will puzzle the Devil himself to find anything else to accuse you of, but remember he may make a great deal of that.*[1]

WHEN MEN ARE EMPLOYED

Apart from the matter of talent, and even to some extent usefulness, just keeping busy will do much to bring one contentment. During the French and Indian war, Franklin was commissioned by the Governor and asked to take charge of the Northwestern frontier, which was infested by the enemy, and provide for the defense of the inhabitants by raising troops and building a line of forts. He raised 560 men to go with him, his son being his aide-de-camp, and marched to Gnadenhut, a village settled by the Moravians and recently razed by a band of Indians. The morning after their arrival, they began work and quickly erected a fort in one day, after which it rained for the next six. This week in Gnadenhut allowed Franklin to observe a very interesting aspect of human nature:

This gave me occasion to observe that, *when men are employed, they are best contented;* for on the days they worked they were good natured and cheerful and, with the consciousness of having done a good day's work, they spent the evening jollily; but on our idle days they were mutinous and quarrelsome, finding fault with their pork, the bread, etc., and in continual ill-humor, which put me in mind of a sea-captain, whose rule it was to keep his men constantly at work, and, when his mate once told him that they had done everything, and there was nothing further to employ them about, "Oh," says he, "make them scour the anchor."[2]

To a friend who seemed to be unhappy, Franklin offered this advice:

Pray learn, if you have not already learnt, like me, to be pleased with other people's pleasures, and happy with their happiness, when none occur of your own; and then perhaps you will not so soon be weary of the place you chance to be in, and so fond of rambling to get rid of your *ennui*. I fancy you have hit upon the right reason of your being weary of St. Omer's, viz., that you are out of temper, which is the effect of full living and idleness. *A month in Bridewell, beating hemp, upon bread and water, will give you health and spirits, and subsequent cheerfulness and contentment with every other situation.* I prescribe that regimen for you, my dear, in pure good-will, without a fee.[3]

THE WASTE OF LIFE

In a piece published in the Pennsylvania Gazette, titled "The Waste of Life", Franklin presented the view that even the food an idler eats more fully answers the nature of its creation than does the idler himself. In reading it, we can easily see why those who squander time have so little reason to feel good about themselves, and how they deny themselves the satisfactions of achievement:

Anergus was a gentleman of a good estate; he was bred to no business and could not contrive how to waste his hours agreeably; he had no relish for any of the proper works of life, nor any taste at all for the improvement of the mind; he spent generally ten hours of the four-and-twenty in his bed; he dozed away two or three more on his couch, and as many were dissolved in good liquor every evening if he met with company of his own humor. Five or six of the rest he sauntered away with much indolence; the chief business of them was to contrive his meals, and to feed his fancy beforehand with the promise of a dinner and supper; not that he was so absolute a glutton, or so entirely devoted to appetite, but chiefly because he knew not how to employ his thoughts better he let them rove about the sustenance of his body. Thus he had made a shift to wear off ten years since the paternal estate fell into his hands; and yet, according to the abuse of words in our day, he was called a man of virtue, because he was scarce ever known to be quite drunk, or was his nature much inclined to lewdness.

One evening as he was musing alone, his thoughts happened to take a most unusual turn, for they cast a glance backward and began to reflect on his manner of life. He bethought himself what a number of living beings had been made a sacrifice to support his carcass, and how much corn and wine had been mingled with those offerings. He had not quite lost all the arithmetic that he had learned when he was a boy, and he set himself to compute what he had devoured since he came to the age of man.

"About a dozen of feathered creatures, small and great, have, one week with another," said he, "given up their lives to prolong mine, which in ten years amounts to at least six thousand.

"Fifty sheep have been sacrificed in a year, with half a hecatomb of black cattle, that I might have the choicest part offered weekly upon my table. Thus a thousand beasts out of the flock and the herd have been slain in ten years' time to feed me, besides what the forest has supplied me with. Many hundreds of fishes have, in all their varieties, been robbed of life for my repast, and of the smaller fry as many thousands.

"A measure of corn would hardly afford me fine flour enough for a month's provision, and this arises to above six score bushels; and many hogsheads of ale and wine and other liquors have passed through this body of mine, this wretched strainer of meat and drink.

"And what have I done all this time for God or man? What a vast profusion of good things upon a useless life and a worthless liver! *There is not the meanest creature among all these things which I have devoured but hath answered the end of its creation better than I. It was made to support human nature, and it hath done so. Every crab and oyster I have eat, and every grain of corn have I devoured, hath filled up its place in the rank of beings with more propriety and honor than I have done. O shameful waste of life and time!"*

In short, he carried on his moral reflections with so just and severe a force of reason as constrained him to change his whole course of life, to break off his follies at once and to apply himself to gain some useful knowledge when he was more than thirty years of age. He lived many following years with the character of a worthy man and an excellent Christian; he performed the kind offices of a good neighbor at home, and made a shining figure as a patriot in the senate-house; he died with a peaceful conscience, and the tears of his country were dropped upon his tomb.

The world that knew the whole series of his life stood amazed at the mighty change. They beheld him as a wonder of reformation, while he himself confessed and adored the Divine power and mercy which had transformed him from a brute to a man.

But this was a single instance; and we may almost venture to write a miracle upon it. Are there not numbers of both sexes among our young gentry in this degenerate age, whose lives thus run to utter waste, without the least tendency to usefulness?

When I meet with persons of such a worthless character as this it brings to my mind some scraps of Horace:

There are a number of us creep
Into this world, to eat and sleep;
And know no reason why they're born,
But merely to consume the corn,
Devour the cattle, fowl, and fish
And leave behind an empty dish.
Though crows and Ravens do the same,
Unlucky birds of hateful name,
Ravens or crows might fill their places,
And swallow corn and eat carcasses.
Then, if their tombstone, when they die,
Be n't taught to flatter or to lie,
There's nothing better will be said,
Than that they've eat up all their bread,
Drunk all their drink, and have gone to bed.[4]

NOT MERELY AN IDLE AMUSEMENT

Care in choosing leisure activities is also a component of mental and emotional health. Who has not had the experience of spending an afternoon or evening in diversion and afterwards feeling guilty and discouraged at the waste of time. As foods differ in nutritional value, so also diversions differ in emotional value, those tending to the improvement of the body and mind being the most beneficial.

Someone has wisely said, "There are no uninteresting things, only uninterested people." Franklin was interested in everything. At any given time he might be found electrocuting a turkey to see if the meat would be more tender than if killed otherwise; attempting to raise flame on the surface of water by stirring the muddy bottom of a pond and putting a lit candle to its surface; exploring a stone quarry where workmen had claimed to find a live toad entombed; experimenting with musical tones in glasses filled with water; pondering why it was more difficult for horses to pull barges in a canal with low water; creating a new alphabet or any one of a myriad of other activities. He was constantly busy, both mentally and physically. He was seldom bored and rarely discouraged. There was too much to learn, too much to do, too much to accomplish. To him, leisure was the opportunity to become involved in the things that interested him most.

An example of his thinking may be found in a piece he wrote to encourage people in the study of mathematics. Titled, "On the Usefulness of Mathematics", some excerpts from it read:

> *Mechanical demonstrations are a logic of as much or more use than that commonly learned at schools, serving to a just formation of the mind, enlarging its capacity, and strengthening it so as to render the same capable of exact reasoning, and discerning truth from falsehood in all occurrences, even subjects not mathematical.* For which reason, it is said, the Egyptians, Persians, and Lacedaemonians seldom elected any new kings but such as had some knowledge in the mathematics, imagining those who had not, men of imperfect judgments and unfit to rule and govern. . . .
>
> The usefulness of some particular parts of the mathematics has rendered some knowledge of them very necessary to a great part of mankind, and very convenient to all the rest that are any way conversant beyond the limits of their own callings. . . .
>
> Philosophers do generally affirm that human knowledge to be most excellent which is conversant among the most excellent things. What science then can there be more noble, more excellent, more useful for men, more admirably high and demonstrative, than that of mathematics?[5]

Later in life, he wrote another piece titled, "The Morals of Chess", describing the benefits of that game:

> *The game of chess is not merely an idle amusement. Several very valuable qualities of the mind, useful in the course of human life are to be acquired or strengthened by it, so as to become habits, ready on all occasions.* For life is a kind of chess, in which we have often points to gain, and competitors or adversaries to contend with, and in which there is a vast variety of good and evil

events that are in some degree the effects of prudence or the want of it. By playing at chess, then, we may learn:

1. *Foresight*, which looks a little into futurity and considers the consequences that may attend an action; for it is continually occurring to the player: "If I move this piece, what will be the advantage of my new situation? What use can my adversary make of it to annoy me? What other moves can I make to support it and to defend myself from his attacks?"

2. *Circumspection*, which surveys the whole chessboard, or scene of action; the relations of the several pieces and situations, the dangers they are respectively exposed to, the several possibilities of their aiding each other, the probabilities that the adversary may make this or that move, and attack this or the other piece, and what different means can be used to avoid his stroke, or turn its consequences against him.

3. *Caution*, not to make our moves too hastily. The habit is best acquired by observing strictly the rules of the game, such as, "If you touch a piece, you must move it somewhere; if you set it down, you must let it stand"; and it is therefore best that these rules should be observed, as the game thereby becomes more the image of human life, and particularly of war, in which, if you have incautiously put yourself into a bad and dangerous position, you cannot obtain your enemy's leave to withdraw your troops and place them more securely, but you must abide all the consequences of your rashness.

And, lastly, we learn by chess the habit of not being discouraged by present appearances in the state of our affairs, the habit of hoping for a favorable change, and that of persevering in the search of resources. The game is so full of events, there is such a variety of turns in it, the fortune of it is so subject to sudden vicissitudes, and one so frequently, after long contemplation, discovers the means of extricating one's self from a supposed insurmountable difficulty, that one is encouraged to continue the contest to the last in the hopes of victory by our own skill, or a least of getting a stalemate by the negligence of our adversary. And whoever considers, what in chess he often sees instances of, that particular pieces of success are apt to produce presumption and its consequent inattention, by which the losses may be recovered, will learn not to be too much discouraged by the present success of his adversary, nor to despair of final good fortune upon every little check he receives in the pursuit of it.[6]

Obviously, the above are only intended as examples of ways in which to employ one's leisure time usefully. In a world so full of diverse opportunities for useful endeavor, it can hardly be imagined that anyone who wants to do better has any need to be bored with life or to waste away their days.

In reality, few people come anywhere near close to utilizing the capacities they possess. In his autobiography, Franklin expressed his own belief that even people with modest abilities can accomplish much if they are willing to make the effort.

I have always thought that one man of tolerable abilities may work great changes, and accomplish great affairs among mankind if he first forms a good plan and, cutting off all amusements or other employments that would divert his attention, makes the execution of that same plan his sole study and business.[7]

SMALL CONVENIENCES

There is a proverb which says, "The idle mind is the devil's workshop." Keeping busy, physically and mentally, is a key ingredient of emotional health and happiness. The more useful the activity is, the more satisfying it will be. Since, however, life consists more in performing daily duties than it does in grand events, the following perspective is important to keep in mind.

After commenting in his biography on some proposals he had made for keeping the streets of London clean, Franklin wrote this justification for the importance of his proposal:

Some may think these trifling matters not worth minding or relating but when they consider that though dust blown into the eyes of a single person or into a single shop on a windy day, is but of small importance, yet the great number of the instances in a populous city and its frequent repetitions give it a weight and consequence, perhaps they will not censure very severely those who bestow some attention to affairs of this seemingly low nature. *Human felicity is produced not so much by great pieces of fortune that seldom happen as by little advantages that occur every day.*[8]

Bigelow in *The Works of Benjamin Franklin*, notes this entertaining account of a visit to Dr. Franklin by a Mr. Ellicott:

I found him (Franklin) in his little room among his papers. He received me very politely and immediately entered into conversation about the western country. His room makes a singular appearance, being filled with old philosophical instruments, papers, boxes, tables and stools. About ten o'clock he placed some water on the fire but not being expert through his great age, I desired him to give me the pleasure of assisting him. He thanked me and replied that he ever made it a point to wait upon himself and although he began to find himself infirm, he was determined not to increase his infirmities by giving way to them. After the water was hot I observed his object was to shave himself, which operation he performed without a glass and with great expedition. I asked him if he never employed a barber, he answered: *"No, I think happiness does not consist so much in particular pieces of good fortune which perhaps accidentally fall to a man's lot, as to be able in his old age to do those little things which, being unable to perform himself, would be done by others with a sparing hand."*[9]

To those who wish to climb above the lowlands of despair and discontent to higher ground, there are few paths more accessible and easier to find than that marked by the sign *INDUSTRY.*

FRANKLIN'S FORMULA FOR SUCCESSFUL LIVING
NUMBER NINE

It is not given
to mankind
to have complete control
over the circumstances and events
of their lives.

Upheavals of nature,
conflicts between nations,
accidents, disease, and disappointments
constantly nip at the heels
and hedge up the way
of all who walk planet earth.

Yet in every condition
and circumstance of life
may be seen the good,
as well as the bad.

While we may not
be able to control
all that happens to us,
we can control
what happens inside us.

In every circumstance
may be found
those who are cheerful
and those who are bitter,
those who are pleasant
and those who are hateful.
The difference lies not so much
in the circumstance,
as in the person.

Formula Nine

The control
of our thoughts and feelings
may not come easily,
but with effort
and determination,
little by little,
we can rise above the trials
of mortal existence.

Looking for the good around us,
discovering useful ways
to use our talents,
and keeping ourselves busy,
physically and mentally_
these are sure stays
for emotional well being,
within the grasp
of any who make
the effort to reach.

GUIDING PRINCIPLE NUMBER TEN

LIFE IS IMMEASURABLY MORE SATISFYING TO THOSE WHO GET ALONG WELL WITH OTHERS THAN TO THOSE WHO DO NOT

There are certain kinds of weeds that are particularly unpleasant to be around. Some, like the thistle, while not without beauty, are prickly and can only be handled with gloves, if handled at all. Others, like crabgrass, have very little beauty and are just plain bothersome. These weeds seem to come from nowhere and to grow without any encouragement whatsoever. Most of them are prolific in nature and take over any space in which they can get root. To get rid of them requires a determined effort, generally over a long period of time. For, while we may be able to remove the obvious plants today, there are seeds that continue, like so many time capsules, to sprout and grow despite our best efforts to get rid of them. But, as the experienced gardner knows, it is possible, over time and with the right kind of effort, to eventually eliminate them. Even once they are gone, however, we must keep a careful watch lest they return.

In like manner, there are also certain habits or behaviors that sprout up in our lives that render us unpleasant and sometimes prick and wound the feelings of those around us. These habits also seem to come from nowhere and thrive without any encouragement on our part. They, too, are prolific in nature and will take root wherever the opportunity exists to do so. Neither can they be removed except by determined and continuous effort, sometimes for long periods of time. But like weeds in the garden, they respond to cultivation and, over time, can be removed entirely from our lives.

Of these habits, none are more prevalent nor more distracting than quarreling and faultfinding. In the course of daily life, it sometimes seems as if little, and sometimes not so little, disputes arise from out of nowhere to irritate, aggravate, and torment us. Then, to add fuel to the fire, all around us are so many people doing so many foolish things that we have ample reason, at least in our own minds, to be frequently exasperated and agitated. Needless to say, in this frame of mind it is difficult to be very happy, or for that matter, even to be particularly productive. No matter how much we might wish it otherwise, sour minds cannot breed sweet thoughts, and distracted minds are not noted for their coherence, clarity, or productivity.

Among those things Franklin disliked most were disputes with other people. In his private letters, in satires, and in essays he dealt with problems in human relations arising from contentious dispositions and faultfinding. Often humorous, always perceptive and practical, his comments on getting along with others offer entertaining reading and beneficial counsel.

THE PROBLEMS
OF DISPUTING PEOPLE

21

Differences of opinion are not necessarily detrimental, and may even be beneficial, to well-meaning people in search of truth. To them, such differences are the natural offspring of the imperfections of human reason and represent an opportunity to test and improve their ideas. The fires of conflict are only ignited when differences in opinion are fueled by self-interest and sparked by passion. When disagreements arise between people who have a vested interest in the acceptance of their opinions, conflict is inevitable. When the degree of self-interest is high and the differences are wide, the more difficult the communication process is. In this situation, there are those who tend to become verbally, and sometimes even physically, abusive. Needless to say, such behaviors generally aggravate differences and compound difficulties.

In his writings Franklin dealt particularly with two kinds of situations where people become obnoxious in promoting their views. One situation occurs with those who love to debate as a form of sport, the other with those who become contemptuous or rude to those who disagree with them.

THOSE WHO LOVE TO ARGUE

There are individuals who enjoy argument. Generally they have a talent for expressing themselves and for discomfiting their opponents. Often it is a game to them, much as someone might play at chess. The primary difference is that when two people enter into a game of chess, it is a mutual choice, both understand the rules, and the contest is limited to that particular sphere. Those who love to dispute tend not to limit themselves to specific rules and agreed upon arenas for engaging in their sport. As a consequence they often become obnoxious to others and while they may *win the battle*, they frequently *lose the war*, for *those convinced against their will are of the same opinion still.*

Along those lines Franklin had the following to say about a new governor appointed to Pennsylvania:

> In my journey to Boston this year, I met at New York with our new governor, Mr. Morris, just arrived there from England, with whom I had been before intimately acquainted. He brought a commission to supersede Mr. Hamilton, who, tired with the disputes his proprietary instructions subjected him to, had resigned. Mr. Morris asked me if I thought he must expect as uncomfortable an administration. I said: "No; you may, on the contrary, have a very comfortable one if you will only take care not to enter into any dispute with the Assembly." "My dear friend," says he, pleasantly, "how can you advise my avoiding disputes? You know I love disputing; it is one of my greatest pleasures; however, to show the regard I have for your counsel I promise you I will, if possible, avoid them." He had some reason for loving dispute, being eloquent, an acute sophister and therefore generally successful in argumentative conversation. He had been brought up to it from a boy, his father, as I have heard, accustoming his children to dispute with one another for his diversion while sitting at table after dinner; but I think the practice was not wise for, *in the course of my observation these disputing, contradicting, and confuting people are generally unfortunate in their affairs. They get victory sometimes, but they never get good will, which would be of more use to them.*[1]

Benjamin revealed in his autobiography that, as a boy, he loved to argue and nearly developed this unfortunate style as his own:

> There was another bookish lad in the town, John Collins by name, with whom I was intimately acquainted. We sometimes disputed, and very fond we were of argument, and very desirous of confuting one another, which disputatious turn, by the way, is apt to become a very bad habit, making people often extremely disagreeable in company by the contradiction that is necessary to bring it into practice; and thence, besides souring and spoiling the conversation, is productive of disgusts and perhaps, enmities where you may have occasion for friendship.[2]

THOSE WITH PRICKLY PERSONALITIES

There is another group of people who go through life in a constant state of anger. Seething with hostility at anyone who may differ with them or hinder them in their ambitions, these folks are always in a state of conflict with someone or another. Franklin had an opportunity to meet such a couple on a trip to Canada at the beginning of the war with England. He had been commissioned along with others to go to Canada to solicit support for the American cause. On his return home he had occasion to travel with a Mr. and Mrs. Walker, whom he believed *had a talent for making themselves enemies:*

> Dear Friends: We arrived here safe yesterday evening, having left Mrs. Walker with her husband at Albany, from whence we came down by land. We passed him on Lake Champlain; but he returning overtook us at Saratoga, where they both took such liberties, in taunting at our conduct in Canada, that it came almost to a quarrel. We continued our care of her, however, and landed her safe in Albany with her three wagon loads of baggage, brought thither without putting her to any expense, and parted civilly, though coldly. *I think they*

*both have an excellent talent at making themselves
enemies, and I believe, live where they will, they will
never be long without them.*[3]

During the war, while serving as Minister to France, Franklin
managed maritime affairs for America for a time. John Paul
Jones, commander of the Alliance, experienced a mutiny of
several of his officers, led by his second in command, Captain
Landais. Court Martial proceedings were initiated and Franklin
became very much involved. On one occasion he wrote to
Landais:

> No one has ever learnt from me the opinion I formed
> of you from the inquiry made into your conduct. I kept it
> entirely to myself. I have not even hinted it in my letters
> to America, because I would not hazard giving to
> anyone a bias to your prejudice. By communicating a
> part of that opinion privately to you it can do no harm,
> for you may burn it. I should not give you the pain of
> reading it if your demand did not make it necessary. *I
> think you, then, so impudent, so litigious and
> quarrelsome a man, even with your best friends, that
> peace and good order, and, consequently, the quiet and
> regular subordination so necessary to success, are,
> where you preside, impossible.* These are matters within
> my observation and comprehension; your military opera-
> tions I leave to more capable judges. If, therefore, I had
> twenty ships of war in my disposition, I should not give
> one of them to Captain Landais. The same temper which
> excluded him from the French marine would weigh
> equally with me. Of course I shall not replace him in the
> Alliance.
> I am assured, however, that as captain of a merchant
> ship you have two very good qualities highly useful to
> your owners, viz., economy and integrity; for these I
> esteem you, and have the honor to be, sir, etc.,[4]

Not long afterwards, Landais commandeered the Alliance,
when Jones was ashore on leave, and sailed it to America

without an important shipment of war materials it was supposed
to carry. Needless to say this event created a myriad of problems
for Franklin which sparked this comment from him to a
colleague:

> As to Captain Landais, I have no other powers relating
> to the Alliance, than what are implied in my ministerial
> office. He was instructed strictly by the Admiralty in
> America to obey my orders. He disobeyed them. It is not
> necessary to discuss these matters here. We are account-
> able at home. I am heartily sorry that you have been so
> long detained. I have done everything in my power to
> prevent it. You can have no conception of the vexation
> these maritime affairs occasion me. *It is hard that I, who
> give others no trouble with my quarrels, should be
> plagued with all the perversities of those who think fit to
> wrangle with one another.*[5]

Later, in trying to outfit Jones with another ship, the problems
continued and Franklin wrote to his cousin:

> I was told that if we would obtain the Ariel, she would
> do our business; I joined in the application and we ob-
> tained her. Now she is too little and another is wanted. I
> will have absolutely nothing to do with any new
> squadron project. *I have been too long in hot water,
> plagued almost to death with the passions, vagaries and
> ill humors and madness of other people.* I must have a
> little repose.[6]

After the war was over and Benjamin Franklin had returned to
America, a Mr. Elam tried to enlist his support in a quarrel he
was engaged in with his church. Franklin's response was this
timely counsel:

> Sir: I received your note of the 8th instant, and being
> now, as you observe, retired to a private station, I hope
> to enjoy the repose appertaining to it. I cannot think,
> therefore, of calling, as you propose, you and your

accusers before me, to discuss differences which I have
no authority to judge of or to determine. *I can only give
you my friendly advice, which is to behave peaceably
and respectfully* to the religious society you profess to
be connected with, especially in their public assemblies;
in which case I am persuaded you may quietly enjoy
"that liberty of a freeholder and citizen" which you
desire, without receiving from them the smallest
interruption. *By giving me no further trouble with your
quarrels you will oblige your well-wisher.*[7]

"Unpleasantness" is probably the word that characterizes
association with contentious people the best. Since few people
enjoy being involved in unpleasant situations or with unpleasant
people, the act of disputing with others to carry our view is what
psychologists refer to as *self-defeating behavior*. As passions
flame and hostility increases, resistance to our ideas also
increases, and though we may win for a while by simply
overpowering our opponents, we will generally make enough
enemies in the process to eventually lose whatever we were
trying to gain. Was it not Poor Richard who said:

A Man in a Passion rides a mad Horse. (1749)

Take this remark from Richard *poor and lame,
Whate're's begun in anger ends in shame.* (1734)

Anger *is never without a Reason,
but seldom with a good One.* (1753)

*What signifies your Patience, if you can't find
it when you want it?* (1747)

AVOIDING
CONFLICTS WITH OTHERS 22

There are few things in life that cause more discomfort or unhappiness than conflicts with other people. It is, however, within our ability to minimize both the frequency of those conflicts and the troubles they cause us. To avoid personal disputes, there are at least two things we can do. First, severely restrict our willingness to be offended by what others may say or do. Most of us are too easily offended by those misunderstandings that are so common to human interaction. Second, to the best of our ability, avoid offending others. Of the two, the latter is the more difficult as we cannot always predict how others may react to things we do or say, even when well-intentioned. Even so, there is much we can do to reduce the frequency of any differences we may have, and to speed their resolution when they do occur. To Franklin, personal disputes were so distasteful that he went to great lengths to avoid them. In his writings may be found examples of what he did, and some excellent counsel on what we may do, to avoid such conflicts with others.

HOW TO AVOID BEING OFFENDED BY OTHERS

Someone has said that "whoever is offended when no offense was intended is a fool, and whoever is offended when offense was intended is usually a fool." In his own life Franklin made written resolves to help him avoid this problem:

MODERATION
Avoid extremes; forbear resenting injuries so much as
you think they deserve.

TRANQUILLITY
Be not disturbed at trifles, or at accidents common or
unavoidable.[1]

As we have seen in earlier sections, Franklin believed that:
Censure from friends is more useful than praise.[2]
With personal adversaries, the noblest victory is
obtained by neglect and by shining on.[3]
If we make good use of our enemies, they will do us
more good than harm.[4]
It is not appropriate to enter into controversy to
defend our personal opinions.[5]

These maxims, applied in his life, enabled him to avoid many
unpleasant situations and to benefit from situations that might
otherwise have been detrimental.

While in France, one of Franklin's colleagues in Europe
believed himself to have been slighted by Franklin and became
resentful and highly critical. To him Franklin sent the following
useful suggestion:

DEAR SIR: I received yours late last evening. Present
circumstances, which I will explain to you when I have
the honor of seeing you, prevent my giving it a full
answer now. The reasons you offer had before been all
under consideration. But I must submit to remain some
days under the opinion you appear to have formed, not
only of my poor understanding of the general interests of
America, but of my defects in sincerity, politeness, and
attention to your instructions. These offenses, I flatter
myself, admit of fair excuses, or rather will be found not
to have existed. You mention that *you feel yourself hurt.*
Permit me to offer you a maxim, which through life has
been of use to me, and it may be so to you in preventing
such imaginary hurts. It is: *Always to suppose one's*

friends may be right, till one finds them wrong, rather than to suppose them wrong till one finds them right. You have heard and imagined all that can be said or supposed on one side of the question, but not on the other.[6]

A Parable on Brotherly Love

In this parable written by Benjamin Franklin, the message is clear. Above all other things, a willingness to forgive and forget is the surest means of rising above personal injury and preserving harmonious relationships with those who may have offended us:

1. In those days there was no worker of iron in all the land. And the merchants of Midian passed by with their camels, bearing spices, and myrrh, and balm, and wares of iron.

2. And Reuben bought an axe of the Ishmaelite merchants, which he prized highly, for there was none in his father's house.

3. And Simeon said unto Reuben his brother, "Lend me, I pray thee, thine axe." But he refused, and would not.

4. And Levi also said unto him: "My brother, lend me, I pray thee, thine axe"; and he refused him also.

5. Then came Judah unto Rueben, and entreated him, saying: "Lo, thou lovest me, and I have always loved thee; do not refuse me the use of thine axe."

6. But Reuben turned from him, and refused him likewise.

7. Now it came to pass, that Reuben hewed timber on the banks of the river, and his axe fell therein, and he could by no means find it.

8. But Simeon, Levi, and Judah had sent a messenger after the Ishmaelites, with money, and had bought for themselves each an axe.

9. Then came Reuben unto Simeon, and said: "Lo I have lost mine axe, and my work is unfinished; lend me thine, I pray thee."

10. And Simeon answered him, saying: "Thou wouldest not lend me thine axe, therefore will I not lend thee mine."

11. Then went he unto Levi, and said unto him: "My brother, thou knowest my loss and my necessity; lend me, I pray thee, thine axe."

12. And Levi reproached him, saying: "Thou wouldest not lend me thine axe when I desired it, but I will be better than thou, and will lend thee mine."

13. And Reuben was grieved at the rebuke of Levi, and being ashamed, turned from him, and took not the axe, but sought his brother Judah.

14. And as he drew near, Judah beheld his countenance as it were covered with grief and shame; and he prevented him, saying: "My brother, I know thy loss; but why should it trouble thee? Lo, have I not an axe that will serve both thee and me? Take it, I pray thee, and use it as thine own."

15. And Reuben fell on his neck, and kissed him, with tears, saying: "Thy kindness is great, but thy goodness in forgiving me is greater. Thou art indeed my brother, and whilst I live, will I surely love thee."

16. And Judah said: "Let us also love our other brethren; behold, are we not all of one blood?"

17. And Joseph saw these things, and reported them to his father Jacob.

18. And Jacob said: "Reuben did wrong, but he repented. Simeon also did wrong; and Levi was not altogether blameless.

19. "But the heart of Judah is princely. Judah hath the soul of a king. His father's children shall bow down before him, and he shall rule over his brethren."[7]

Poor Richard had some worthwhile thoughts on not being offended by others. Some of his insights include:

It is better to take many Injuries than to give one. (1735)

Neglect kills Injuries, Revenge increases them. (1749)

Doing *an Injury puts you* below *your Enemy;* Revenging *one makes you but* even *with him;* Forgiving *it sets you* above *him.* (1749)

HOW TO AVOID GIVING OFFENSE TO OTHERS

As a young man, Franklin also formed written resolutions to help him avoid the problem of ever intentionally offending someone:

SINCERITY
Use no hurtful deceit; think innocently and justly; and, if you speak, speak accordingly.

JUSTICE
Wrong none by doing injuries, or omitting the benefits that are your duty.[8]

Additionally Franklin developed communication skills specifically designed to help him avoid confrontations with others. It is interesting to note that he deliberately undertook to develop these skills even though they ran contrary to his natural inclinations. As we can see, these skills not only made his relationships with others more pleasant, but also substantially increased his influence among his fellow men:

> *I made it a rule to forbear all direct contradiction to the sentiments of others, and all positive assertion of my own.* I even forbid myself, agreeably to the old laws of our Junto, the use of every word or expression in the language that imported a fixed opinion, such as *certainly, undoubtedly,* etc., and I adopted, instead of them, *I conceive, I apprehend, or I imagine* a thing to be so or so; *or it so appears to me at present.* When another asserted something that I thought an error, I denied

myself the pleasure of contradicting him abruptly, and of showing immediately some absurdity in his proposition; and in answering I began by observing that in certain cases or circumstances his opinion would be right, but in the present case there appeared or seemed to me some difference. *I soon found the advantage of this change in my manner; the conversations I engaged in went on more pleasantly. The modest way in which I proposed my opinions procured them a readier reception and less contradiction; I had less mortification when I was found to be in the wrong, and I more easily prevailed with others to give up their mistakes and join with me when I happened to be in the right.*

And this mode, which I at first put on with some violence to natural inclination, became at length so easy, and so habitual to me, that perhaps for these fifty years past no one has ever heard a dogmatical expression escape me. And to this habit (after my character of integrity) I think it principally owing that I had early so much weight with my fellow citizens when I proposed new institutions, or alterations in the old, and so much influence in public councils when I became a member; for I was but a bad speaker, never eloquent, subject to much hesitation in my choice of words, hardly correct in language, yet I generally carried my points.[9]

To an unnamed friend, Benjamin sent this valuable counsel:

Dear Sir: I hope your gout will be of service to you, as I have always found mine to be to me. I return the piece. And since you seem to wish for my advice, though without asking for it, I will give it. Do not publish the piece immediately. Let it lie by you at least a twelvemonth, then reconsider it, and do what you find proper. Such personal public attacks are never forgiven. You both have children, and the animosity may be entailed to the prejudice of both sides. With great esteem and affection, I am ever yours.[10]

Best of the Argument and Best of the Dispute

When a young friend shared with him an experience where she gave up an argument to preserve a friendship, Franklin provided her with this reassurance:

> So you see I think you had the best of the argument; and as you notwithstanding gave it up in compliasance to the company, I think you had also the best of the dispute. There are few, though convinced, that know how to give up, even an error, they have been once engaged in maintaining. There is therefore more merit in dropping a contest where one thinks one's self is right; it is at least respectful to those we converse with. *And indeed all our knowledge is so imperfect, and we are from a thousand causes so perpetually subject to mistake and error, that positiveness can scarce ever become even the most knowing; and modesty in advancing any opinion, however plain and true we may suppose it, is always decent, and generally more like to procure assent.* Pope's rule:
> "To speak, though sure, with seeming diffidence"
> is therefore a good one; and, if I had ever seen in your conversation the least deviation from it, I should earnestly recommend it to your observation.[11]

If we were to contemplate the number of people in the world who, during the course of a single day, have their peace of mind disturbed, their feelings hurt, and their tempers soured by the unkind words or inconsiderate actions of others, the value of the above counsel is inestimable. As in managing other thoughts and feelings, the ability to rise above provocations and to avoid irritating others requires determined and disciplined effort. But the reward is significant, both in the personal enjoyment it brings and the greater influence it tends to give us with others.

THE FOLLY

OF FINDING FAULT

THE HANDSOME AND DEFORMED LEG

One of the proper effects of religion is to motivate us to become more perfect by getting rid of our faults, and to make others happy by doing them good. It is amazing, however, how often we get that formula turned around. Many of us would rather, it seems, make ourselves happy and others more perfect. As a result, there is a proneness in human nature to observe and to criticize those imperfections we may see in those around us. Franklin addressed this problem in an essay he titled "The Handsome and Deformed Leg."

> *There are two sorts of people in the world, who, with equal degrees of health and wealth, and the other comforts of life, become, the one happy, and the other miserable. This arises very much from the different views in which they consider things, persons, and events; and the effect of those different views upon their own minds.*
>
> In whatever situation men can be placed, they may find conveniences and inconveniences; in whatever company, they may find persons and conversations more or less pleasing; at whatever table, they may meet with meats and drinks of better and worse taste, dishes better and worse dressed; in whatever climate, they will find

good and bad weather; under whatever government, they may find good and bad laws, and good and bad administration of those laws; in whatever poem, or work of genius, they may see faults and beauties; in almost every face, and every person, they may discover fine features and defects, good and bad qualities.

Under these circumstances, the two sorts of people above mentioned fix their attention; those who are disposed to be happy, on the conveniences of things, the pleasant parts of conversation, the well-dressed dishes, the goodness of the wines, the fine weather, etc., and enjoy all with cheerfulness. *Those who are to be unhappy, think and speak only of the contraries.* Hence they are continually discontented with themselves, and, by their remarks, sour the pleasures of society, offend personally many people, and make themselves everywhere disagreeable. If this turn of mind was founded in nature, such unhappy persons would be the more to be pitied. *But as the disposition to criticize and to be disgusted is perhaps taken up originally by imitation, and is unawares grown into a habit which, though at present strong, may, nevertheless, be cured, when those who have it are convinced of its bad effects on their felicity, I hope this little admonition may be of service to them, and put them on changing a habit which, though in the exercise it is chiefly an act of imagination, yet has serious consequences in life, as it brings on real griefs and misfortunes.* For, as many are offended by, and nobody loves, this sort of people, no one shows them more than the most common civility and respect, and scarcely that; and this frequently puts them out of humor, and draws them into disputes and contentions. If they aim at obtaining some advantage in rank or fortune, nobody wishes them success, or will stir a step, or speak a word, to favor their pretensions. If they incur public censure or disgrace, no one will defend or excuse, and many join to aggravate, their misconduct and render them completely odious. If these people will not change this bad habit, and condescend to be pleased

with what is pleasing, without fretting themselves and
others about the contraries, it is good for others to avoid
an acquaintance with them; which is always
disagreeable, and sometimes very inconvenient,
especially when one finds one's self entangled in their
quarrels. An old philosophical friend of mine was grown
from experience, very cautious in this particular, and
carefully avoided any intimacy with such people. He
had, like other philosophers, a thermometer to show him
the heat of the weather, and a barometer to mark when it
was likely to prove good or bad; but there being no
instrument invented to discover, at first sight, this
unpleasing disposition in a person, he for that purpose
made use of his legs, one of which was remarkably
handsome, the other, by some accident, crooked and
deformed. If a stranger, at the first interview, regarded
his ugly leg more than his handsome one, he doubted
him. If he spoke of it, and took no notice of the
handsome leg, that was sufficient to determine my
philosopher to have no further acquaintance with him.
Everybody has not this two-legged instrument; but every
one, with a little attention, may observe signs of that
carping, fault-finding disposition, and take the same
resolution of avoiding the acquaintance of those affected

with it. *I therefore advise those critical, querulous, discontented, unhappy people, that, if they wish to be respected and beloved by others, and happy in themselves, they should leave off looking at the ugly leg.*[1]

WHAT GREAT DIFFERENCE IS THERE?

In a satire titled, "On Scandal", Franklin considered some reasons he believed the tendency to find fault and to criticize is so common:

I am a young girl about thirty-five, and live at present with my mother. I have no care upon my head of getting a living, and therefore find it my duty, as well as inclination, to exercise my talent at *censure*, for the good of my country-folks. There was, I am told, a certain generous emperor, who, if a day had passed over his head in which he had conferred no benefit on any man, used to say to his friends, in Latin, *diem perdidi*, that is, it seems, *I have lost a day.* I believe I should make use of the same expression, if it were possible for a day to pass in which I had not, or missed, an opportunity to scandalize somebody; but, thanks be praised, no such misfortune has befell me these dozen years.

Yet, what ever good I may do, I cannot pretend that I at first entered into the practice of this virtue from a principle of public spirit; for I remember that, when a child, I had a violent inclination to be ever talking in my own praise; and being continually told that it was ill manners, and once severely whipped for it, the confined stream formed for itself a new channel, and I began to speak for the future in the disparise of others. This I found more agreeable to company, and almost as much so to myself; *for what great difference can there be between putting yourself up, or putting your neighbor down? Scandal, like other virtues, is in part its own reward, as it gives us the satisfaction of making ourselves appear better than others, or others no better than ourselves.*[2]

BEING FORBID TO PRAISE THEMSELVES

In a letter to a friend, Franklin suggested that people who are discouraged from praising themselves, often develop a tendency to criticize others:

What you mention concerning the love of praise is indeed very true; it reigns more or less in every heart; though we are generally hypocrites in that respect, and pretend to disregard praise, and our nice, modest ears are offended, forsooth, with what one of the ancients calls *the sweetest kind of music*. This hypocrisy is only a sacrifice to the pride of others, or to their envy; both which, I think, ought rather to be mortified. . . .

One of the Romans, I forget who, justified speaking in his own praise by saying: *Every freeman had a right to speak what he thought of himself, as well as of others.* That this is a natural inclination appears in that all children show it, and say freely: *I am a good boy; Am I not a good girl?* and the like, till they have been frequently chid [chided], and told their trumpeter is dead, and that it is unbecoming to sound their own praise, etc. But naturan expellas furca, tamen usque recurret. *Being forbid to praise themselves, they learn instead to censure others, which is only a roundabout way of praising themselves; for condemning the conduct of another, in any particular, amounts to as much as saying: I am so honest, or wise, or good, or prudent, that I could not do or approve of such an action.* This fondness for ourselves, rather than malevolence to others, I take to be the general source of censure and backbiting; and I wish men had not been taught to dam up natural currents, to the overflowing and damage of their neighbors' grounds.

Another advantage, me thinks, would arise from freely speaking our good thoughts of ourselves, viz.: if we were wrong in them, somebody or other would readily set us right; but now, while we conceal so carefully our vain, erroneous self-opinions, we may carry them to our grave, for who would offer physic to a man that seems to be in health? and the privilege of recounting freely our own good actions might be an inducement to the doing of them, that we might be enabled to speak of them without being subject to be justly contradicted or charged with falsehood; whereas now, as we are not allowed to mention them, and it is an uncertainty whether others will take due notice of them or not, we are perhaps the more indifferent about them; so that, upon the whole, I wish the out-of-fashion practice of praising ourselves would, like other old fashions, come round into fashion again. But this I fear will not be in our time, so we must even be contented with what little praise we can get from one another.[3]

ALL OF US HAVE WISDOM

After the war with England was over, many well-meaning people in Europe had plenty of advice for the new nation. Franklin wrote to the President of Congress:

I am much pestered with applications to make such
inquiries, and often obliged to promise that I will
transmit them; but I would not wish you to take more
trouble than to ask questions of the members of
Congress, or others that fall in your way, and
communicate to me their answers, if of any importance.
I have also multitudes of projects sent to me, with
requests that I would lay them before Congress. They
are plans and schemes of governments, legislation,
education, defense, manufacturers, commerce, etc.,
formed by people who have great goodwill to us, but are
totally ignorant of our affairs and circumstances;
whence their projects are, for the most part, wild and impracticable, or unfit to be presented to Congress, as not
pertaining to their jurisdiction. I have therefore not forwarded them; but now and then send some of them for
your amusement, if you should have any leisure, *that*

you may see how people make shoes for feet they have never measured.[4]

In giving personal advice, many people often make shoes for feet they have never measured. This tendency to assume we know what is best for others is delightfully illustrated in a letter from Benjamin to his sister. He had just returned to America from several long years in France. Upon returning home, it was Benjamin's plan to retire from public life. He was eighty years old and longing for leisure. The Pennsylvania Assembly had other ideas, however, and he was elected President of the Assembly shortly after he returned. His sister doubted his wisdom in accepting this responsibility at his age. His answer reflects both wisdom and affectionate humor:

> I do not wonder at your blaming me for accepting the government. *We have all of us wisdom enough to judge what others ought to do or not to do in the management of their affairs*, and it's possible I might blame you as much if you were to accept the offer of a young husband. My example may teach you not to be too confident in your own prudence, as it teaches me not to be surprised at such an event should it really happen.[5]

So it is that the tendency to find fault, to criticize, or to judge what others should do is a frequent disturber of human relationships. This intruder comes so frequently and is so familiar to us all that we tend to accept, and sometimes even welcome, his presence when we should be saying, "Begone! You are no friend of mine. You disrupt my family, you disturb my friendships, and you detract from my happiness and peace of mind. Get thee away from me thou foul habit. I want nothing to do with you."

CULTIVATING FRIENDSHIPS

The pleasures of good friends and peaceful relationships with others are so great that a prudent person will cultivate them in every way possible.

Franklin, being a prudent person, tried to find ways in his own life to develop friendships with those who might otherwise be his enemies and to strengthen his relationships with those who were already his friends.

HE THAT HAS ONCE DONE YOU A KINDNESS

In his autobiography, Franklin shared this example of turning a potential opponent into a lifelong friend:

My first promotion was my being chosen, in 1736, clerk of the General Assembly. The choice was made that year without opposition; but the year following, when I was again proposed (the choice, like that of the members, being annual), a new member made a long speech against me in order to favor some other candidate. I was, however, chosen, which was the more agreeable to me as, besides the pay for the immediate service as clerk, the place gave me a better opportunity of keeping up an interest among the members, which secured me the business of printing the votes, laws,

paper money and other occasional jobs for the public
that, on the whole were very profitable.

I therefore did not like the opposition of this new
member who was a gentleman of fortune and education,
with talents that were likely to give him, in time, great
influence in the House which, indeed, afterward
happened. I did not, however, aim at gaining his favor
by paying any servile respect to him but, after some
time, took this other method. Having heard that he had
in his library a certain very scarce and curious book I
wrote a note to him expressing my desire of perusing
that book and requesting he would do me the favor of
lending it to me for a few days. He sent it immediately
and I returned it in about a week with another note
expressing strongly my sense of the favor. When next
we met in the House he spoke to me (which he had
never done before), and with great civility; and he ever
after manifested a readiness to serve me on all
occasions, so that we became great friends and our
friendship continued to his death. This is another
instance of the truth of an old maxim I had learned,
which says, "*He that has once done you a kindness will
be more ready to do you another than he whom you
yourself have obliged.*" And it shows how much more
profitable it is prudently to remove, than to resent,
return, and continue inimical proceedings.[1]

Opposed to detraction and criticism, Franklin's approach to
human relations was carefully considered. In one of his Busy-
Body articles, Franklin examined, at some length, the tendency
of some to ridicule the failings and shortcomings of others. He
then provided an example of a different kind of person, one
whose interest was to build up his friends:

How different from this character is that of the good-
natured, [cheerful] Eugenius. . . . Eugenius takes more
delight in applying the wit of his friends than in being
admired himself; and *if anyone of the company is so
unfortunate as to be touched a little too nearly, he will*

make use of some ingenious artifice to turn the edge of the ridicule another way, choosing rather to make himself a public jest than be at the pain of seeing his friend in confusion.[2]

This same kind of thinking may be seen in a letter written over fifty years later to John Paul Jones. His counsel to this famous naval commander could well benefit anyone:

I approve much of your humanity and prudence, but am sorry that in the letter to Dr. Bancroft you complain of your friends, who are in no fault. They spare you, and have not even hinted that if you had stayed on board where your duty lay, instead of coming to Paris, you would not have lost your ship. Now you blame them as having deserted you in recovering her. Though relinquishing to prevent mischief was a voluntary act of your own, for which you have credit, *hereafter, if you should observe, on occasion, to give your officers and friends a little more praise than is their due, and confess more fault than you can justly be charged with, you will only become the sooner for it, a great captain. Criticizing and censuring almost everyone you have to do with, will diminish friends, increase enemies, and thereby hurt your affairs.*[3]

I COULD SCARCE HAVE BEEN SO PROUD

One of the reasons Benjamin Franklin was beloved by so many is because he loved so many. Although any form of flattery disgusted him, he was not at all backward in expressing affection to his friends. The following excerpts from some of his letters are exemplary of his depth of affection for others and provide a self-evident demonstration of how one may secure friendships of a lasting kind. To a friend in England, Franklin wrote this good-natured jest:

Dear Straney: I am here in my way to New England, where I expect to be till towards the end of summer. I have writ to you lately, and have nothing to add. 'Tis against my conscience to put you to the charge of a shilling for a letter that has nothing in it to any purpose; but as I have [written] to some of your acquaintance by this opportunity, I was afraid you would not forgive me if I did not write also to you. This is what people get by not being always as good-natured as they should be. *I am glad, however, that you have this fault; for a man without faults is a hateful creature.* He puts all his friends out of countenance; but I love you exceedingly.[4]

To another he wrote this delightful letter:

The *Tatler* tells us of a girl who was observed to grow suddenly proud, and none could guess the reason, till it came to be known that she had on a pair of new silk garters. Lest you should be puzzled to guess the cause, when you observe any thing of the kind in me, I think I will not hide my new garters under my petticoats, but take the freedom to show them to you, in a paragraph of our friend Collinson's last letter, viz. _But I ought to mortify, and not indulge, this vanity; I will not transcribe the paragraph, yet I cannot forbear.

"If any of thy friends," says Peter, "Should take notice that thy head is held a little higher up than formerly, let them know: when the grand monarch of France strictly commands the Abbe Mazeas to write a letter in the politest terms to the Royal Society, to return the King's thanks and compliments in an express manner to Mr. Franklin of Pennsylvania, for his useful discoveries in electricity, and application of the pointed rods to prevent the terrible effects of thunder-storms, I say, after all this, is not some allowance to be made, if thy crest is a little elevated? There are four letters containing very curious experiments on thy doctrine of points and its verifications, which will be printed in the new *Transactions*. I think, now I have stuck a feather in thy cap, I may be allowed to conclude in wishing thee long to wear it. Thine, P. Collinson."

On reconsidering this paragraph, I fear I have not so much reason to be proud as the girl had; for a feather in the cap is not so useful a thing, or so serviceable to the wearer, as a pair of good silk garters. *The pride of man is very differently gratified; and had his Majesty sent me a marshal's staff, I think I could scarce have been so proud of it as I am of your esteem. . . .*[5]

When Franklin was leaving England after his first trip on Pennsylvania business, he wrote the following to a friend:

My Dear Lord: I am now waiting here only for a wind to waft me to America, but cannot leave this happy island and my friends in it without extreme regret, though; I am going to a country and a people that I love. I am going from the old world to the new; and I fancy I feel like those who are leaving this world for the next: grief at the parting; fear of the passage; hope of the future. These different passions all affect their minds at once; and these have tendered me down exceedingly. It is usual for the dying to beg forgiveness of their surviving friends, if they have ever offended them.

Can you, my Lord, forgive my long silence, and my not acknowledging till now the favor you did me in sending me your excellent book? Can you make some allowance for a fault in others which you have never experienced in yourself; for the bad habit of postponing from day to day what one every day resolves to do to-morrow? —a habit that grows upon us with years, and whose only excuse is we know not how to mend it.[6]

Some of the most touching of Benjamin Franklin's letters were written near the end of his life. This affectionate exchange between himself and President George Washington, just six months before Franklin's death, is an example of the goodness of these two men and the kind of relationships we might all strive to have with others. Franklin wrote to Washington:

Dear Sir: My malady renders my sitting up to write rather painful to me; but I cannot let my son-in-law, Mr. Bache, part for New York without congratulating you by him on the recovery of your health, so precious to us all, and on the growing strength of our new government under your administration. For my own personal ease I should have died two years ago; but, though those years have been spent in excruciating pain, I am pleased that I have lived them, since they have brought me to see our present situation. I am now finishing my eighty-fourth year, and probably with it my career in this life; but, in whatever state of existence I am placed hereafter, if I retain any memory of what has passed here, I shall with it retain the esteem, respect, and affection with which I have long been, my dear friend, yours most sincerely,
                                    B. Franklin[7]

Within the week, Washington replied:

Dear Sir: The affectionate congratulations on the recovery of my health, and the warm expressions of personal friendship, which were contained in your letter of the 16th instant, claim my gratitude. And the consideration that it is written when you are afflicted with a painful malady greatly increases my obligation for it.

Would to God, my dear sir, that I could congratulate you upon the removal of that excruciating pain under which you labor, and that your existence might close with as much ease to yourself as its continuance has been beneficial to our country and useful to mankind; or, if the united wishes of a free people, joined with the earnest prayers of every friend to science and humanity, could relieve the body from pain or infirmities, that you could claim an exemption on this score. But this cannot be, and you have within yourself the only resource to which we can confidently apply for relief, a philosophic mind.

If to be venerated for benevolence, if to be admired for talents, if to be esteemed for patriotism, if to be beloved for philanthropy, can gratify the human mind, you must have the pleasing consolation to know that you have not lived in vain. And I flatter myself that it will not be ranked among the least grateful occurrences of your life to be assured that, so long as I retain my memory, you will be recollected with respect, veneration, and affection by your sincere friend,
George Washington[8]

Like a beautiful flower garden or a bountiful vegetable garden, good friendships must be cultivated. The ability to make others feel good about themselves does not come naturally to most of us. To praise without flattering, to criticize without offending, to encourage without belittling, to express affection without being effusive, these are all skills or habits that must be acquired. They spring forth from seeds of caring and consideration and can only thrive when such weeds as faultfinding and blaming are thoroughly removed.

FRANKLIN'S FORMULA FOR SUCCESSFUL LIVING
NUMBER TEN

"Mankind are all of a family",
wrote Franklin,
all children
of that being who gave us life.

It is folly,
said he,
for us to be on ill terms
with those whom we must live.

Yet,
within most of us
are certain
destructive tendencies,
which if not removed
tend to divide and alienate
large segments of the human family.

Among these are the tendencies
to criticize,
to find fault,
and to dispute,
one with another.

Like weeds in a garden,
these bad habits
crowd out and overcome
the more useful plants of
appreciation,
respect,
and consideration.

When that happens,
our lives,
like a garden full of weeds,
provide neither beauty
nor nourishment
to those around us.

In his life,
Benjamin Franklin
developed written resolves
intended
to help him
avoid conflicts with others.

He further
developed specific communication skills
and attitudes
designed to improve his ability
to function well with others.

Speak modestly,
do not put self above others,
do not be easily offended,
do not retaliate injuries,
try not to offend others,
look for the good in both friend and foe,
be cheerful and pleasant,
and freely express affection
to friends and loved ones.

These were the maxims
of Franklin's life
and those, he believed,
most likely to produce good will and
lasting friendships.

GUIDING PRINCIPLE
NUMBER ELEVEN

OF ALL HUMAN RELATIONSHIPS, THE MOST
ENDURING AND SATISFYING
ARE THOSE OF FAMILY

In the Divine plan, it was ordained that entrance to mortal life be through the door of a mother's womb. But, in bringing forth life, a woman is not without the man, and only together are they able to do that which neither can do alone. It was also ordained for each person to be brought forth as an infant, helpless and dependent upon those who gave it life. Both parents were given mutual responsibility for the protection and nurturing of their offspring. It was further ordained that, upon reaching maturity, each child should leave the home of his parents, find a companion, marry, and build a family of his own. This is the Divine plan for perpetuating the human species. In it may be found the fountains of human happiness. In its misuse may also be found bitter pools of despair and misery.

To both the man and the woman were given desires for union, which are among the strongest of human bonds when combined with mutual respect, consideration, and fidelity; and when given expression in procreation. Ties of family link together generations and extend even beyond life itself. In family life are to be found identity and purpose, hope and aspiration, love and affection. It is in the family that the basic values of society are transmitted from one generation to another. It is here that children first learn selflessness, honesty, industriousness, frugality, self-esteem and other virtues necessary to their happiness and well being. It is here they are taught how to get along with others and to work for common goals. It is in the family that children develop those habits and attitudes that largely determine the kind of people they will be.

The importance of marriage and family, both to society and to individual happiness, was not lost to Benjamin Franklin. In his own life, Franklin enjoyed a happy marriage and knew both the joys and sorrows of child rearing. In his travels, he nearly always took a child or grandchild with him. He always found occasion to visit relatives and to seek out information on his ancestors. The most difficult years of Franklin's life were those when he was away from his wife and family. As he wrote to his wife from England, "It is true, the regard and friendship I meet with from persons of worth, and the conversations of ingenious men, give me no small pleasure; but, at this time of life, domestic comforts afford the most solid satisfaction, and my uneasiness at being absent from my family, and longing desire to be with them, make me often sigh in the midst of cheerful company."[1] In another letter he wrote, "I have a thousand times wished you with me, and my little Sally."[2]

Some of Franklin's sagest and most poignant writings had to do with marriage and family. He believed that a man and woman complement each other, not only in the capacity to bring forth children, but also by the very nature of their talents and dispositions. He believed that the better family members get along, the more respected they would be by others. In a world which sometimes seems to have lost sight of the great purpose and blessings of family, his wisdom and counsel may be of great benefit.

GOOD MARRIAGES

In our modern society, the institution of marriage is under a great deal of stress. Of all the miseries of misguided self-interest, perhaps none are more prevalent than those associated with broken marriage vows. To Franklin, the importance of marriage was more than merely hypothetical. He believed there were important and practical reasons for people to marry.

LIKE 1/2 PAIR OF SCISSORS

Happily married himself for nearly forty-five years, Benjamin Franklin was a great advocate of marriage and family throughout his life. From France he wrote the following to a friend:

> The account you give me of your family is pleasing, except that your eldest son continues so long unmarried. I hope he does not intend to live and die in celibacy. The wheel of life, that has rolled down to him from Adam without interruption, should not stop with him. I would not have one dead, unbearing branch in the genealogical tree of the Sargents. *The married state is, after all our jokes, the happiest, being conformable to our natures. Man and woman have each of them qualities and tempers, in which the other is deficient, and which in union contribute to the common felicity. Single and*

separate, they are not the complete human being; they are like the odd halves of scissors: they cannot answer the end of their formation.[1]

To another friend he commented:

I am glad to hear that Mr. Fitzmaurice is married, and has an amiable lady and children. It is a better plan than he once proposed, of getting Mrs. Wight to make him a wax-work wife to sit at the head of his table. For after all wedlock is the natural state of man. *A bachelor is not a complete human being. He is like the odd half of a pair of scissors, which has not yet found its fellow, and therefore is not even half so useful as they might be together.*[2]

GOOD MARRIAGES

To his wife, Franklin wrote the following from London:

The accounts you give me of the marriages of our friends are very agreeable. *I love to hear of every thing that tends to increase the number of good people.* You cannot conceive how shamefully the mode here is a single life. One can scarce be in the company of a dozen men of circumstance and fortune, but what it is odds that you find on inquiry eleven of them are single. The great complaint is the excessive expensiveness of English wives.[3]

Writing to a young friend who requested his opinion on marriage, Benjamin offered this useful advice:

Dear Jack: You desire, you say, my impartial thoughts on the subject of an early marriage, by way of answer to the numberless objections that have been made by numerous persons to your own. You may remember, when you consulted me on the occasion, that I thought

youth on both sides to be no objection. Indeed, from the
marriages that have fallen under my observation, I am
rather inclined to think that early ones stand the best
chance of happiness. The temper and habits of the young
are not yet become so stiff and uncomplying as when
more advanced in life; they form more easily to each
other, and hence many occasions of disgust are removed.
And if youth has less of that prudence which is
necessary to manage a family, yet the parents and elder
friends of young married persons are generally at hand
to afford their advice, which amply supplies that defect;
and by early marriage youth is sooner formed to regular
and useful life; and possibly some of those accidents or
connexions that might have injured the constitution, or
reputation, or both, are thereby happily prevented.

Particular circumstances of particular persons may
possibly sometimes make it prudent to delay entering
into that state; but in general, when nature has rendered
our bodies fit for it, the presumption is in nature's favor,
that she has not judged amiss in making us desire it.
Late marriages are often attended, too, with this further
inconvenience, that there is not the same chance that the
parents shall live to see their offspring educated. "*Late
children,*" says the Spanish proverb, "*are early
orphans.*" A melancholy reflection to those whose case
it may be! With us in America, marriages are generally
in the morning of life; our children are therefore
educated and settled in the world by noon; and thus, our
business being done, we have an afternoon and evening
of cheerful leisure to ourselves; such as our friend at
present enjoys. By these early marriages we are blessed
with more children; and from the mode among us,
founded by nature, every mother suckling and nursing
her own child, more of them are raised. Thence the swift
progress of population among us, unparalleled in
Europe.

In fine, I am glad you are married, and congratulate
you most cordially upon it. You are now in the way of
becoming a useful citizen; and you have escaped the

unnatural state of celibacy for life, the fate of many
here, who never intended it, but who, having too long
postponed the change of their condition, find at length
that it is too late to think of it, and so live all their lives
in a situation that greatly lessens a man's value. An odd
volume of a set of books bears not the value of its
proportion to the set. What think you of the odd half of a
pair of scissors? It cannot well cut any thing; it may
possibly serve to scrape a trencher.

Pray make my compliments and best wishes
acceptable to your bride. I am old and heavy, or I should
ere this have presented them in person. I shall make but
small use of the old man's privilege, that of giving
advice to younger friends. *Treat your wife always with
respect; it will procure respect to you, not only from
her, but from all that observe it. Never use a slighting
expression to her, even in jest, for slights in jest, after
frequent bandyings, are apt to end in angry earnest. Be
studious in your profession and you will be learned. Be
industrious and frugal, and you will be rich. Be sober
and temperate, and you will be healthy. Be in general
virtuous, and you will be happy. At least you will, by
such conduct, stand the best chance for such
consequences.* I pray God to bless you both; being ever
your affectionate friend,

B. Franklin[4]

Poor Richard had an additional bit of advice:

*Keep your eyes wide open before marriage,
half shut afterwards.* (1738)

In a letter to his sister, Benjamin commented on the prospects
of his nephew getting married:

I don't doubt but Benny will do very well when he
gets to work; but I fear his things from England may be
so long a coming as to occasion the loss of the rent.
Would it not be better for you to move into the house?

Perhaps not, if he is near being married. I know nothing
of that affair but what you write me, except that I think
Miss Betsy a very agreeable, sweet-tempered, good girl,
who has had a housewifely education, and will make, to
a good husband, a very good wife. Your sister and I have
a great esteem for her; and if she will be kind enough to
accept of our nephew, we think it will be his own fault if
he is not as happy as the married state can make him.
The family is a respectable one, but whether there be
any fortune I know not; and as you do not inquire about
this particular, I suppose you think with me, that where
every thing else desirable is to be met with, that is not
very material. If she does not *bring* a fortune, she will
help to *make* one. *Industry, frugality, and prudent
economy in a wife, are to a tradesman, in their effects, a
fortune*; and a fortune sufficient for Benjamin, if his
expectations are reasonable. We can only add that if the
young lady and her friends are willing, we give our
consent heartily, and our blessing.[5]

The most obvious way in which a man and woman complement each other is, of course, in child bearing. Less obvious, but
perhaps more important is the manner in which they can
complement each other in child rearing. Men and women tend to
view similar situations through different eyes. Depending upon
the wisdom of the couple, that can be a source of contention and
disagreement or it can be the means by which they are able to
arrive at better decisions. As we have seen in previous sections,
human reason is an unreliable guide to human behavior. We all
have need to examine things from different perspectives and to
consider opinions other than our own. A married couple who
share common objectives and understand each other are better
able to assist one another in the achievement of worthwhile
goals than anyone else. Additionally, by assuming different roles
in the family and by supporting each other in the execution of
their differing responsibilities, the duties of family life are made
easier and substantially more enjoyable. In a good marriage, the
additive value of a husband and wife is much greater than the
sum of one plus one.

Benjamin Franklin's marriage to Deborah Read has all the makings of a delightful romance story. At the age of seventeen, Benjamin ran away from an oppressive apprenticeship to his brother in Boston. He first went to New York, but unable to find work there he went on to Philadelphia. Of his arrival in Philadelphia Benjamin wrote the following in his autobiography:

> I was dirty from my journey; my pockets were stuffed out with shirts and stockings, and I knew no soul nor where to look for lodging. I was fatigued with travelling, rowing, and want of rest; I was very hungry; and my whole stock of cash consisted of a Dutch dollar, and about a shilling in copper.
> . . .I walked up the street, gazing about till near the market-house I met a boy with bread. I had made many a meal on bread, and, inquiring where he got it, I went immediately to the baker's he directed me to. . . . I asked for a three-penny loaf, and was told they had none such. So not considering or knowing the difference of money, and the greater cheapness nor the names of his bread, I bade him give me three-penny worth of any sort. He gave me, accordingly, three great puffy rolls. I was surprised at the quantity, but took it, and, having no room in my pockets, walked off with a roll under each

arm, and eating the other. Thus I went up Market-street
as far as Fourth-street, passing by the door of Mr. Read,
my future wife's father; when she, standing at the door,
saw me, and thought I made, as I certainly did, a most
awkward, ridiculous appearance.[1]

Eventually, Benjamin came to board in the Read home. His
courtship with Miss Read, however, was interrupted when
Governor Keith offered to set him up in his own printing house
if he would go to England to get the necessary equipment.:

I had made some courtship during this time to Miss
Read. I had a great respect and affection for her, and had
some reason to believe she had the same for me; but, as I
was about to take a long voyage, and we were both very
young, only a little above eighteen, it was thought most
prudent by her mother to prevent our going too far at
present, as a marriage, if it was to take place, would be
more convenient after my return, when I should be, as I
expected, set up in my business. Perhaps, too, she
thought my expectations not so well founded as I
imagined them to be.[2]

After Benjamin left, Governor Keith fell through on his end of
the bargain, leaving young Franklin stranded in England. While
there Benjamin committed a serious mistake:

I immediately got into work at Palmers, then a famous
printing house in Bartholomew Close, and here I continued near a year. I was pretty diligent, but spent with
Ralph a good deal of my earnings in going to plays and
other places of amusement. We had together consumed
all my pistoles, and now just rubbed on from hand to
mouth. He seemed quite to forget his wife and child, and
I, by degrees, my engagements with Miss Read, to
whom I never wrote more than one letter, and that was
to let her know I was not likely soon to return. This was
another of the great errata of my life, which I should
wish to correct if I were to live it over again.[3]

When Benjamin finally returned to Philadelphia, some two years after leaving, he found things had changed:

> We landed in Philadelphia on the 11th of October where I found sundry alterations. Keith was no longer governor, being superseded by Major Gordon. I met him walking the streets as a common citizen. He seemed a little ashamed at seeing me, but passed without saying anything. I should have been as much ashamed at seeing Miss Read, had not her friends despairing with reason of my return after the receipt of my letter, persuaded her to marry another, one Rogers, a potter, which was done in my absence. With him, however, she was never happy, and soon parted from him, refusing to cohabit with him or to bear his name, it being now said that he had another wife. He was a worthless fellow, though an excellent workman, which was the temptation to her friends. He got into debt, ran away in 1727 or 1728, went to the West Indies, and died there.[4]

"All's well that ends well", however, and Benjamin's story has a happy ending:

> A friendly correspondence as neighbors and old acquaintances had continued between me and Mrs. Read's family, who all had a regard for me from the time of my first lodging in their house. I was often invited there and consulted in their affairs, wherein I sometimes was of service. I pitied poor Miss Read's unfortunate situation, who was generally dejected, seldom cheerful, and avoided company. I considered my giddiness and inconsistency when in London as in a great degree the cause of her unhappiness, though the mother was good enough to think the fault more her own than mine, as she had prevented our marrying before I went thither, and persuaded the other match in my absence. Our mutual affection was revived, but there were now great objections to our union. The match was indeed looked upon as invalid, a preceding wife being

said to be living in England; but this could not easily be proved, because of the distance; and, though there was a report of his death, it was not certain. Then, though,it should be true, he had left many debts, which his successor might be called upon to pay. We ventured, however, over all these difficulties, and I took her to wife, September 1st, 1730. *None of the inconveniences happened that we had apprehended; she proved a good and faithful helpmate, assisted me much by attending the shop; we throve together, and have ever mutually endeavored to make each other happy.* Thus I corrected that great erratum as well as I could.[5]

After forty-three years of "mutually endeavoring to make each other happy," Benjamin was able to write to his wife:

It seems but the other day since you and I were ranked among the boys and girls, so swiftly does time fly! *We have, however, great reason to be thankful, that so much of our lives has passed so happily; and that so great a share of health and strength remains, as to render life yet comfortable.*

I received your kind letter of November 16th by Sutton. The apples are not yet come on shore, but I thank you for them. Captain All was so good as to send me a barrel of excellent ones, which serve me in the mean time. I rejoice to hear that you continue well. But you have so used me to have something pretty about the boy [Franklin's grandson], that I am a little disappointed in finding nothing more of him than that he is gone up to Burlington. Pray give in your next, as usual, a little of his history.[6]

Starting with little, Benjamin and his wife worked together and over time their condition improved:

We have an English proverb that says: "He that would thrive, must ask his wife." It was lucky for me that I had one as much disposed to industry and frugality as

myself. She assisted me cheerfully in my business,
folding old linen rags for the paper makers, etc., etc. We
kept no idle servants, our table was plain and simple, our
furniture of the cheapest. For instance, my breakfast was
a long time bread and milk, (no tea), and I ate it out of a
twopenny earthen porringer, with a pewter spoon. But
mark how luxury will enter families, and make a
progress, in spite of principle: being called one morning
to breakfast, I found it in a China bowl, with a spoon of
silver! They had been bought for me without my knowledge by my wife, and had cost her the enormous sum of
three-and-twenty shillings, for which she had no other
excuse or apology to make, but that she thought her
husband deserved a silver spoon and a china bowl as
well as any of his neighbors. This was the first appearance of plate and China in our house, which afterward, in a course of years, as our wealth increased, augmented gradually to several hundred pounds in value.[7]

Franklin's biographers seem able to discover all kinds of faults
in his wife, but he appears to have been unaware of them.
Perhaps that was another key to the happiness he enjoyed with
her. Some twenty-five years after their marriage, Benjamin
wrote the following to a young friend:

The cheeses, particularly one of them, were excellent.
All our friends have tasted it, and all agree that it
exceeds any English cheese they ever tasted. Mrs.
Franklin was very proud, that a young lady should have
so much regard for her old husband, as to send him such
a present. We talk of you every time it comes to table.
She is sure you are a sensible girl, and a notable
housewife, and talks of bequeathing me to you as a
legacy; but I ought to wish you better, and hope she will
live these hundred years; *for we are grown old together,
and if she has any faults, I am so used to them that I
don't perceive them*; as the song says,

> Some faults we have all, and so has my Joan,
>> But then they're exceedingly small;
> And, now I'm grown used to them, so like my own,
>> I scarcely can see them at all;
>>> My dear friends,
>> I scarcely can see them at all.

Indeed, I begin to think she had none, as I think of you.
And since she is willing I should love you, as much as
you are willing to be loved by me, let us join in wishing
the old lady a long life and a happy.[8]

One of the seeming incongruities of Benjamin's marriage to
Debbie was the apparent disparity between their intellectual
capacities. Many of his biographers use examples of her poor
spelling and his use of the words "Dear Child" in addressing her
as evidence that he felt himself somewhat above her. That this
disparity was more apparent than real, however, may be seen in
the following letter from Deborah to Benjamin:

> My Dear Child: —the bairer of this is the Son of Dr.
> Phinis Bond his only son and a worthey young man he is
> a going to studey the Law he desired a line to you I
> believe you have such a number of worthey young
> Jentelmen as ever wente to gather I hope to give you
> pleshuer to see such a numbe of fine youthes from your
> one countrey which will be an Honour to thar parentes
> and Countrey.
>> I am my Dear child your ffeckshonot
>> wife D. Franklin[9]

While there are those who only see the poor spelling and never
recognize the noble sentiments expressed in the above letter,
Franklin never seems to have been troubled in the least by the
poor spelling of others. As he expressed in a letter to his sister
some years after his wife's death:

> You need not be concerned, in writing to me, about
> your bad spelling; for, *in my opinion, as our alphabet*

*now stands, the bad spelling, or what is called so, is
generally the best, as conforming to the sound of the
letters and of the words.* To give you an instance. A
gentleman received a letter, in which were these words:
*Not finding Brown at hom, I delivered your meseg to his
yf.* The gentleman, finding it bad spelling, and therefore
not very intelligible, called his lady to help him read it.
Between them they picked out the meaning of all but the
yf, which they could not understand. The lady proposed
calling her chambermaid, "because Betty," says she,
"has the best knack at reading bad spelling of any one I
know." Betty came, and was surprised that neither sir
nor madam could tell what *yf* was. "Why," says she, "*yf*
spells *wife*; what else can it spell?" And, indeed, it is a
much better, as well as shorter method of spelling *wife*,
than *doubleyou, i, ef, e*, which in reality spell
doubleyifey.[10]

Indeed, Franklin had so much respect for his wife's judgment,
that he once wrote to his daughter:

Human reason, my dear daughter, must be a very
uncertain thing, since two sensible persons, like you and
me, can draw diametrically opposed conclusions from
the same premises. I think reason is a blind guide; true
and sure instinct would be worth much more. All
inferior animals, put together, do not commit as many
mistakes in the course of a year, as a single man within a
month, even though this man claims to be guided by
reason. This is why, as long as I was fortunate enough to
have a wife, I had adopted the habit of letting myself be
guided by her opinion in difficult matters, for women, I
believe, have a certain feel, which is more reliable than
our reasonings.[11]

As the lives of Benjamin and Debra Franklin illustrate, if a
man and woman care for each other, share common values,
overlook each other's faults, and are frugal and industrious in
their affairs, they can hardly fail of thriving together.

THE MORE AFFECTIONATE

RELATIONS ARE   27

I WILL LOVE THAT SIDE BEST

In Benjamin Franklin's view of family life there is much of benefit to both parents and children in our day. As an advocate of harmonious human relationships, he felt very strongly about the importance of family members getting along with each other. At the death of a brother, Franklin wrote to his sister:

> As our number diminishes, let our affection to each other rather increase; for, besides it being our duty, it is our interest, *since the more affectionate relations are to each other, the more they are respected by the rest of the world.*[1]

When a quarrel arose between his sister and his brother's widow, Benjamin sent his sister this advice:

> Above all things I dislike family quarrels, and when they happen among my relations, nothing gives me more pain. If I were to set myself up as a judge of those subsisting between you and brother's widow and children, how unqualified must I be, at this distance, to determine rightly, especially having heard but one side. They always treated me with friendly and affectionate regard; you have done the same. What can I say between

you, but that I wish you were reconciled, and that *I will love that side best that is most ready to forgive and oblige the other?* You will be angry with me here, for putting you and them too much upon a footing; but I shall nevertheless be, dear sister, your truly affectionate brother.[2]

AMONG THE CHINESE, HONOR ASCENDS

One of the great and serious problems afflicting many homes today is the lack of respect children have for their parents. Unfortunately, one of the natural effects resulting from the disintegration of family life in contemporary society has been an accompanying disrespect for the preceding generation. In this context, the following excerpt from a letter by Franklin to his daughter offers some refreshing perspectives on the reasons for and the importance of keeping the fifth commandment, "Honor thy father and thy mother."

Shortly after the war with England was over, an organization was formed in America consisting of those officers who had fought in the war. Called the Cincinnati, it was a controversial organization that some feared might lead to the creation of an elite class in America. In writing to his daughter on this subject, Franklin expressed some highly relevant thoughts about how children can honor their parents:

> *I suppose those who disapprove of it have not hitherto given it much opposition, from a principle somewhat like that of your good mother, relating to punctilious persons, who are always exacting little observances of respect: that, "if people can be pleased with small matters, it is a pity but they should have them."*
> In this view, perhaps, I should not myself, if my advice had been asked, have objected to their wearing their ribands and badges themselves according to their fancy, though I certainly should to the entailing it as an honor on their posterity. For honor, worthily obtained (as that, for example, of our officers), is in its nature a personal thing, and incommunicable to any but those who had

some share in obtaining it. *Thus among the Chinese, the most ancient, and from long experience the wisest of nations, honor does not descend, but ascen*ds. If a man, from his learning, his wisdom, or his valor, is promoted by the emperor to the rank of Mandarin, his parents are immediately entitled to all the same ceremonies of respect from the people that are established as due the Mandarin himself; on the supposition that it must have been owing to the education, instruction, and good example afforded him by his parents, that he was rendered capable of serving the public.

*This ascending honor is therefore useful to the state, as it encourages parents to give their children a good and virtuous educa*tion. But the descending honor, to a posterity who could have no share in obtaining it, is not only groundless and absurd, but often hurtful to that posterity, since it is apt to make them proud, disdaining to be employed in useful arts, and thence falling into poverty, and all the meannesses, servility, and wretchedness attending it; which is the present case with much of what is called the noblesse in Europe. . . .

I wish, therefore, that the Cincinnati, if they must go on with their project, would direct badges of their order to be worn by their fathers and mothers, instead of handing them down to their children. It would be a good precedent, and might have good effect. *It would also be a kind of obedience of the [fifth] commandment, in which God enjoins us to honor our father and mother, but has nowhere directed us to honor our children. And certainly no mode of honoring those immediate authors of our being can be more effectual, that that of doing praiseworthy actions, which reflect honor on those who gave us our education; or more becoming, than that of manifesting, by some public expression or token, that it is to their instruction and example we ascribe the merit of those actions.*[3]

I ENJOY AMONG THEM THE PRESENT HOUR

In all cases where children are brought into the world by willing parents, the children have ample cause to respect their parents. While a parent may hope for the best, there is considerable risk in bringing children into the world. Apart from the physical risk to a mother in child bearing, there is no assurance loving parents will not be exposed to all manner of heartache and anguish in the child-rearing process, and, in fact, there is some likelihood they will. Franklin commented on this to a friend as follows:

As to my domestic circumstances, of which you kindly desire to hear something, they are at present as happy as I could desire them. I am surrounded by my offspring, a dutiful and affectionate daughter in my house, with six grandchildren, the eldest of whom you have seen, who is now at a college in the next street, finishing the learned part of his education; the others promising, both for parts and good dispositions. What their conduct may be when they grow up and enter the important scenes of life, I shall not live to see, and I cannot forsee. *I therefore enjoy among them the present hour, and leave the future to Providen*ce.

He that raises a large family does, indeed, while he lives to observe them, stand, as Watts says, a broader mark for sorrow; but then he stands a broader mark for pleasure to*o. When we launch our little fleet of barks into the ocean, bound to different ports, we hope for each a prosperous voyage; but contrary winds, hidden shoals, storms, and enemies come in for a share in the disposition of events, and though these occasion a mixture of disappointment, yet, considering the risk where we can make no insurance, we should think ourselves happy if some return with success*.[4]

In the home where love, mutual respect, kindness, forgiveness, consideration, and helpfulness reside, happiness is a resident member and not just an occasional visitor.

LESSONS FROM HIS FATHER

Of all the things a parent may do to assure a child's success, nothing is more important than teaching correct principles. If parents leave children to their own devices and whatever instruction circumstance may provide, all of which are terribly unreliable in leading to proper understanding and correct behavior, the children are seriously handicapped in their bid for happiness. There are two ways parents may teach, by precept and by example. Benjamin learned from his own father in both of those ways. Of his father, Franklin wrote:

> He had an excellent constitution of body, was of middle stature, but well set, and very strong; he was ingenious, could draw prettily, was skilled a little in music, and had a clear, pleasing voice, so that when he played psalm tunes on his violin and sung withal, as he sometimes did in an evening after the business of the day was over, it was extremely agreeable to hear. He had a mechanical genius too, on occasion, was very handy in the use of other tradesmen's tools; *but his great excellence lay in a sound understanding and solid judgment in prudential matters, both in private and public affairs.* In the latter, indeed, he was never

employed, the numerous family he had to educate and the straitness of his circumstances keeping him close to his trade; but I remember well his being frequently visited by leading people, who consulted him for his opinion in affairs of the town or of the church he belonged to, and showed a good deal of respect for his judgment and advice: he was also much consulted by private persons about their affairs when any difficulty occurred, and frequently chosen an arbitrator between contending parties. *At his table he liked to have, as often as he could, some sensible friend or neighbor to converse with, and always took care to start some ingenious or useful topic for discourse, which might tend to improve the minds of his children. By this means he turned our attention to what was good, just, and prudent in the conduct of life; and little or no notice was ever taken of what related to the victuals on the table, whether it was well or ill dressed, in or out of season, of good or bad flavor, preferable or inferior to this or that other thing of the kind, so that I was brought up in such a perfect inattention to those matters as to be quite indifferent what kind of food was set before me, and so unobservant of it that to this day if I am asked I can scarcely tell a few hours after dinner what I dined upon.* This has been a convenience to me in travelling, where my companions have been sometimes very unhappy for want of a suitable gratification of their more delicate, because better instructed, tastes and appetites.[1]

FRANKLIN'S SONS

Benjamin Franklin knew something of the sorrows of raising a family. His second son died of smallpox when only four years old. As seen in a letter written to his sister many years later, Benjamin still felt the loss of this son:

All who have seen my grandson agree with you in their accounts of his being an uncommonly fine boy, which brings often afresh to my mind the idea of my son

Franky, though now dead thirty-six years, whom I have
seldom since seen equaled in everything, and whom to
this day I cannot think of without a sigh.[2]

Franklin's first son, William, became a casualty of the Revolu-
tionary War, not in death, but in relationship. Benjamin and
William enjoyed a close relationship for nearly forty-five years.
Then, as Governor of New Jersey, William became a loyalist to
England, siding against his father's cause. As the crisis between
the two countries grew, Benjamin counseled William:

I know your sentiments differ from mine on these
subjects. You are a thorough government man, which I
do not wonder at, nor do I aim at converting you. *I only
wish you to act uprightly and steadily, avoiding that
duplicity which in Hutchinson, adds contempt to
indignation.* If you can promote the prosperity of your
people, and leave them happier than you found them,
whatever your political principles are, your memory will
be honored.[3]

Ultimately war broke out. As a loyalist, William was captured
and sent to Connecticut as a prisoner. Upon his word not to
become involved in the war, William was given considerable
freedom to move about. Shortly after, Benjamin went to France
as a representative of the United States, taking Temple,
William's son, with him as an aide. Concerning William,
Benjamin wrote to a friend from France:

You enquire what is become of my son, the Governor
of New Jersey. As he adhered to the party of the king,
his people took him prisoner, and sent him under guard
into Connecticut, where he continues; but is allowed a
district of some miles to ride about, upon his parole of
honor not to quit that country. I have with me here his
son, a youth of about seventeen, whom I brought with
me partly to finish his education, having a great affection for him, and partly to have his assistance as a secre-
tary, in which capacity he is very serviceable to me.[4]

Unfortunately, William took advantage of the leniency afforded him and became involved in espionage for the British. In doing so, he violated his pledge of honor not to engage in any warlike activities. To Benjamin, who above all things abhorred duplicity, and who saw armies of mercenaries burning towns and killing civilians in what he considered a wicked and unjust war, it was a bitter pill. After the war, his son wrote from England wishing to revive their relationship. Franklin responded:

Dear Son: I received your letter of the 22d ultimo, and am glad to find that you desire to revive the affectionate intercourse that formerly existed between us. It will be very agreeable to me; indeed, *nothing has ever hurt me so much*, and affected me with such keen sensations, as to find myself deserted in my old age by my only son; and not only deserted, but to find him taking up arms against me in a cause wherein my good fame, fortune, and life were all at stake. You conceived, you say, that your duty to your king and regard for your country required this. I ought not to blame you for differing in sentiment with me in public affairs. Our opinions are not in our own power; they are formed and governed much by circumstances that are often as inexplicable as they are irresistible. Your situation was such that few would have censured your remaining neuter, though there are natural duties which precede political ones, and cannot be extinguished by them.

This is a disagreeable subject. I drop it; and we will endeavor, as you propose, mutually to forget what has happened relating to it, as well as we can. . . .

I shall be glad to see you when convenient, but would not have you come here at present. You may confide to your son the family affairs you wished to confer upon with me, for he is discreet; and I trust that you will prudently avoid introducing him to company that it may be improper for him to be seen with. I shall hear from you by him; and letters to me afterwards will come safe under cover directed to Mr. Ferdinand Grand, banker, at Paris. *Wishing you health, and more happiness than it*

seems you have lately experienced, I remain your
affectionate father,[5]

FRANKLIN'S DAUGHTER

As the following excerpts from various letters to his daughter
demonstrate, Franklin's counsel was tender and instructive.
Enroute to England, on his second trip to represent the colonies
in the growing conflict with England, a journey from which he
was not to return for ten long years, Benjamin wrote to her:

My Dear Child, the natural prudence and goodness of
heart God has blessed you with makes it less necessary
for me to be particular in giving you advice. *I shall*
therefore only say that the more attentively dutiful and
tender you are towards your good mamma, the more you
will recommend yourself to me. But why should I
mention me when you have a so much higher promise in
the commandments that such conduct will recommend
you to the favor of God. You know that I have many
enemies, all indeed on the public account (for I cannot
recollect that I have in a private capacity given just
cause of offense to any one whatever), yet they are
enemies, and very bitter ones, and you must expect their
enmity will extend in some degree to you, so that your
slightest indiscretions will be magnified into crimes in
order the more sensibly to wound and afflict me. It is
therefore the more necessary for you to be extremely
circumspect in all your behavior, that no advantage may
be given to their malevolence.

Go constantly to church, whoever preaches. The act of
devotion in the Common Prayer Book is your principal
business there, and if properly attended to will do more
toward amending the heart than sermons generally can
do. For they were composed by men of much greater
piety and wisdom than our common composers of
sermons can pretend to be, and therefore I wish you
would never miss the prayer days; yet I do not mean you
should despise sermons, even of the preachers you

dislike, for the discourse is often much better than a man, as sweet and clear waters come through very dirty earth. I am the more particular on this head, as you seemed to express a little before I came away some inclination to leave our church, which I would not have you do.

For the rest, I would only recommend to you in my absence to acquire those useful accomplishments, arithmetic and book-keeping. This you might do with ease if you would resolve not to see company on the hours you set apart for those studies.

We expect to be at sea to-morrow if this wind holds, after which I shall have no opportunity of writing to you till I arrive (if it please God I do arrive) in England. I pray that his blessing may attend you, which is worth more than a thousand of mine, though they are never wanting.[6]

Another letter to her, now as Mrs. Sarah Bache, is just as helpful:

Dear Sally: I met with Mr. Bache at Preston where I stayed two or three days, being very kindly entertained by his mother and sisters, whom I liked much. He came to town with me, and is now going home to you. I have advised him to settle down to business in Philadelphia, where he will always be with you. I am of opinion that almost any profession a man has been educated in is preferable to an office held at pleasure, as rendering him more independent, more a free man, and less subject to the caprices of superiors; and I think that in keeping a store, if it be where you dwell, you can be servicable to him, as your mother was to me; for you are not deficient in capacity, and I hope you are not too proud.

You might easily learn accounts, and you can copy letters, or write them very well upon occasion. By industry and frugality you may get forward in the world, being both of you yet young; and then what we may leave you at our death will be a pretty addition, though

of itself far from sufficient to maintain and bring up a
family. It is of more importance for you to think
seriously of this, as you may have a number of children
to educate. Till my return you need be at no expense for
rent, as you are all welcome to continue with your
mother; and indeed it seems to be your duty to attend
her, as she grows infirm, and takes much delight in your
company and the child's. This saving will be a help in
your progress; and for your encouragement I can assure
that there is scarce a merchant of opulence in your town
whom I do not remember a young beginner with as little
to go on with, and no better prospects than Mr. Bache.

I hope you will attend to what is recommended to you
in this letter, it proceeding from sincere affection, after
due consideration, with the knowledge I have of the
world and my own circumstances. I am much pleased
with the account I receive from all hands of your dear
little boy. I hope he will be continued a blessing to us
all. It is a pleasure to me that the little things I sent you
proved agreeable. I am ever, my dear Sally, your
affectionate father,[7]

THE COMFORT OF MY DECLINING YEARS

Of the little fleet of barks Benjamin and his wife launched into
the ocean of life, Sarah was the one that safely returned, although more literally it was he that returned to her. Benjamin's
wife died when he was in England, just before the outbreak of
the war. After the war was over, and estranged from his son, it
was with his daughter and her family that he most wanted to be.
Notwithstanding the risk of an ocean voyage to a man of his age
and health, and several offers of places to live in Europe, he
determined to return home. Writing to his daughter and son-in-
law, he said:

The desire, however, of spending the little remainder
of my life with my family is so strong as to determine
me to try at least whether I can bear the motion of the
ship. If not, I must get them to set me on shore

somewhere in the Channel, and content myself to die in Europe.[8]

Once home, nestled in the bosom of his family, Benjamin Franklin was able to enjoy the fruits of a long life well lived. To one friend he wrote:

> I too have a daughter, who lives with me and is the comfort of my declining years, while my son is estranged from me by the part he took in the late war, and keeps aloof, residing in England, whose cause he espoused; whereby the old proverb is exemplified:
>
> "My son is my son till he gets him a wife;
> But my daughter's my daughter all the days of her life."[9]

To another he wrote:

> I am again surrounded by my friends, with a fine family of grandchildren about my knees, and an affectionate good daughter and son-in-law to take care of me.[10]

And again to another:

> But, though I could not leave that dear nation (France) without regret, I certainly did right in coming home. I am here in my niche in my own house, in the bosom of my family, my daughter and grandchildren all about me, among my old friends, or the sons of my friends, who equally respect me, and who all speak and understand the same language with me. . . .[11]

As with most grandparents, the joy of Benjamin Franklin's declining years was his family and most especially his grandchildren. From his example we may learn how blessed are those who, in their old age, are enfolded in the bosom of a loving posterity.

FRANKLIN'S FORMULA FOR SUCCESSFUL LIVING
NUMBER ELEVEN

There are few blessings in life
comparable to that
of a good marriage
and a good family.

In the tender love
of a faithful companion,
may be found the strength
and courage
to live
and fight
another day.

In the responsibility
of protecting,
feeding,
teaching,
and caring for children
may be found
the purpose
to live
and fight
another day.

In the joy of sharing
each other's success,
and in the comfort
of sharing each other's sorrows,
may be found the reward
for having lived
and having fought
another day.

But,
like any other form of happiness,
family life
must be firmly established
on the foundation of virtue.

Patience, gentleness, kindness,
industry, frugality, selflessness,
temperance, cleanliness, chastity,
silence, sincerity, humility,
order, resolution, justice—
what virtue is there
that does not have
an application in the home.

To those who are virtuous,
home can be heaven on earth;
to those who are not,
it can be a living hell.

Next to the
inner recesses
of our own mind,
nothing touches us deeper
than the environment
of home
and family.

GUIDING PRINCIPLE
NUMBER TWELVE

IN THE PROCESS OF AGING AND DYING, THE FRUITS OF A VIRTUOUS LIFE ARE MOST SENSIBLY FELT

A graphic representation of an individual's capacities over the course of a long life will normally be shaped much like the curve of a bell. When a new born infant comes into its mother's arms, it is totally dependent with little capacity for either thought or action. During the course of a normal life these capacities increase, little by little, until somewhere near what we call middle age. Then, little by little, these capacities begin to decrease until the person eventually dies. This process, of course, takes place over many years, and will vary in its effects from person to person. The primary variable, however, is simply time. The mortal experience, as we now know it, is limited and, if not cut short beforehand, will eventually be accompanied by a decline in either mental or physical capacity or perhaps both.

In this process there may be found great purpose. One such purpose is to tie families together so as to insure, insofar as possible, that children are properly taught and that bonds of affection are properly developed within the family. It is a foolish parent who fails to love and teach a child properly, for apart from the difficulties and unhappiness the parent may experience while the child is growing, the parent also cuts off the greatest source of comfort old age can afford. Old age is often accompanied by ill health and the death of dear friends and loved ones. It may be complicated by financial problems and poor living conditions. The loss of capacity may induce feelings of uselessness and being unwanted. The loss of lifetime associates and family members may bring on feelings of loneliness and isolation. To those who have been so blessed, there is no other source of happiness and pleasure comparable to the tender affections of loving children and the joy of being near grandchildren.

Irrespective, however, of whether one has been blessed with affectionate offspring or not, a virtuous life can substantially mollify the effects of physical and mental deterioration associated with aging. The same is true of any other form of injury or handicap. Similarly, in the death of a virtuous person, whether it comes early or late, whether it comes sudden or slow, may be found experiences that transcend the difficulties of the process. There is something glorious in a life well lived that may be sensibly felt at the time of the persons death. It may be described as a spiritual experience accompanied by a sweet and comforting peacefulness.

Benjamin Franklin's attitudes toward the process of aging and death are both instructive and inspiring. When he was young, he had a respect and appreciation for the elderly. He also realized that the time would likely come when he too would be old and that, in many respects, the benefits of a virtuous life would be more sensibly felt in his declining years than in any other. He was to experience the blessing of that realization. From temperance, he enjoyed health; from industry and frugality, he experienced financial ease and a wide range of interests to keep him actively employed; from cheerfulness and selflessness he was rewarded with loving family and friends; and from honesty, chastity, and sincerity he was blessed with a clear conscience and peace of mind.

As we now gain an intimate view of this good man's personal experience in aging and dying, we can observe the fruits of a long life lived in service to others.

RESPONSIBILITY TO THE OLD

The responsibility of the young to care for the old was one Franklin took seriously. He believed that the faithful discharge of this duty would not only bring happiness to the elderly, but also to those who served them. At the death of his mother, he wrote this tender note of appreciation to his sister and her husband for their care of his mother:

> Dear Brother and Sister:
> I received yours with the affecting news of our good mother's death. I thank you for your long continued care of her in her old age and sickness. Our distance made it impracticable for us to attend her, but you have supplied all. She has lived a good life, as well as a long one, and is happy.[1]

Some ten years later, he wrote to his wife from England concerning the death of her mother:

> My Dear Child:
> I condole with you most sincerely on the death of our good mother, being extremely sensible of the distress and affliction it must have thrown you into. Your

comfort will be, that no care was wanting on your part towards her, and that she had life as long as this life could afford her any rational enjoyment. It is, I am sure, a satisfaction to me, that I cannot charge myself with having ever failed in one instance of duty and respect to her during the many years that she called me son.[2]

In a letter to his sister Jane respecting the care of another sister, Benjamin provided some important insight into the problems of aging and the kinds of things we might do to help make life easier for them:

As *having their own way* is one of the greatest comforts of life to old people, I think their friends should endeavor to accommodate them in that, as well as in any thing else. When they have long lived in a house, it becomes natural to them; they are almost as closely connected with it as the tortoise with his shell; they die, if you tear them out of it; old folks and old trees, if you remove them, it is ten to one that you kill them; so let our good old sister be no more importuned on that head. We are growing old fast ourselves, and shall expect the same kind of indulgences; if we give them, we shall have a right to receive them in our turn.

And as to her few fine things, I think she is in the right not to sell them, and for the reason she gives, that they will fetch but little; when that little is spent, they will be of no further use to her; but perhaps the expectation of possessing them at her death may make that person tender and careful of her, and helpful to her to the amount of ten times their value If so, they are put to the best use they possibly can be.

I hope you visit sister as often as your affairs will permit, and afford her what assistance and comfort you can in her present situation. *Old age, infirmities, and poverty, joined, are afflictions enough. The neglect and slights of friends and near relations should never be added.* People in her circumstances are apt to suspect this sometimes without cause; *appearances should therefore be attended to, in our conduct to them, as well as realities.*[3]

To a young friend, Franklin sent the following counsel:

I see very clearly the unhappiness of your situation, and that it does not arise from any fault in you. I pity you most sincerely. I should not, however, have thought of giving you advice on this occasion, if you had not requested it, believing, as I do, that your own good sense is more than sufficient to direct you in every point of duty to others and yourself. If, then, I should advise you to anything that may be contrary to your own opinion, do not imagine that I shall condemn you if you do not follow such advice. I shall only think that, from a better acquaintance with circumstances, you form a better judgment of what is fit for you to do.

Now, I conceive with you, that _____, both from her affection to you, and from the long habit of having you with her, would really be miserable without you. Her temper, perhaps, was never of the best; and, when that is the case, age seldom mends it. Much of her unhappiness must arise from thence; and since wrong turns of mind, when confirmed by time, are almost as little in our power to cure as those of the body, I think with you that her case is a compassionable one.

If she had, through her own imprudence, brought on herself any grievous sickness, I know you would think it your duty to attend and nurse her with filial tenderness, even were your own health to be endangered by it. *Your apprehension, therefore, is right, that it may be your duty to live with her, though inconsistent with your happiness and your interest; but this can only mean present interest and present happiness; for I think your future, greater, and more lasting interest and happiness will arise from the reflection that you have done your duty, and from the high rank you will ever hold in the esteem of all that know you, for having persevered in doing that duty under so many and great discouragements.*

My advice, then, must be, that you return to her as soon as the time proposed for your visit is expired; and that you continue, by every means in your power, to make the remainder of her days as comfortable to her as possible. Invent amusements for her, be pleased when she accepts of them, and patient when she perhaps peevishly rejects them. I know this is hard, but I think you are equal to it; not from any servility of temper, but from abundant goodness. In the meantime, all your friends, sensible of your present uncomfortable situation, should endeavor to ease your burden, by acting in concert with you, and to give her as many opportunities as possible of enjoying the pleasures of society, for your sake.

Nothing is more apt to sour the temper of aged people, than the apprehension that they are neglected; and they are extremely apt to entertain such suspicions. It was therefore that I proposed asking her to be of our late party; but, your mother disliking it, the motion was dropped. . . . Not but that I was sensible her being with us might have lessened our pleasure, but I hoped it might have prevented you some pain.

In fine, nothing can contribute to true happiness that is inconsistent with duty; nor can a course of action, conformable to it, be finally without an ample reward. For God governs; and he is good. I pray him to direct you; and indeed, you will never be without his direction, if you humbly ask it, and show yourself always ready to obey it. Farewell, my dear friend, and believe me ever sincerely and affectionately yours.[4]

FRANKLIN'S OWN EXPERIENCE IN AGING

The Loss of Friends

Franklin's own aging experience can provide us with some useful insights into the problems of aging and suggests some attitudes that may be helpful in coping with those problems. One of the greatest trials elderly people experience is the loss of friends through death. As Benjamin wrote to a friend:

Dear Sir: It is a long time since I have had the
pleasure of hearing from you. The intelligence you were
used to favor me with was often useful to our affairs. . . .
Our excellent Mr. Winthrop, I see, is gone. He was one
of those old friends, for the sake of whose society I
wished to return and spend the small remnant of my
days in New England. A few more such deaths will
make me a stranger in my own country. *The loss of
friends is the tax a man pays for living long himself. I
find it a heavy one.*[5]

To another friend he wrote:

My very dear friend: I received your kind letter,
enclosing one from Miss Kitty Shipley, informing me of
the good Bishop's decease, which afflicted me greatly.
My friends drop off one after another, when my age and
infirmities prevent my making new ones; and, if I still
retained the necessary activity and ability, I hardly see
among the existing generation where I could make them
of equal goodness. So that the longer I live I must expect
to be the more wretched. *As we draw nearer the
conclusion of life nature furnishes us with more helps to
wean us from it, among which one of the most powerful
is the loss of such dear friends.*[6]

The Loss of Health
Another tax one pays in aging is the loss of health. In the
following letters, Franklin expressed some useful perspectives:

You will forget me quite, my dear old friend, if I do
not write to you now and then.
I still exist, and still enjoy some pleasure in that existence, though now in my seventy-ninth year. Yet I feel
the infirmities of age come on so fast, and the building
to need so many repairs, that in a little time the owner
will find it cheaper to pull it down and build a new one.
I wish, however, to see you first, but I begin to doubt the
possibility.[7]

You kindly enquire after my health. I have not, of late, much reason to boast of it. *People that will live a long life and drink to the bottom of the cup must expect to meet with some of the dregs. However, when I consider how many more terrible maladies the human body is liable to, I think myself well off that I have only three incurable ones: the gout, the stone, and old age*; and, those notwithstanding, I enjoy many comfortable intervals, in which I forget all my ills, and amuse myself in reading or writing, or in conversation with friends, joking, laughing, and telling merry stories, as when you first knew me, a young man about fifty.[8]

PRODUCTIVITY IN OLD AGE

For many people, the later years are the most productive and satisfying of their lives. Possessed with wisdom gained from years of experience, free from the responsibilities of family, and untroubled with fears of failure, they discover within themselves the ability to do many useful and important things. While not everyone may have the opportunity to be engaged in negotiating treaties and writing constitutions, there is much in Benjamin Franklin's life to suggest some possibilities for those who are able to retain a reasonable share of mental and physical capacity in their old age. As Franklin expressed to a friend, some of his most productive years were after the age of seventy:

You are now seventy-eight, and I am eighty-two; you tread fast upon my heels; but, though you have more strength and spirit, you cannot come up with me till I stop, which now must be soon; for I am grown so old as to have buried most of the friends of my youth, and I now often hear persons whom I knew as children, called *old* Mr. such-a-one, to distinguish them from their sons now men grown and in business; so that, by living twelve years beyond David's period, I seem to have intruded myself into the company of posterity, when I ought to have been abed and asleep. *Yet, had I gone at*

seventy, it would have cut off twelve of the most active
years of my life; employed too in matters of the greatest
importance; but whether I have been doing good or
mischief is for time to discover. I only know that I
intended well, and I hope all will end well.[9]

In a letter to a friend in England, Benjamin described, with
characteristic good humor, his life in Philadelphia after returning
from France. At this time he was in his eightieth year:

The companions of my youth are indeed almost all
departed, but I find an agreeable society among their
children and grandchildren. I have public business
enough to preserve me from *ennui*, and private
amusement besides in conversation, books, my garden,
and cribbage. Considering our well-furnished, plentiful
market as the best of gardens, I am turning mine, in the
midst of which my house stands, into grass plots and
gravel walks, with trees and flowering shrubs. Cards we
sometimes play here, in long winter evenings; but it is as
they play at chess, not for money, but for honor, or the
pleasure of beating one another. This will not be quite a
novelty to you, as you may remember we played
together in that manner during the winter at Passy. I
have indeed now and then a little compunction in re-
flecting that I spend time so idly; but another reflection
comes to relieve me, whispering: *"You know that the*
soul is immortal; why then should you be such a niggard
of a little time, when you have a whole eternity before
you?" So, being easily convinced, and, like other
reasonable creatures, satisfied with a small reason,
when it is in favor of what I have a mind to, I shuffle the
cards again, and begin another game.[10]

Some useful things to do, a cheerful disposition, the blessings
of a clear conscience, and the opportunity to be near loved ones
are the surest comforts of old age. They are natural fruits of a
virtuous life.

ALL WHO ARE BORN
MUST DIE

30

THE EXPECTATION OF DEATH

To those who believe in the eternal nature of man, and who have lived virtuously here, the prospect of dying holds no fear. In leaving France to return home, and conscious of his advanced age, Franklin wrote to a friend:

> I have continued to work till late in the day; it is time I should go home and go to bed.[1]

Shortly after arriving home in Philadelphia, he wrote to a friend in England:

> You will kindly expect a word or two concerning myself. My health and spirits continue, thanks to God, as when you saw me. The only complaint I then had does not grow worse, and is tolerable. I still have enjoyment in the company of my friends, and, being easy in my circumstances, have many reasons to like living. *But the course of nature must soon put a period to my present mode of existence. This I shall submit to with the less regret, as, having seen during a long life a good deal of this world, I feel a growing curiosity to be acquainted with some other; and can cheerfully, with*

filial confidence, resign my spirit to the conduct of that great and good Parent of mankind, who created it, and who has so graciously protected and prospered me from my birth to the present hour.[2]

Three years later, and one year before is own death, his friend died. He wrote to the man's daughter:

Your reflections on the constant calmness and composure attending his death are very sensible. *Such instances seem to show that the good sometimes enjoy in dying a foretaste of the happy state they are about to enter.*
According to the course of years, I should have quitted this world long before him. I shall, however, not be long in following. I am now in my eighty-fourth year, and the last year has considerably enfeebled me; so, that I hardly expect to remain another. You will then, my dear friend, consider this as probably the last line to be received from me, and as taking a leave.[3]

In the following description of Franklin's death by John Bigelow, there is something splendid. Perhaps it is the fortitude with which he bore the pain of his last year. Perhaps it is the alertness of mind he retained to the end. Perhaps it is the enjoyment of family and friends he never lost. Perhaps it is the cheerfulness and humor which he maintained through it all. Whatever it is, it is surely a witness that, in the death of a virtuous person there is much to be admired.

During the greatest part of his life Dr. Franklin had enjoyed almost uninterrupted good health. In the year 1735, indeed, he had an attack of pleurisy, which ended in a suppuration of the left lobe of the lungs. But from this, as well as from another attack of the same kind, he recovered completely.
As he advanced in years, however, he became subject to fits of the gout, to which, in 1782, a nephritic colic was superadded. From this time, he was also affected with the stone, as well as the gout; and for the last

twelve months of his life, these complaints confined him almost entirely to his bed.

"Notwithstanding his distressed situation," his grandson tells us, "neither his mental faculties nor his natural cheerfulness ever forsook him. His memory was tenacious to the very last. . . . A remarkable instance of which is, that he learned to speak French with considerable facility after he had attained the age of seventy!"

In the beginning of April, 1790, he was attacked with a fever and pain in his breast, which terminated his existence. The following account of his last illness was written by his friend and physician, Dr. Jones:

"The stone, with which he had been afflicted for several years, had for the last twelve months confined him chiefly to his bed; and during the extremely painful paroxysms, he was obliged to take large doses of laudanum to mitigate his tortures—still, in the intervals of pain, he not only amused himself with reading and conversing cheerfully with his family, and a few friends who visited him, but was often employed in doing business of a public as well as a private nature, with various persons who waited on him for that purpose; and in every instance displayed, not only that readiness and disposition of doing good, which was the distinguishing characteristic of his life, but the fullest and clearest possession of his uncommon mental abilities; and not infrequently indulged himself in those *jeux d'esprit* and entertaining anecdotes, which were the delight of all who heard him.

"About sixteen days before his death he was seized with a feverish indisposition, without any particular symptoms attending it, till the third or fourth day, when he complained of a pain in the left breast, which increased till it became extremely acute, attended with a cough and laborious breathing. During this state when the severity of his pains drew forth a groan of complaint, he would observe—that he was afraid he did not bear them as he ought—acknowledged his grateful sense of the many blessings he had received from that Supreme

Being, who had raised him from small and low beginnings to such high rank and consideration among men—
and made no doubt but his present afflictions were
kindly intended to wean him from a world, in which he
was no longer fit to act the part assigned him. In this
frame of body and mind he continued till five days before his death, when his pain and difficulty of breathing
entirely left him, and his family were flattering themselves with the hopes of his recovery, when an inpost-
humation, which had formed itself in his lungs, suddenly
burst, and discharged a great quantity of matter, which
he continued to throw up while he had sufficient
strength to do it; but, as that failed, the organs of respir-
ation became gradually oppressed—a calm lethargic
state succeeded—and, on the 17th of April, 1790, about
eleven o'clock at night, he quietly expired, closing a
long and useful life of eighty-four years and three
months."

In a letter from Dr. Rush to Dr. Price, dated at Philadelphia a week after Franklin's death, the writer says:

"The papers will inform you of the death of our late
friend Dr. Franklin. The evening of his life was marked
by the same activity of his moral and intellectual powers
which distinguished its meridian. His conversation with
his family upon the subject of his dissolution was free
and cheerful. A few days before he died, he rose from
his bed and begged that it might be made up for him so
that he might die in a decent manner. His daughter told
him that she hoped he would recover and live many
years longer. He calmly replied, 'I hope not.' Upon
being advised to change his position in bed that he might
breathe easy, he said, 'A dying man can do nothing
easy.'"

. . . . Mrs Hewson, writing to one of Dr. Franklin's
oldest friends in England, thus spoke of her own and the
nation's loss:

"We have lost that valued, that venerable, kind friend,
whose knowledge enlightened our minds, and whose
philanthropy warmed our hearts. But we have the

consolation to think, that, if a life well spent in acts of universal benevolence to mankind, a grateful acknowledgement of Divine favor, a patient submission under severe chastisement, and an humble trust in Almighty mercy, can insure the happiness of a future state, our present loss is his gain. I was the faithful witness of the closing scene, which he sustained with that calm fortitude which characterized him through life. No repining, no peevish expression, ever escaped him during a confinement of two years, in which, I believe, if every moment of ease could be added together, would not amount to two whole months. When the pain was not too violent to be amused, he employed himself with his books, his pen, or in conversation with his friends; and upon every occasion displayed the clearness of his intellect and the cheerfulness of his temper. Even when the intervals from pain were so short, that his words were frequently interrupted, I have known him to hold a discourse in a sublime strain of piety. I say this to you because I know it will give you pleasure.

"I never shall forget one day that I passed with our friend last summer. I found him in bed in great agony; but when that agony abated a little, I asked if I should read to him. He said, yes; and the first book I met with was Johnson's *Lives of the Poets*. I read the *Life of Watts*, who was a favorite author with Dr. Franklin; and, instead of lulling him to sleep, it roused him to a display of the powers of his memory and his reason. He repeated several of Watts' Lyric Poems, and decanted upon their sublimity in a strain worthy of them and their pious author. It is natural for us to wish that an attention to some ceremonies had accompanied that religion of the heart, which I am convinced Dr. Franklin always possessed; but let us, who feel the benefit of them, continue to practice them, without thinking lightly of that piety, which could support pain without a murmur, and meet death without terror."[4]

FRANKLIN'S FORMULA FOR SUCCESSFUL LIVING
NUMBER TWELVE

In the sunset of life,
as the shades of night
begin to draw down
around us,
the effects of a virtuous life
may be
most sensibly felt.

In the reflection
of a long life
spent in meaning well,
and in having done
one's best
to help others along the way,
lies the one solid pleasure
that remains,
as the sun goes down.

In the submission
to God's will
and the laws of nature,
may be found
the tranquillity of mind
that brings peace
and contentment,
as the night comes on.

In the rectitude
of one's heart
may be found
the well grounded expectation
of happiness hereafter,
as we close our eyes
and go to sleep.

For,
all who are born
must die,
and whether our lives
are long
or short,
the greatest blessing
of a virtuous heart
is the calm assurance
that when the light
of mortality goes out,
another light goes on;
a brighter, clearer light
in a happier future state
where we can continue
learning forever, and
where all that is wrong here
will be made right
by that good Parent
of mankind.

CHAPTER NOTES

ABBREVIATIONS:

> *WBF* - Bigelow, John, *The Works of Benjamin Franklin*,
> New York: G. P. Putman's Sons, 1904, 12 vols.
> Phil. - Philadelphia
> PG - Pennsylvania Gazette
> WM - Weekly Mercury

PREFACE

1 BF to Lord Kames, London, 3 May 1760, *WBF* 3:257

2 Autobiography, *WBF* 1:200-201

3 Clark, R.B., *A Biography, Benjamin Franklin* New York: Random House, Inc., 1983, p.41

4 See 3

5 Fleming, T., *The Man Who Dared the Lightning, A New Look At Benjamin Franklin*, New York: Wm. Morrow and Co., Inc., 1971, p.22

6 Fleming, T., *The Founding Fathers, Benjamin Franklin, A Biography in His Own Words,* New York: Newsweek, 1972, p.59

INTRODUCTION

1 Preface, *WBF* 1:vi

2 BF to Mrs. Abiah Franklin, no date, *WBF* 2:271

3 BF to Samuel Mather, Passy, 12 May 1784, *WBF* 10:321

4 Mather, C., *Essays to do Good*, Boston: Lincoln & Edmands, 1808, p.32

GUIDING PRINCIPLE NUMBER ONE

Chapter 1. BE CAREFUL WHAT YOU WANT, YOU MAY GET IT

1 BF to Madame Brillon, 1779, *WBF* 7:366

2 BF to Madame Brillon, 1778, *WBF* 7:363

3 Busy-Body III, WM, Tuesday, 18 Feb. 1728-9, *WBF* 1:347

Chapter 2. THOSE WHO LOVE THEMSELVES RIGHTLY
    1   Dialogue Concerning Virtue and Pleasure, PG, 23 June 1730, *WBF* 1:396
    2   See 1, *WBF* 1:396
    3   See 1, *WBF* 1:398
    4   See 1, *WBF* 1:398
    5   See 1, *WBF* 1:400
    6   A Second Dialogue Between Philocles and Horatio
Concerning Virtue and Pleasure, PG, 9 July 1730, *WBF* 1:403

Chapter 3. HAPPINESS, A UNIVERSAL DESIRE
    1   Autobiography, *WBF* 1:153
    2   Queries on Happiness, *WBF* 1:338
    3   On True Happiness, PG, 20 Nov. 1735, *WBF* 2:7

GUIDING PRINCIPLE NUMBER TWO

Chapter 4. A METHOD FOR PROGRESSING
    1   BF to Mary Stevenson, Craven Street, 11 June 1760, *WBF* 3:267
    2   Autobiography, *WBF* 1:188
    3   Autobiography, *WBF* 1:190
    4   Autobiography, *WBF* 1:195
    5   Autobiography, *WBF* 1:197

GUIDING PRINCIPLE NUMBER THREE
    1   BF to Ezra Stiles, Phil., 9 Mar. 1790, *WBF* 12:185
    2   Autobiography, *WBF* 1:205

Chapter 5. THERE IS ONE GOD WHO MADE ALL THINGS
    1   Autobiography, *WBF* 1:150
    2   Autobiography, *WBF* 1:185
    3   A Lecture on the Providence of God in the Government of the World, no date, *WBF* 9:241
    4   See 3, *WBF* 9:243
    5   See 3, *WBF* 9:244
    6   See 3, *WBF* 9:245
    7   See 3, *WBF* 9:246
    8   See 3, *WBF* 9:247

Chapter 6. HE OUGHT TO BE WORSHIPPED
    1   Articles of Belief and Acts of Religion, 20 Nov. 1728, *WBF*
1:319
    2   Motion for Prayers in the Convention, July 1787, *WBF* 11:376
Chapter 7. THE MOST ACCEPTABLE SERVICE OF GOD
    1   BF to Josiah Franklin, Phil., 13 Apr. 1738, *WBF* 2:65
    2   A Narrative of the Late Massacres in Lancaster County of a
Number of Indians, Friends of This Province, by Persons Unknown,
With Other Observations on the Same, 1764, *WBF* 4:31
    3   See 2, *WBF* 4:45
    4   BF to Mr. Small, Phil., 28 Sept. 1787, *WBF* 11:362
    5   BF to John Ingenhousz, Passy, 2 Oct. 1781, *WBF* 9:31
    6   BF to Deborah Franklin, London, 4 June 1765, *WBF* 4:155
    7   BF to Benjamin Webb, Passy, 22 Apr. 1784, *WBF* 10:308
    8   BF to Jane Mecom, Phil., 28 July 1743, *WBF* 2:66
    9   BF to Jane Mecon, London, 16 Sept. 1758, *WBF* 3:242
   10 BF to Joseph Huey, Phil., 6 June 1756, *WBF* 3:132

Chapter 8. THE SOUL IS IMMORTAL
    1   On True Happiness, *WBF* 2:7
    2   BF to Edward and Jane Mecom, Phil., 14 Nov. 1752, *WBF*
2:381
    3   BF to Miss E. Hubbard, Phil., 23 Feb. 1756, *WBF* 3:127
    4   BF to James Hutton, Passy, 7 July 1782, *WBF* 9:377
    5   BF to Miss Catherine Greene, Phil., 15 Apr. 1764, *WBF* 4:8
    6   BF to George Whately, Passy, 23 May 1785, *WBF* 11:45
    7   BF to Alexander Small, Phil., 19 Feb. 1787, *WBF* 11:303

GUIDING PRINCIPLE NUMBER FOUR

Chapter 9. HUMAN REASON, AN UNRELIABLE GUIDE
    1   Autobiography, *WBF* 1:80
    1   Autobiography, *WBF* 1:244
    3   BF to Mary Stevenson (Hewson), Paris, 14 Sept. 1767, *WBF*
4:312
    4   BF to John Winthrop, London, 2 July 1768, *WBF* 5:9
    5   BF to Benjamin Vaughan, Phil., 31 July 1786, *WBF* 11:272
    6   BF to Thomas Cushing, London, 15 Feb. 1774, *WBF* 6:287

Chapter 10. HOW TO THINK RIGHTLY
1   Rules for a Club Established for Mutual Improvement, 1728, *WBF* 1:334
2   BF to Peter Collinson, Phil., Sept. 1753, *WBF* 2:432
3   BF to John Ingenhousz, 1782, *WBF* 9:231
4   BF to John Lining, Phil., 18 Mar. 1755, *WBF* 3:69
5   See 4, *WBF* 3:73
6   BF to Peter Collinson, Phil., 25 Aug. 1755, *WBF* 3:80
7   BF to Mary Stevenson, London, 13 Sept 1760, *WBF* 3:271
8   Autobiography, *WBF* 1:47
9   Autobiography, *WBF* 1:48
10 Autobiography, *WBF* 1:184
11 See 1, *WBF* 1:331
12 BF to Cadwaller Colden, Phil., 28 Nov. 1745, *WBF* 2:121,124
13 Poor Richard's Almanac, 1734, *WBF* 2:44
14 BF to Mary Stevenson, Craven Street, 16 May 1760, *WBF* 3:263
15 The Right of Impressing Seamen, Remarks on Judge Fosters Argument in Favor of the Right, 1762, *WBF* 4:349
16 See 14, *WBF* 4:350
17 See 14, *WBF* 4:358
18 BF to Dr. Priestly, London, 19 Sept. 1772, *WBF* 5:371

GUIDING PRINCIPLE NUMBER FIVE

Chapter 11. HOW LITTLE WE KNOW OUR OWN GOOD
1   BF to Joseph Priestly, Passy, 8 Feb. 1760, *WBF* 8:176
2   BF to Georgiana Shipley, London, 26 Sept. 1772, *WBF* 5:373
3   On Government - No. II, PG, 8 Apr. 1736, *WBF* 2:15
4   BF to Cadwaller Colden, Phil., 27 Nov. 1747, *WBF* 2:206
5   Preface by British Editor to the Votes and Proceedings of the Freeholders and Other Inhabitants of the Town of Boston, 1772, *WBF* 5:393
6   Impolicy of War, 1784, *WBF* 10:299
7   BF to Joseph Priestly, Phil., 3 Oct. 1775, *WBF* 7:85
8   BF to Lord Howe, Phil., 20 July 1776, *WBF* 7:137
9   BF to Marquis de Lafayette, Passy, 19 Aug. 1779, *WBF* 8:115
10 BF to Lafayette, Passy, 4 May 1781, *WBF* 8:412
11 BF to John Adams, Passy, 31 Mar. 1782, *WBF* 9:172

Chapter 12. THE POWER OF SELFLESSNESS
1 Autobiography, *WBF* 1:206
2 BF to Wm. Franklin, London, 19 Aug. 1772, *WBF* 5:349
3 BF to a friend, Passy, 14 Oct. 1777, *WBF* 7:231
4 BF to Jane Mecom, London, 30 Dec. 1770, *WBF* 5:221
5 BF to Wm. Carmichael, Passy, 24 Aug. 1782, *WBF* 9:20
6 BF to Reverend M_, London, 30 Mar. 1762, *WBF* 12:281
7 BF to William Smith, Phil., 3 May 1753, *WBF* 2:406
8 Autobiography, *WBF* 1:53
9 Autobiography, *WBF* 1:181

GUIDING PRINCIPLE NUMBER SIX
1 On True Happiness, *WBF* 2:7
2 Autobiography, *WBF* 1:201

Chapter 13. WHERE TRUTH IS NOT
1 Autobiography, *WBF* 1:43
2 On Smuggling and its Various Species, London Chronicle, 24 Nov. 1767, *WBF* 4:324
3 Preface to the Speech of Joseph Galloway, 1764, *WBF* 4:73
4 See 2, *WBF* 4:74
5 See 2, *WBF* 4:76
6 See 2, *WBF* 4:79,80
7 BF to Joseph Galloway, London, 17 Feb. 1768, *WBF* 4:397
8 BF to Joseph Galloway, London, 13 Mar. 1768, *WBF* 4:426
9 BF to Richard Price, Passy, 9 Oct. 1780, *WBF* 8:310
10 BF to Richard Price, Passy, 16 Aug. 1784, *WBF* 10:408
11 Speech in Convention, On the Subject of Salaries, 1787, *WBF* 11:366

Chapter 14. THE POWER OF A GOOD CONSCIENCE
1 Autobiography, *WBF* 1:294
2 Franklin's Account of the Negotiations in London for Effecting a Reconciliation Between Great Britain and the American Colonies, 22 Mar. 1775, *WBF* 7:24
3 See 2, *WBF* 7:71
4 Journal of Trip from England, 23 July - 11 Oct. 1726, *WBF* 1:112

5 BF to Charles Thomson, London, 27 Sept. 1766, *WBF* 4:240
6 BF to Jane Mecom, no date, *WBF* 5:77,
7 BF to Joseph Galloway, London, 2 Dec. 1772, *WBF* 5:399
8 BF to Wm. Franklin, London, 5 Jan. 1774, *WBF* 6:268
9 Dr. Priestly to Editor of *Monthly Magazine*, Northumberland, 10 Nov. 1802, *WBF* 6:295
10 David Hartley to BF Paris, 23 Apr. 1778, *WBF* 7:292
12 Note by John Bigelow, *WBF* 7:293
13 BF to Juliana Ritchie Paris, 19 Jan. 1777, *WBF* 7:170
14 BF to John Jay, Passy, 6 Jan. 1784, *WBF* 10:261

GUIDING PRINCIPLE NUMBER SEVEN
1 Autobiography, *WBF* 1:238

Chapter 15. THE FOIBLE OF MANKIND
1 BF to Thomas Cushing, London, 13 Jan. 1772, *WBF* 12:326
2 Observations Concerning the Increase of Mankind and the Peopling of Countries, 1751, *WBF* 2:344
3 BF to Peter Collinson, Phil., 9 May 1753, *WBF* 2:408
4 On the Price of Corn and Management of the Poor, London Chronicle, 1766, *WBF* 4:347
5 Busy Body - VIII, WM, Tuesday 27 Mar. 1729, *WBF* 1:366
6 BF to Benjamin Vaughan, Passy, 26 July 1784, *WBF* 10:376
7 BF to Wm. Strahan, Phil., 2 June 1750, *WBF* 12:251

Chapter 16. THE WAY TO WEALTH
1 The Way to Wealth As Clearly Shown in the Preface of an Old Almanac Entitled "Poor Richard Improved", 1758, *WBF* 2:27
2 Advice to a Young Tradesman, 1748, *WBF* 2:236

GUIDING PRINCIPLE NUMBER EIGHT
1 BF to Benjamin Vaughan, Phil., 31 July 1786, *WBF* 11:272

Chapter 17. PRESERVING HEALTH THROUGH NUTRITION AND EXERCISE
1 Autobiography, *WBF* 1:191
2 Autobiography, *WBF* 1:52
3 Autobiography, *WBF* 1:95
4 Autobiography, *WBF* 1:97

4 BF to Captain Landais, Passy, 12 Mar. 1780, *WBF* 8:200
5 BF to M. Wharton, Passy, 17 June 1780, *WBF* 8:255
6 BF to Johnathan Williams, Passy, 17 June 1780, *WBF* 8:267
7 BF to Mr. Elam, Phil., 10 Nov. 1788, *WBF* 12:11

Chapter 22. AVOIDING CONFLICT WITH OTHERS
1 Autobiography, *WBF* 1:190
2 BF to William Smith, Phil., 3 May 1753, *WBF* 2:407
3 See 2: *WBF* 407
4 BF to John Jay, Passy, 6 Jan. 1784, *WBF* 10:261
5 BF to a friend, Passy, 14 Oct. 1777, *WBF* 7:231
6 To Ralph Izard, Passy, 29 Jan. 1778, *WBF* 7:244
7 A Parable on Brotherly Love, 1774, *WBF* 6:368
8 Autobiography, *WBF* 1:190
9 Autobiography, *WBF* 1:202
10 BF to _____, Phil., 22 Nov. 1786, *WBF* 11:291
11 BF to Mary Stevenson, Craven Street,1769, *WBF* 5:126

Chapter 23. THE FOLLY OF FINDING FAULT
1 The Handsome and Deformed Leg, 1779, *WBF* 7:379
2 On Scandal, 1745, *WBF* 2:140
3 BF to Jared Eliot, Phil., 11 Sept. 1751, *WBF* 2:352
4 BF to Charles Thomson, Passy, 14 June 1784, *WBF* 10:338
5 BF to Jane Mecom, Phil., 14 Jan. 1786, *WBF* 11:223

Chapter 24. CULTIVATING FRIENDSHIPS
1 Autobiography, *WBF* 1:215
2 Busy Body - II, WM, 11 Feb. 1728-9, *WBF* 1:346
3 BF to John Paul Jones, Passy, 5 July 1780, *WBF* 8:271
4 BF to Wm. Strahan, Woodbridge, N.J., 10 June 1763, *WBF* 3:455
5 BF to Jared Eliot, Phil., 12 Apr. 1753, *WBF* 2:401
6 BF to Lord Kames, Portsmouth, 17 Aug. 1762, *WBF* 3:423
7 BF to George Washington, Phil., 16 Sept. 1789, *WBF* 12:137
8 George Washington to BF, New York, 23 Sept. 1789, *WBF* 12:139

GUIDING PRINCIPLE NUMBER ELEVEN
1   BF to Deborah Franklin, London, 21 Jan. 1758, *WBF* 3:212
2   BF to Deborah Franklin, London,19 Feb. 1758, *WBF* 3:217

Chapter 25. GOOD MARRIAGES
1   BF to John Sargent, Passy, 27 Jan. 1783, *WBF* 10:81
2   BF to Thomas Jordan, Phil., 18 May 1787, *WBF* 11:330
3   BF to Deborah Franklin, London, 27 June 1760, *WBF* 3:269
4   BF to John Alleyne, Craven Street, 9 Aug. 1768, *WBF* 5:28
5   BF to Jane Mecom, Woodbridge, N.J., 21 May 1757, *WBF*
3:182

Chapter 26. WE THROVE TOGETHER
1   Autobiography, *WBF* 1:64
2   Autobiography, *WBF* 1:82
3   Autobiography, *WBF* 1:91
4   Autobiography, *WBF* 1:141
5   Autobiography, *WBF* 1:170
6   BF to Deborah Franklin, London, 6 Jan. 1773, *WBF* 6:62
7   Autobiography, *WBF* 1:185
8   BF to Catherine Ray, Phil., 11 Sept. 1755, *WBF* 3:88
9   Deborah Franklin to BF, 11 Oct. 1770, *WBF* 5:214
10 BF to Jane Mecom, Phil., 4 July 1786, *WBF* 11:262
11 Lopez, C., *Mon Cher Papa, Franklin and the Ladies of Paris,*
New Haven: Yale Univ. Press, 1966, p.82

Chapter 27. THE MORE AFFECTIONATE RELATIONS ARE
1   Bigelow note re. letter from BF to sister, 1756, *WBF* 3:129
2   BF to Jane Mecom, New York, 30 May 1757, *WBF* 3:193
3   BF to Sarah Bache, Passy, 26 Jan. 1784, *WBF* 10:274
4   BF to Dr. Shipley, Phil., 24 Feb. 1786, *WBF* 11:234

Chapter 28. FRANKLIN'S FAMILY
1   Autobiography, *WBF* 1:43
2   BF to Jane Mecom, London, 13 Jan. 1772, *WBF* 5:276
3   BF to Wm. Franklin, London, 6 Oct. 1773, *WBF* 6:222
4   BF to Dr. Priestly ?,1778, *WBF* 7:349
5   BF to Wm. Franklin, Passy, 16 Aug. 1784, *WBF* 10:403
6   BF to Sarah Franklin, Reedy Island, 8 Nov. 1764,*WBF* 4:18

7 BF to Sara Bache, London, 29 Jan. 1772, *WBF* 5:298
8 BF to Mr. and Mrs. Bache, Passy, 10 May 1785, *WBF* 11:39
9 BF to Mather Byles, Phil., 1 June 1788, *WBF* 11:399
10 BF to William Hunter, Phil., 24 Nov. 1786, *WBF* 11:289
11 BF to the Abbe Morellet, Phil., 22 Apr. 1787, *WBF* 11:326

GUIDING PRINCIPLE NUMBER TWELVE

Chapter 29. PEOPLE WHO LIVE LONG

1 BF to Edward and Jane Mecom, Phil., 21 May 1752, *WBF* 2:374
2 BF to Deborah Franklin, London, 24 Mar. 1762, *WBF* 3:401
3 BF to Jane Mecom, New York, 19 Apr. 1757, *WBF* 3:180
4 BF to Mary Stevenson, London, Oct. 1768, *WBF* 5:46
5 BF to Samuel Cooper, Passy, 27 Oct. 1779, *WBF* 8:152
6 BF to Richard Price, Phil., 31 May 1789, *WBF* 12:73
7 BF to Mary Hewson (Stevenson), Passy, 19 Mar. 1784, *WBF* 10:295
8 BF to Mrs. Partridge, Phil., 25 Nov. 1788, *WBF* 12:16
9 BF to George Whately, Phil., 18 May 1787, *WBF* 11:333
10 BF to Mary Hewson, Phil., 6 May 1786, *WBF* 11:254

Chapter 30. THE EXPECTATION OF DEATH

1 BF to Mary Hewson, St.Germain, 13 July 1785, *WBF* 11:81
2 BF to Dr. Shipley, Phil., 24 Feb. 1786, *WBF* 11:235
3 BF to Catherine Shipley, Phil., 27 Apr. 1789, *WBF* 12:72
4 Note by John Bigelow, *WBF* 12:195

INDEX